KW-761-285

Contents

Introduction

From 2 to 4 September 1998 – as part of the events and activities commemorating the 50th Anniversary of the Universal Declaration of Human Rights, following the appeal to the international community made by the United Nations – the Council of Europe organised in Strasbourg a European regional colloquy, entitled "'In our hands': the effectiveness of human rights protection 50 years after the Universal Declaration". Its first session was devoted to this commemoration. The colloquy was designed not only to commemorate this anniversary, but also to examine progress, problems and priorities in Europe in the implementation of the Vienna Declaration and Programme of Action adopted by the World Conference on Human Rights in 1993, building on the results of the interregional meeting organised by the Council of Europe in January 1993 in preparation for the World Conference, "Human Rights at the Dawn of the 21st Century" (January 1993). In its second part, the colloquy is intended consequently to be substantive and to look at the achievements to date and progress still to be made in human rights protection and promotion in Europe five years after the World Conference on Human Rights.

Its six themes are divided in two groups: the first group deals with selected current challenges, the second with effective action to protect and promote human rights.

By way of introduction, here is an outline of some key questions discussed during the colloquy under each of these six themes.

I – Effective action to protect and promote human rights

Theme 1: Protection: effective action at the national level

Notwithstanding the vital role played by international mechanisms, the effective protection of human rights begins and ends at the national level; it concerns the role of the judicial system, ombudsmen and similar institutions, national human rights institutions, but also that of parliaments, executive authorities and non-governmental organisations. The development of a genuine "human rights culture" is essential on this point of view, but this also presupposes the existence of a national "human rights infrastructure", and some important issues remain to be addressed.

Is the judicial system able to play to the full its role in protecting human rights by providing effective remedies? What about access to justice, independence of the courts, the crucial role of the public prosecution in making criminal remedies effective, implementation of judgments, application of international and European human rights standards? What obstacles arise? How can they be removed?

The legislature has an important responsibility for ensuring that national law conforms to constitutional and international human rights standards, thus avoiding future human rights violations. Are human rights considerations given proper attention in the legislative process? What "checks" can be developed to ensure that this is the case?

Ombudsmen and national institutions for the promotion and protection of human rights can complement the action of the courts. The United Nations, the Council of Europe and other international organisations encourage the establishment of such independent bodies which now exist in a number of states. However, not all member states have created them. What are the main obstacles in this respect and what are the conditions for the effective functioning of such non-judicial bodies?

Non-governmental organisations (NGOs) undoubtedly form part of an effective national infrastructure for the protection of human rights. Are the conditions fulfilled which allow them to act in a genuine partnership in this respect? What are the main problems encountered in practice? How can they be solved?

Theme 2: Protection: effective action at the international level

Let us take a critical look at the operation of the essential mechanisms and instruments of the Council of Europe: the European Convention on Human Rights, the European Social Charter, the European Convention for the Prevention of Torture and Inhuman or Degrading Treatment or Punishment, the Framework Convention for the Protection of National Minorities, mechanisms established by the Committee of Ministers and the Parliamentary Assembly for monitoring compliance with commitments by member states. What is the status of ratifications by member states of United Nations and Council of Europe treaties?

To what extent will the future Council of Europe commissioner for human rights contribute to the effectiveness of Council of Europe action in promoting and protecting human rights?

Theme 3: The promotion of human rights: information, education and training

Effective protection of human rights cannot be achieved without a genuine "human rights culture" in society. What support role can the Council of Europe play for the promotion of human rights information and education? Can a national plan of action for human rights education be established in each member state by the year 2000? Is this not an obvious area for partnership, bringing together the creativity and closeness to people of local NGOs with a government's networks and resources, in relation to (formal and informal) education, training, and general dissemination of information and promotion of awareness of human rights?

Practical campaigns can remind the public of why we have a human rights framework and the horrors such a framework must prevent. How can the media, and others in positions of influence, be encouraged to contribute to such campaigns? How can governments, intergovernmental and non-governmental institutions work together to make the basic human rights material accessible for the citizen in his/her language?

Doesn't a government which accepts its full responsibility for human rights protection have to ensure that this acceptance pervades the machinery of its administration? How can foreign ministries ensure that information about treaty obligations and other international standards are translated into a commitment from interior and justice ministries or other parts of government with operational responsibilities affecting human rights? How can parliamentarians ensure that the national legislature is similarly informed? What role could national institutions for the promotion and protection of human rights, human rights institutes, professional associations, usefully play in this regard?

It seems essential to give a new impetus to action at the national level and to explore ways of generating political commitment and financial support for education and training initiatives and for the widest possible distribution of basic human rights information in the different languages of Europe.

II – Current challenges

Theme 4: Prevention of and responses to structural or large-scale human rights violations

The system of the European Convention on Human Rights has traditionally focused on providing effective redress for human rights violations which are of an individual character, not on general structural problems, which may amount to situations of massive violations of human rights.

On the basis of the experience of the United Nations, OSCE, etc. relating to large-scale and persistent human rights violations, what methods of prevention and types of responses are most effective? In what type of situations? What factors determine the effectiveness of an international action?

For dealing with such violations, which avenues are already in place within the Council of Europe? What are the possibilities under its existing treaty mechanisms? Can satisfactory and effective mechanisms for prevention of and responses to such violations be attained through adaptation of those existing avenues? Should new mechanisms/procedures be developed?

Theme 5: Social rights: the challenge of indivisibility and interdependence

The World Conference on Human Rights reaffirmed that all human rights are universal, indivisible and interdependent and interrelated. It also stressed the importance of fighting extreme poverty and social exclusion, protecting vulnerable groups and reaffirmed the obligations of states in social fields such as education, health and social support.

For the Council of Europe, the European Social Charter and the Revised Social Charter of 1996 constitute the key human rights instruments protecting fundamental social rights and might review progress made in strengthening the protection of social rights and ensure that they are taken as fully-fledged human rights and are an indivisible part of human rights protection at national and European levels. Are not the entry into force of the Revised Social Charter and the collective complaints mechanism significant of recent developments in this field? What about the fully implementation of the Action Plan adopted at the Second Council of Europe Summit of Heads of State and Government?

Theme 6: Effective implementation of women's rights

In most cases, the principle of equality between women and men is now protected in law. However, the definition of equality used is often a very narrow one of *de jure* equality. Inequalities persist in practice. A critical assessment of measures and strategies designed to remove these inequalities is warranted. Should the effectiveness of human rights instruments not be reviewed from a gender perspective? And what steps could be envisaged to realise the potential value of these instruments as a tool for the protection of the rights of women? What would this mean for the human rights instruments and their organs?

What about ways to ensure that women's human rights are fully respected and implemented? And how to combat the continuing affront to the dignity and integrity of women? Are the human rights instruments of the Council of Europe adequately equipped? Are they efficiently apprised of such problems? What measures should be adopted to combat violence against women and trafficking in human beings for sexual exploitation? How to remove any obstacles to their implementation?

Taking stock of the current, overall state of affairs in the different member states, the colloquy focused on lessons to be learned since 1993, and forward-looking in nature, it attempts to find ways and means of resolving outstanding problems in partnership. The reader is referred to the six excellent papers of the colloquy's rapporteurs, and to Ms Hanna Suchocka's outstanding General Report.

In this volume are also the recommendations drawn up by non-governmental organisations at a forum held the day before the colloquy, the effect of which was felt in the colloquy's outcome, together with certain written contributions presented by participants.

We should like to thank all those who contributed greatly to the success of the Colloquy. Let us also extend our warm gratitude to the Chair of the Organising Committee of the Colloquy, Mr Christian Strohal, and to its members, Messrs Jean-Claude Couvreur, Vitaliano Esposito, Carsten Carlsen, Ms Heddy Astrup, Messrs Krzysztof Drzewicki, Miroslaw Łuczka, Gabriel Micu, Oleg Malguinov, Ms Meral Çelikcan, Messrs Pierre Boulay, Adama Dieng, and Martin Eaton.

Furthermore, we should like to pay our last respects to Mr Ernst Ametistov, Judge at the Constitutional Court of the Russian Federation, who was to chair a discussion group but was unable for health reasons. To our great regret, we were informed that Mr Ametistov died few days after the colloquy.

Directorate of Human Rights

Message of the colloquy

presented by Daniel Tarschys,
Secretary General of the Council of Europe

Message

adopted on the occasion of the 50th anniversary
of the Universal Declaration of Human Rights
by the participants at the colloquy

"In our hands – The effectiveness of human rights protection 50 years after the Universal Declaration" (Strasbourg, 2 September 1998)

We are here to commemorate the 50th anniversary of the Universal Declaration of Human Rights. Wanting to reaffirm our profound commitment to that Declaration, participants from the forty member states of the Council of Europe and several non-member states have adopted the following message. We ask the Secretary General of the Council of Europe to disseminate it as widely as possible:

Fifty years ago, the General Assembly of the United Nations adopted the Universal Declaration of Human Rights. Over the half-century since that visionary step, governments and individuals worldwide have achieved a great deal in promoting respect for fundamental freedoms.

Still, all of us – and each of us – could do more to safeguard human rights. And we must do more if we want to give this anniversary real meaning.

The human family cannot live together in freedom, justice and peace unless each member recognises – and more importantly, defends – the equal dignity of every other member. That is the principle that underpins the Universal Declaration of Human Rights, and it is a principle no less true today than it was on December 10th 1948, when the United Nations adopted the Declaration.

As a common standard of achievement for all peoples and all nations, the Universal Declaration was, and remains today, an indispensable and undeniable basis for the international protection of human rights. It has given birth to the human rights protection systems of the United Nations, the Council of Europe and other organisations in different regions of the world.

But it has not by any means prevented all violations.

In many parts of the world, including our own, serious breaches of human rights mean that this 50th anniversary cannot be an occasion only for celebration. We must use it to take a critical look at human rights standards, and at the ways we promote and apply them, so as to do a better job. That job will not be finished until everybody enjoys his or her rights in full.

Aware of the important responsibility that each of us bears in this respect, we take this as an opportunity to pay special attention to ways of improving human rights in Europe.

The Universal Declaration continues to be a beacon and a source of hope for people whose fundamental rights are denied – people who are persecuted, who are tortured, or who live in abject poverty for example. It stands out as an unambiguous proclamation that human rights are universal, indivisible, and interdependent, and that every government is obliged by law to prevent, or at least remedy, any violation of those rights. Every government must answer for this at the international level.

We are convinced that the Universal Declaration remains as alive and valid as the century draws to a close as it was fifty years ago. We are also convinced that the best way of building a free, just and peaceful world is for everyone to abide by the Declaration and the international and regional human rights standards adopted since 1948.

We call on everyone, governments and parliaments, intergovernmental and non-governmental organisations, national human rights institutions and individuals, to do something real to commemorate this anniversary: to release political prisoners, stop torture, strengthen human rights laws, promote ordinary citizens' understanding of what human rights are. That way we will not just be commemorating the Universal Declaration, we will be taking a step towards achieving its aims.

This concerns all of us; it is in our hands.

Message adopted by the colloquy participants, embracing governmental experts from member states of the Council of Europe as well as from several non-member states, representatives from the various human rights bodies of the Council of Europe, other international and regional organisations, national Ombudsmen and national institutions for the promotion and protection of human rights, human rights institutes, non-governmental organisations and individuals active in the human rights field.

Programme

Strasbourg, 2-4 September 1998

Opening ceremony

Opening address by Mr Daniel Tarschys, Secretary General of the Council of Europe

Statement by Ms Mary Robinson, United Nations High Commissioner for Human Rights

First session – Commemoration of the 50th anniversary of the Universal Declaration of Human Rights

Chair: Mr Daniel Tarschys, Secretary General of the Council of Europe

Personal statements on the impact and continuing relevance of the Universal Declaration of Human Rights

- Mr Miguel Angel Martínez (Spain)
- Ms Hina Jilani (Pakistan)
- Mr Jiří Dienstbier (Czech Republic)
- Mr Adama Dieng, Secretary General, International Commission of Jurists, Geneva (Switzerland)

Statement on "The Universal Declaration of Human Rights and the establishment of a European public order in the field of human rights", by the Chairmanship of the Committee of Ministers

- Mr Stelios Perrakis, Secretary General for European Affaires, Ministry of Foreign Affairs, Athens (Greece)

Reading out and adoption of the Message of the Colloquy on the occasion of the 50th anniversary of the Universal Declaration of Human Rights

- Mr Daniel Tarschys, Secretary General of the Council of Europe

Second session – Current challenges

Plenary presentation of introductory reports on Themes 1-3
Chair: Mr Pierre-Henri Imbert, Director of Human Rights of the Council of Europe

Theme 1: Prevention of and responses to structural or large-scale human rights violations
Rapporteur: Mr Vojin Dimitrijević, Professor of International Law and International Relations, University of Belgrade; Director of the Belgrade Centre for Human Rights (Federal Republic of Yugoslavia)

Theme 2: Social rights: the challenge of indivisibility and interdependence
Rapporteur: Mr Aalt-Willem Heringa, Professor of Public Law, University of Maastricht (Netherlands)

Theme 3: Effective implementation of women's rights
Rapporteur: Ms Katarina Tomaševski, Danish Centre for Human Rights, Copenhagen (Denmark)

Discussion of themes 1-3 in parallel discussion groups

Discussion Group 1: Prevention of and responses to structural or large-scale human rights violations
Chair: Mr Christian Strohal, Director of Human Rights, Ministry for Foreign Affairs, Vienna (Austria)

Written contribution presented by Mr Peter Jambrek, Judge at the European Court of Human Rights, on the topic "Individual complaints v. structural violence; reactive and proactive role of the Strasbourg Court of Law"

Discussion Group 2: Social rights: the challenge of indivisibility and interdependence
Chair: Ms Nathalie Prouvez, International Commission of Jurists, Geneva (Switzerland)

Discussion Group 3: Effective implementation of women's rights
Chair: Mrs Elena Poptodorova, First Vice-Chairman of the Committee on Equal Opportunities for Women and Men, Parliamentary Assembly of the Council of Europe, Member of the National Assembly, Sofia (Bulgaria)

Reception given by the Secretary General of the Council of Europe

Third session – Effective action to protect and promote human rights

Plenary presentation of introductory reports on Themes 4-6
Chair: Mr Pierre-Henri Imbert, Director of Human Rights of the Council of Europe

Theme 4: Protection: effective action at the national level
Rapporteur: Mr Régis de Gouttes, Avocat Général à la Cour de Cassation, Paris (France)

Theme 5: Protection: effective action at the international level
Rapporteur: Mr Jeremy McBride, Professor, Institute of European Law, University of Birmingham (United Kingdom)

Theme 6: The promotion of human rights: information, education and training
Rapporteur: Ms Kaija Gertnere, former Director of the Latvian Human Rights Office, Riga (Latvia)

Discussion of themes 4-6 in parallel discussion groups

Discussion Group 4: Protection: effective action at the national level
Chair: Mr Egbert Myjer, Deputy Procurator-General, Court of Appeal, Amsterdam

Discussion Group 5: Protection: effective action at the international level
Chair: Mr Thór Viljhálmsson, Vice-President of the European Court of Human Rights

Discussion Group 6: The promotion of human rights: information, education and training
Chair: Mr Viacheslav Bakhmin, Executive Director, Open Society Institute, Moscow

Reception offered by the Mayor of Strasbourg and the President of the Bas-Rhin Regional Council, Pavillon Joséphine (Orangerie park)

Closing session – Presentation of the reports

Plenary session: reports by the rapporteurs for Themes 1-6
Chair: Mr Pierre-Henri Imbert, Director of Human Rights of the Council of Europe

Theme 1: Prevention of and responses to structural or large-scale human rights violations
Rapporteur: Mr Vojin Dimitrijević, Professor of International Law and International Relations, University of Belgrade; Director of the Belgrade Centre for Human Rights (Federal Republic of Yugoslavia)

Theme 2: Social rights: the challenge of indivisibility and interdependence
Rapporteur: Mr Aalt-Willem Heringa, Professor of Public Law, University of Maastricht (Netherlands)

Theme 3: Effective implementation of women's rights
Rapporteur: Ms Katarina Tomaševski, Danish Centre for Human Rights, Copenhagen (Denmark)

Theme 4: Protection: effective action at the national level
Rapporteur: Mr Régis de Gouttes, Avocat Général à la Cour de Cassation, Paris (France)

Theme 5: Protection: effective action at the international level
Rapporteur: Mr Jeremy McBride, Professor, Institute of European Law, University of Birmingham (United Kingdom)

Theme 6: The promotion of human rights: information, education and training
Rapporteur: Ms Kaija Gertnere, former Director of the Latvian Human Rights Office, Riga (Latvia)

Presentation of the conclusions and recommendations of the Colloquy
General Rapporteur: Mrs Hanna Suchocka, Minister of Justice, Warsaw (Poland)

Close of the Colloquy by Mr Daniel Tarschys, Secretary General of the Council of Europe

Opening ceremony

Opening speeches

Daniel Tarschys
Secretary General of the Council of Europe

It is a great pleasure for me to welcome you all at this colloquy. It is a special source of satisfaction to note that you have come in such large numbers, from so many member and non-member states and from such a wide variety of backgrounds, to join us in this European event to commemorate the 50th anniversary of the Universal Declaration of Human Rights and to discuss some key themes relating to the protection of human rights in Europe. Mrs Robinson, we are particularly honoured and pleased to welcome you in our midst, as High Commissioner for Human Rights, but also as an old friend of the Council of Europe.

Allow me to share with you a number of thoughts on the purpose and context of this meeting.

Fifty years ago, the vision, wisdom and commitment of great men and women such as René Cassin, and Franklin Delano and Eleanor Roosevelt led to the adoption by the United Nations General Assembly of the first ever universal instrument proclaiming human rights in general. In the wake of the second world war and the horrors that humanity had suffered, this signalled the beginning of a new era in which the prevailing spirit was one of "never again". It was this very same spirit, this resolve to achieve a better, more peaceful and just world through international co-operation based on respect for fundamental principles of respect for human rights, which inspired the foundation of the Council of Europe only six months after the proclamation of the Universal Declaration.

As you know, much of our European human rights protection system was inspired by and is deeply indebted to the Universal Declaration. Already in 1950, the European Convention on Human Rights was adopted by European governments resolved "to take the first steps for the collective enforcement of certain of the rights stated in the Universal Declaration". Other such rights were added in subsequent years, in protocols to the Convention and in the European Social Charter. The Council of Europe therefore has a natural duty to make its own contribution to the worldwide commemorations taking place in this Human Rights Year. This colloquy is meant to do precisely that, and this morning's session will allow us to listen to reflections on the impact and continued relevance of the Universal Declaration, culminating in the solemn adoption of the colloquy's Message to the outside world.

But the aim of this meeting is wider than that.

Too often, human rights are no more than the object of empty talk, of solemn affirmations without substance. Official celebrations tend to be the perfect occasion for such talk; and when they are about human rights, the risk of misplaced self-satisfaction and hollow statements is even higher. Fortunately, this Human Rights Year is also marked by the five-year review of the follow-up to the Declaration and Programme of Action of the World Conference on Human Rights. We believe that, by critically taking stock of the effectiveness of human rights protection in Europe, we can make the 50th anniversary both meaningful and practical. This regional colloquy gives us all the opportunity to assess together the implementation of the World Conference texts, to evaluate progress made and the problems that remain to be solved in Europe, and to set our priorities for future action accordingly. The themes of this colloquy have been chosen so as to allow for comprehensive debates.

Where do we stand in Europe?

Over the last fifty years, we have witnessed momentous change for the better. Dictatorships have fallen and made way for democracies, first in western Europe during the 1970s. Then the countries in central and eastern Europe have shrugged off the yoke of communist oppression, and are seeking to establish democratic systems. Europe today is definitely more united around common values of freedom and the rule of law than it was fifty years ago. In the framework of the Council of Europe, we have been able to develop advanced legal systems, alongside political mechanisms, for the protection of human rights which more and more permeate and interact with national protection systems, thus providing the foundations for a cohesive protective structure for the benefit of the populations of our forty member states.

It is undeniable that much progress has been achieved. None the less, we must have the honesty to acknowledge that the solemn vow "never again" has not prevented horrors here in Europe. They occur even as we speak.

Five years ago, as we met here at a meeting which contributed to the preparations of the World Conference on Human Rights, the war in Bosnia-Herzegovina raged on, forming the setting for atrocious human rights violations. Today, we witness the deep suffering which is being inflicted on the population of Kosovo, where probably hundreds of thousands of civilians have been forced out of their homes. But also in Northern Ireland, Abkhazia, Nagorno-Karabach and Chechnya we have seen the tragic results of conflicts, in the form of immense human suffering. By any standards, it is clear that the international community has not succeeded in preventing widespread abuses of human rights here and in other continents – be they acts of the authorities or of non-state actors.

So we have some uneasy questions to ask ourselves.

Why, despite all efforts deployed by international and regional organisations since the adoption of the Universal Declaration, have we failed to protect adequately the basic rights of all human beings?

Why, despite the creation of elaborate international mechanisms for the protection of human rights, is it impossible for us to escape the conclusion that violations of such basic rights as the right to life or the right not to be subjected to torture continue to occur, also in member states of the Council of Europe?

Why is it that, also in our European societies, so many human beings – think of the poor, aliens – do not enjoy human rights to the full? Do we have sufficient tools for addressing the difficult problem of structural human rights violations?

Are we serious enough when we affirm the indivisibility of all human rights, social, economic and cultural as well as civil and political? Do we invest enough in long-term strategies to prevent human rights violations through non-legal measures such as training, education and awareness-raising?

How do we cope with pernicious phenomena such as discrimination, racism and intolerance *vis-à-vis* minorities? Why is equality between women and men still not a reality in our societies?

Our colloquy must address these questions and try to come up with some answers – but it must do more. For me, there are two key expressions in the title of this meeting.

The first is the notion of "effectiveness". Our debates should be guided by the overriding concern for "effectiveness" of our efforts to protect and promote human rights. Indeed, the questions I just posed can all be summed up as follows: why, in many cases, have our efforts been ineffective?

The second is the expression "in our hands". All of us, governments, non-governmental organisations, national institutions, international and regional organisations, must learn lessons from the past, to recognise our successes and our failures, and assume our respective responsibilities to bring the full enjoyment of human rights by everyone closer to realisation. This requires a concerted effort and co-operation by all. Governments should also realise that the work of NGOs and the role of civil society in general are indispensable.

By critically following governmental action, by raising public awareness of human rights and of human rights violations, by influencing public opinion and lobbying governments and parliaments, these non-governmental actors can act as a powerful force for change. Placed at the heart of our societies, they are well equipped to articulate and demand respect for human rights values wherever these risk being neglected or even openly violated. In a democratic state, public authorities should listen to the voices of civil society and indeed provide channels for communication and consultation, such as national human rights institutions. The national judicial system and ombudsmen have a key role to play in upholding human rights standards and protecting the rights of individuals.

At the European level, the Council of Europe has over the last forty-nine years acted as an institutional framework for co-operation between the member states and as the home of several human rights protection mechanisms which also serve as a constant reminder that human rights are not a matter of domestic affairs but one which involves duties of states to their populations for which they are accountable internationally. Co-operation and human rights supervision: both are essential characteristics of our work. They may at first sight seem difficult to reconcile, but in fact they are complementary, provided the appropriate institutional separation of powers is observed between the organs of intergovernmental co-operation and the human rights treaty mechanisms. Both ultimately contribute to reinforcing the common values of democracy, human rights and the rule of law in the European family of states and thus, at the macro-level, to democratic security in Europe and, and the micro-level, to better respect for human dignity of each member of our societies.

As was said, much has been achieved. The impact of the European Convention on Human Rights and the Strasbourg case-law on the law and practice of the States Parties is impressive and we are about to inaugurate the new permanent Court of Human Rights. The relaunch of the European Social Charter is beginning to produce its first results which should be part of a wider effort to reinforce the protection of social rights. The Committee for the Prevention of Torture has been widely acclaimed for its achievements in a relatively short period of time and the recent entry into force of the Framework Convention for the Protection of National Minorities is a promising development which will hopefully contribute, through its implementation and monitoring mechanism, to more tolerant and stable societies in which cultural diversity is cherished. In a different way, the European Commission against Racism and Intolerance makes its own contribution to that same ultimate aim.

Discussions are under way in the Committee of Ministers on the mandate of a Council of Europe Commissioner for Human Rights.

Efforts of the Parliamentary Assembly and the Committee of Ministers have resulted in a situation where capital punishment is now regarded as incompatible with human rights. Formal abolition or a moratorium is in place in all of the forty member States. 1998 is so far the first year in European history when no single execution has taken place in this area.

While much has been done and still is being done, allow me to share with you also some critical reflections on the work and the mechanisms of the Council of Europe. I think this colloquy is a good occasion to ask ourselves some frank questions about priorities.

If our core human conventions are not to erode into empty flagships, difficult but fundamental choices are indispensable. We sense already a widening gap between the demands placed on the Council of Europe in this area and the means put at its disposal. These and other questions concerning the role, working structures and priorities of the Council of Europe are being examined by a Committee of Wise Persons which will make recommendations to the Committee of Ministers. I would personally welcome it if the results of this colloquy could be taken into account also in this ongoing process of reflection.

Finally, I would like to offer you some tentative ideas on the nature and focus of future action by the Organisation in the area of human rights.

Certainly, there may still be a need for further standard-setting in this field, either to address new challenges or to fill certain lacunae in existing instruments. But I tend to agree with the view shared by most human rights experts that the main emphasis should now be placed on implementation of existing standards. There are many ways in which this Organisation could contribute to that and I will mention just a few of them.

First of all: a better follow-up in intergovernmental committees to problems identified by the human rights organs of the Council of Europe. This obviously requires courage and willingness on the part of member states also to identify and address – through dialogue and co-operation – questions that relate to individual countries. In this respect, we must stand ready and enhance our capacity to offer assistance to member states to resolve such problems, especially where they are of a structural or large-scale nature.

Secondly: the number of human rights mechanisms and monitoring bodies in place within the Council of Europe has increased considerably in recent years and it would seem advisable to find ways of improving possibilities for coherence and the gradual development of a truly comprehensive "system" of human rights protection. This will favour a better implementation and avoid situations where a multitude of disparate demands are being placed on member states under different conventions. Furthermore, it is a practical expression of the indivisibility of human rights also for the individual, who, after all, cares very little whether his rights are guaranteed in this or the other convention, as long as they are respected and effectively protected.

Thirdly: further improve the interaction and dialogue between national structures (courts, ombudsmen, national human rights institutions, NGOs) and the various human rights institutions of the Council of Europe. This will help construct the "cohesive protective structure" which I referred to before.

Fourthly: the implementation of judgments of the European Court of Human Rights deserves more attention so as to ensure that the full consequences of these judgments are drawn.

Finally, we should not make the mistake of regarding human rights as the exclusive domain of lawyers, policy-makers and legal mechanisms. Our experience in assisting democratisation in central and eastern European countries has once more confirmed that human rights education and awareness are essential tools for changing mentalities and for promoting a democratic human rights culture in society. Here, concrete strategies must be implemented and much work remains to be done, also by the Council of Europe, first and foremost in co-operation with civil society.

I have spoken at some length about the Council of Europe and some of the challenges it faces in the human rights field. Naturally, this is close to my heart and my daily preoccupations, and I certainly hope that during this colloquy you will take a critical look at our own performance and come up with suggestions for improvements. However, I must stress that, as is borne out by the title of this colloquy, debates over the next three days should address the role and responsibilities of all categories of participants, governmental and non-governmental, national and international.

Fifty years ago, we said "Never again". Perhaps today, fifty years on, we must add a second motto to guide our efforts to reach a full realisation of human rights: "Never enough". We never do enough in the area of human rights protection and promotion. There will always be individuals and governments seeking to deny or destroy the fundamental rights of an individual. In many other cases, their action may have the unintentional effect of interfering with those rights. Therefore, constant vigilance is called for, but also a concerted effort to take effective measures, both at the national level and in the framework of organisations like the Council of Europe. I believe that, over the next three days, we have an excellent opportunity to rethink the effectiveness of our efforts so far and to come up with imaginative and constructive proposals for ensuring that we do better in the future.

I declare open this colloquy with the wish that your debates be guided by honest dialogue, constructive criticism and, last but not least, by a productive mixture of both realism and imagination.

Mary Robinson

United Nations High Commissioner
for Human Rights

A few years ago, I served – for my sins – as General Rapporteur of the Interregional preparatory meeting hosted by the Council of Europe for the World Conference on Human Rights. At the time, I noted the support for creating the Office of the United Nations High Commissioner for Human Rights, but had no inkling that a few years later I would fill this position and embark on one of the most challenging experiences of my life. At that time I urged that the greatest challenge – the greatest failure – was to address gross violations of human rights. It is a theme I shall revisit today.

We are gathered to mark the fifty years that have elapsed since the adoption of the Universal Declaration of Human Rights and to envisage possible future action. We must not forget that 1998 also marks the stock-taking review of the Vienna Declaration and Programme of Action. These inter-related events present us with the opportunity to reflect on the international efforts to promote and protect human rights. But more important, these events challenge us, whether in the United Nations, in regional organisations such as the Council of Europe, in governments or non-governmental entities, to recommit ourselves to the work still to be done to ensure that human rights truly become a reality in the lives of people everywhere.

The Universal Declaration of Human Rights has the great merit of being the first worldwide legal instrument to gather together a set of principles embodying the fundamental rights and freedoms of the human being, recognised by the international community and based on the dignity and equality of the human race. Written in the present tense, the Declaration has continually given its message new life. Indeed, the European Convention itself was envisaged as a way to translate the Declaration into a binding instrument at the European level. It has extended its reach to all parts of the world and has served as a model for domestic constitutions and laws, regulations and policies, and practices of governance that protect human rights. Its provisions have supplied countless reference points for national courts, parliaments, governments, lawyers and non-governmental organisations, proof that the Universal Declaration speaks to our diverse world. Many of the provisions of the Declaration have become part of customary international law, which is binding on all states whether or not they are signatories to one or more multilateral conventions concerning human rights. Thus what started its existence as a solemn but non-binding proclamation of rights and freedoms has, at least in some respects, acquired through state practice the status of universal law.

We now see with greater clarity that the rights enshrined in the Universal Declaration as the birthright of each human being are also the unifying principles which should inform every strategic action of the United Nations – from sustainable development to peace and security, from humanitarian assistance to democracy and peace.

These tasks were greatly facilitated by the development of a close-knit network of international intergovernmental organisations, especially the United Nations, but also its specialised agencies and regional international organisations, which offered the international community a new institutional framework for the development of co-operation among states. But what is new is that the framework provided by the international organisations brings together not just states as the main subjects in this legal order, but also other leading actors in international society which have proved very effective when it comes to codifying the international rules necessary for the recognition and subsequent application of human rights in international law.

The 50th anniversary motto – "all human rights for all" expresses the challenge which we face as we approach a new century. Though the Declaration today is our common proclamation of human rights, it has not yet become our common call to action. We must draw on the inspiration of the individuals who joined together to produce one of the great documents of our human history. To reach its goals, we must work together to advance equally all the rights the Universal Declaration declares.

We have to acknowledge, sadly, that the commemoration of the 50th Anniversary of the Universal Declaration of Human Rights is not a cause for celebration. We must see in the prevalence of conflicts and widespread human rights violations in the world today and the ensuing enormous human suffering which they cause, a measure of our past failures. Graça Machel, the Secretary-General's expert on the impact of armed conflict on children, reported in 1996 that more than two million children had been killed in conflicts in the previous decade – the overwhelming majority of these in internal conflicts. She alluded to the "desolate moral vacuum" created by modern conflict, a "space devoid of the most basic human values".

The abuses prevalent in modern conflicts are appalling; and they are not just distant problems, but tragic realities also for European peoples, most recently in Kosovo. They encompass widespread assaults on the right to life – massacres, direct and indiscriminate attacks on civilians, killing of prisoners, starvation. Torture is common, as are measures attacking people's freedom of movement – forcible relocations, mass expulsions, denial of the right to seek asylum or the right to return to one's home. Women and girls are raped by soldiers and are abducted into forced prostitution, and children are recruited to be soldiers. Tens of thousands of people detained in connection with conflicts "disappear", usually killed and buried in secret, leaving their families with the torment of not knowing their fate. Thousands of others are arbitrarily detained, never brought to trial or, if they are, subject to grossly unfair procedures. Civilian homes and property, schools, health centres and crops are deliberately destroyed. Those who try to assist civilians by providing humanitarian aid are attacked. Insofar as such abuses are occurring in Europe they interrogate Europe's integrity and commitment to the values of the Council of Europe.

In an age of global communication, and media coverage, these abuses are known to us all. Even if some conflicts are neglected by our media, we cannot plead ignorance. A few minutes searching on the Internet brings to light detailed information on such abuses in any serious conflicts in the world today. The problem is not lack of information, but a lack of appropriate action. In an era when threats to human security are coming from new and more diverse forms of conflicts, the challenge of conflict prevention goes to the very heart of the shared mission of the United Nations and regional organisations such as the Council of Europe. To meet this challenge, there is a critical need to develop a culture of prevention. Conflict prevention should focus not only on tense ethnic or political disputes, but also on chronic underdevelopment, grinding poverty, mass unemployment, widespread illiteracy and systematic inequalities of income or opportunities.

We must insist on respect for civil and political rights and the building of democratic societies – so that grievances and disputes can be resolved peacefully, so that a free press and an active civil society can be a check on the corrupt or unlawful exercise of state power, and so that the state's judicial system operates fairly and police or security personnel who abuse their power are brought to justice. But equally, we must insist that due attention be given to economic, social and cultural rights, that adequate health care, education, and housing are seen not as the privileges of a few, but fundamental needs that must be addressed effectively if justice and stability are to be attained. Mass illiteracy and poverty are human rights issues no less than freedom of expression, and the wilful disregard of the former is as likely to sow the seeds of conflict as the denial of the latter.

The drafters of the Universal Declaration perceived the close connection between violations of human rights and national and international peace. Unfortunately, over the past fifty years we have often lost sight of this connection. This is even more tragic when we consider that acting on recognition of this inherent connection could have been pivotal in preventing massive violations of human rights which in recent years we have witnessed here on the continent of Europe, as elsewhere, and against which we pledged "never again". Early warning and preventive action, aimed at deterring such human rights violations and defusing situations which may lead to humanitarian disasters, is invaluable. The necessary efforts – comprehensive and sustained – on the part of the United Nations and other inter-governmental actors must not only be carefully planned, they must also be mutually re-enforcing. This implies the need for a common framework for our action.

I was pleased to participate, with Daniel Tarschys, Secretary General of the Council of Europe, in the third conference between the United Nations and regional organisations in New York this July under the chairmanship of the United Nations Secretary General on "Co-operation for conflict prevention". The meeting examined the potential for greater interaction and co-operation between the United Nations and regional organisations in the field of conflict prevention. Participants reviewed how the United Nations and regional organisations were responding to this challenge, and identified areas of possible future interaction and collaboration. This implies, on the one hand, looking at "structural prevention" – namely, the need to address the economic, social, ethnic and other root causes of conflict, and to promote greater respect for human rights, maintenance of the rule of law and strengthening of democratic institutions. It means, as well, looking at "operational prevention", which encompasses the traditional forms of conflict prevention and "early warning". It was noted that prevention is a continuum that ranges from early warning, through preventive diplomacy, preventive disarmament (particularly of small arms), preventive deployment, and on to peace-building, both before and after conflicts.

The focus should be on how the United Nations and regional organisations, with their strengths and capabilities in the area of conflict prevention, can work together to achieve greater complementarity as mutually reinforcing institutions, making use of their comparative advantages. It is also essential to understand that a key to conflict prevention lies with member states and their support for early external involvement to defuse disputes and crises.

Beyond rhetoric, we must now develop specific modalities for more effective co-operation in the field of conflict prevention that are both practical and implementable. While recognising that no single model of co-operation between the United Nations and regional organisations will cover all eventualities, possible approaches envisage measures for more regular consultation at the working level, including in the context of early warning; more systematic co-ordination of preventive activities in the field, including joint assessment missions, as appropriate; the development of common indicators for early warning and benchmarks for economic, social and cultural rights; better flows of information; exchange of liaison officers; visits and joint training of staff; building specific links to civil society (including the media and professional groups) to increase awareness of the value of prevention; and similar measures to be determined on a case-by-case basis.

As High Commissioner for Human Rights, and recognising the catalytic role of my office, I am particularly keen to strengthen the linkages with regional organisations. I intend to take this opportunity to further develop joint action and common commitments between my office and the various departments within the Council of Europe. The relevant activities of both organisations should be complementary. Among the issues we can address within this common framework are violence against women, advisory services, racism and intolerance, human rights education and awareness, and national human rights institutions.

In the months ahead we should recommit ourselves to reaching all people with the message of the Universal Declaration: the message that human rights belong to every individual, the message that all human rights, be they civil, cultural, economic, political or social must be equally protected if any is to be ensured. The message that together we all must take responsibility for human rights.

The Universal Declaration of Human Rights, the covenants and the conventions on human rights which have been adopted by the United Nations and regional organisations, in particular the Council of Europe, over the past half-century are clear evidence of what can be accomplished when the international community works together for a common purpose. They are both the inspiration and the challenge to us as we face into the next half-century.

First Session: Commemoration of the 50th anniversary of the Universal Declaration of Human Rights

Personal statements on the impact and continuing relevance of the Universal Declaration of Human Rights

Miguel Ángel Martínez

I. Introduction

I should first like to congratulate the Council of Europe, and congratulate all of us, in fact, for the excellent initiative of this colloquy. I should also like straight away to express my gratitude for my invitation to attend and for the opportunity this gives me to address you.

My necessarily brief contribution will comprise a number of thoughts which derive from my personal experience. It will give the views of someone of what is called the age of reason, which is practically the same age as that of the Universal Declaration of Human Rights. Someone who has spent much of his life actively fighting for freedom, dignity and justice, in other words fighting for human rights.

II. Time to take stock

The 50th anniversary of the Universal Declaration of Human Rights is an appropriate time for many initiatives, and in particular, doubtless, for ratifying all our commitments in this field. But it is also, perhaps more than anything else, an almost compulsory opportunity to take stock so as to make a strict appraisal of the point we have reached where respect for human rights in the contemporary world is concerned. For me personally, knowing what we have achieved seems vital, specifically so that we can reaffirm where we wish to go. But if we are to be fully aware of the point we have reached, we also need to look back to where we have come from. In other words, we need to know what path we have been following over the past fifty years.

Well, it is precisely at this time that I shall allow myself to state unreservedly that never before has there been great, such far-reaching, such real and such generalised respect for human rights and effective enjoyment of those rights. I should like to add, as well, that never have the prospects of possible improvements to the situation been so favourable as they are now.

I must immediately admit that, as I make these two affirmations, my friends and my activist companions, in particular, are surprised and even, to some extent, scandalised. Sometimes they think that I am quite simply wrong, and that what I say does not correspond to reality. They often tell me that what I am saying is inappropriately expressed, and even immorally inappropriate, and that it in any case is harmful to "our cause". Of course, I reply to all of this that my affirmations seem easy to verify. Perhaps I am still rather too ingenuous, but I continue to believe that the truth is never inappropriate and certainly not immorally inappropriate.

III. The theory of the half-full, half-empty glass

It seems undeniable to me that in an ever increasing number of cases (although sadly, not yet in all cases) we see before us glasses which some people would describe as half-full while others would say that they are half-empty. Rather than getting embroiled in this debate – although I shall come back to it briefly – I prefer to emphasise that these two visions of one and the same reality do coincide: for one thing, there is some water in the glass, in many glasses, in an increasing number of glasses. For another, there is a lot of space to be filled, a statement which applies to all the glasses concerned, to a greater or a lesser extent.

On this point, I am forced to remind others, who are less optimistic or less positive than I am, of an inevitable truth, namely that we are very numerous, and in fact we are in a majority, unable to put the question whether the glass is half-empty or half-full. And this quite simply because a large number of us have known, have suffered, this glass of respect for human rights in a completely empty state ... very many of us have experienced what it meant gradually to fill it up to its present level. The price of this was much effort and many sacrifices.

Thus my initial affirmation has never been interpreted as an expression of triumphalism or self-satisfaction, and must certainly not be taken to imply that our work is finished. On the contrary, it should constitute a serious statement of the reality, and we must also be aware that, where human rights are concerned, and where the general fight for freedom or for democracy is concerned, there have never been any miracles, no random events and no gifts; there have been only hard-won conquests, won through much conviction, constancy, courage and commitment.

The fact that relative progress has been made, a fact which I invite you to share with me, will be particularly valued insofar as we are able to draw from it self-confidence and the necessary impetus to continue to march forward. In other words, to continue to fill the glass, or the glasses, before us, meeting a never-ending challenge.

IV. Constant progress

I should nevertheless like to put to you some specific arguments on which I base my opinion that the story of human rights over these fifty years has been a story of progress. I would even dare to say that is the history of the progress of humankind, or the most contemporary chapter of this history, the background, as ever, being the Universal Declaration. In each of the eight points I am going to draw to your attention to identify all the progress we have made, I feel that there are strands that can be taken further in order to develop our present and future activity.

1. The number of countries, territories and of millions of women and men effectively in geopolitical contexts where respect for human rights, as described in the Universal Declaration, is operating reasonably, has grown constantly over the past fifty years. Whatever reference criteria are applied, this number, just of states, has tripled at least over this period.

   Of course this must not blind us – quite the contrary – to the fact that too many countries remain, too many territories and too many millions of women and men who are still far from being covered by the standards due to them in this essential aspect of their life. It is up to us to inform them, to motivate them and to support them.

2. Another great innovation as compared to the relatively recent past, in terms of the progress recorded, seems to be the fact that, precisely in the countries and territories – or rather, in most of them – the respect for human rights is not yet the custom, social awareness and the resulting mobilisation with a view to finally achieving this respect have become a constant. The women and men of these states realise that they are entitled to respect for their human rights and are less and less welling to accept that they do not enjoy it.

   Of course this must not conceal the fact that there are still many large population groups here and there who have not reached this level of awareness, or whose attitude is of a certain resignation; they, for one reason or another, do not attach priority to claiming their human rights.

3. One of the areas in which the most progress has been made, in my opinion, is that of the very concept of human rights, which has been constantly updated, enlarged and fleshed out. This applies first and foremost to the most pioneering countries in this field. The initially fairly limited definition has been enlarged to cover economic and social rights, cultural rights, the specific rights of children, women and migrants, the rights of national minorities and so on, in the wide-ranging catalogue of human rights. Such important elements as equality and education have made progress in some places, helping to highlight and to broaden citizens' effective access to the benefits of human rights.

   This is another field in which one should never feel satisfied and take the view that the target has been reached. The progress recorded in certain countries, furthermore, should rub of on others as rapidly as possible and move into neighbouring areas. International, regional or other bodies should play a vital part in this action.

4. So now I come to the fourth glass, one which has seen its contents considerably increased during the period under review, and this is the glass of the machinery set up to ensure that human rights are protected, at national or international level. I shall not go into detail, but the very history of the Council of Europe, which is on the verge of celebrating its own golden jubilee, is a better illustration that of any

other example of this effort. It is a history crowned with success, in moving forward and in perfecting the formulae, text and systems which will ensure that human rights are effectively and efficiently restored to the people they were designed to protect.

Yet this is another area where a huge amount remains to be done, remains for us to do.

5. A relatively new element, and one which seems extremely important in terms of progress in comparison to the previous situation, is the fact that human rights have successfully entered into international law, both in practice and in theory. This is only a recent phenomenon, a fact that should not be forgotten. National sovereignty can no longer be relied on by states telling others that they should not interfere. On the contrary, doctrine is becoming ever more precise: not only is there a right to interfere in such "affairs" but there is a duty.

   It is nonetheless true that some states still remain on the fringes of the international community and constitute anachronisms in this respect. It will be our responsibility not only to bring them back to the centre of the community, but also to devise, discuss and set up systems which are capable of bringing into practice the progress which is necessary for this doctrine to be consolidated.

6. Another weighty argument, bringing grist to the mill of the progress recorded in respect of the protection of human rights, is precisely the setting up of the Office of the United Nations High Commissioner for Human Rights and the start of its activities, and the increasing influence of this institution. The appointment to head it of a figure like Mrs Mary Robinson can but considerably increase the role and the credibility of the Commission.

   It will also be necessary for society, and more particularly its institutions – I am thinking particularly of parliament – to give vigorous, non-politically based support to the action of both the Commission and the High Commissioner.

7. I should not like to leave this area of my argument without saying something about the international court to deal with crimes against humanity, the setting up of which has just been proposed at the Rome conference. Although the role which this court will have to play will be rather broader, I consider that it will comprise another instrument which will make a contribution to respect for human rights, also helping to bring to justice people who have perpetrated indescribable violations of those rights. The setting up of this court, a court for which we have been campaigning for decades at the Inter-Parliamentary Union, is another non-negligible step forward in the field under consideration.

   Yet we are well aware that the task before us in this field remains huge. It can, however, be summed up in few words: to ensure that the court exists and actually operates. In other words, first and foremost, states which believe they can have the rule of law while at the same time placing themselves on the fringes of international law must be brought before it. We must accept and obtain acceptance everywhere for a court where everyone will be able to have a say, but where nobody will have personal control ... these are very large challenges, indeed.

8. The last full glass that I wished to describe to you is that of progress which I have recorded in terms of the growing recognition of the universal nature – of the universality, in short – of human rights. It seems to me that this universal nature is less and less disputed to different levels. For one thing it is becoming clear that human rights cannot allow reservations, exceptions or modulations in the light of so-called cultural, geographical or other traditions or characteristics. Furthermore, it is becoming clear that in an increasingly globalised society, human rights affect all of us, together. There may be an acceptable respect for human rights in one place, while in another – right next door – such rights are flouted.

   I say this is clear, and it is for many, for all of us. But it will be less so for others. This is another challenge facing us, and we must understand that the universality of human rights also requires universal participation, as we draw up definitions and bring matters up to date. There must also be checks of what works and what does not in this field.

V. Conclusion

1. Nowadays, the impression might well sometimes be given that human rights are being systematically violated more or less everywhere, and perhaps even more than they ever were in the past. This impression derives from the media-based nature of our society, with violations of this kind being highlighted on a daily basis, with emphasis frequently being laid on the most abhorrent aspects, coverage also being systematic – although capriciously selected, with much being made of one thing, while others are overlooked or even hidden, in the light of interests which are far less clear than the much-wanted transparency.

   In fact, I maintain that even the worst of these violations, with all the others, are nothing new. Sadly, they already existed in the past, but quite simply less was said about them and people were less expected to know about them. I believe personally that this spotlighting of shortcomings, inadequacies and, above all, flagrant violations in the human rights sphere should be turned into something positive in order to offer more opposition to them and combat them, but, of course, this should be done without regarding such matters as disasters, and even less with a feeling of resigned fatalism in this area.

   The fact which is indisputable is that, where human rights are concerned, a huge amount remains to be done, by which I mean that the concept itself needs to be more closely defined and broadened, so that the benefit of human rights can be extended to all population groups, so that every single person effectively enjoys their human rights. In this field, more than in any other, the Olympic motto seems to me to be fully appropriate: "faster, higher, stronger". Nor should it be forgotten that the effort must be constant in the human rights sphere, as in cycling, for if cyclists stop pedalling, they fall off.

   It is clear that we face challenges which need a new awareness and increasing mobilisation by our societies, by which I mean on the part of associations and, in particular, of institutions.

In this respect, parliaments must shoulder a huge responsibility, so that they may be seen by citizens to have a role as effective and efficient guardians of respect for human rights. It is up to parliaments to do everything possible to raise people's awareness, to adopt relevant legislation, to ratify the corresponding international legal instruments and to promote solid international co-operation, all with a view to the constant strengthening of human rights everywhere. The Inter-Parliamentary Union, of which I chair the Council, is carrying out increasingly vigorous action in this field, and I invite you to read the document which reflects the main aspects of this activity. In this context, I should also like to tell you that the progress to which I referred not long ago is quite clearly apparent within the IPU. Where, a few years ago, talking about human rights immediately led to numerous reservations and was regarded by some people as a provocation, this is now out of the question; with the exception of a few states, which are increasingly isolated examples, there is now no doubt that the states of the world now have on their parliaments' agendas human rights as a priority responsibility, one which cannot be rejected and has therefore been taken on.

2. I told you right at the outset that my contribution would be a personal statement, that of a Spanish citizen, that of someone who has had to fight for human rights in his own country. The paradox was that Spain was part of the so-called "free world", while people of my generation were sent to prison precisely because they wished to enjoy those human rights which are supposed to be characteristic of the rule of law. Well my experience, I can tell you, is that of a Spaniard who has seen how this battle could be won in his society.

   My statement is also that of a European who has fought hard to ensure that the values of freedom and democracy, and particularly the human rights standards which we wanted for our Europe, should not remain confined in one part of the continent, but should stretch out to all Europeans, particularly those in the centre and east of our shared Europe. In this context, too, it was my privilege to head the Parliamentary Assembly of the Council of Europe, which received, not so much fifteen or so states, but, much more importantly, over two hundred million fellow citizens, men and women who were becoming Europeans for good, precisely at the time when they were all becoming covered by the European Convention on Human Rights.

   However, my statement is necessarily also one of a citizen of the world – that of a Spaniard and of a European who is a citizen of the world – and, as such, I am aware that, particularly where human rights are concerned, there is no barrier at the borders of either Spain or Europe. I realise that my Spain and my Europe bear a heavy burden of responsibility to show solidarity with the rest of the world, particularly with what is sometimes referred to as the South. This solidarity is of course a philosophical one, but it is also a physical and mechanical one. It is one which presupposes a full understanding that, as globalisation continues, fighting for the human rights of people elsewhere and everywhere is tantamount to fighting for our own human rights in our own homeland.

   This is the point we have reached. More particularly, this is the point I have reached in my responsibilities as President of the Inter-Parliamentary Union: we know that we are all fighting one and the same battle. Thanks to institutions such as the United Nations High Commissioner for Refugees and the Council of Europe, and particularly to personalities and friends like Mary Robinson and like all of you, we shall continue to find the conviction, tenacity, imagination and strength which are necessary, and victory will be ours. We shall overcome.

Hina Jilani

Defence of human rights: the Asian perspective

As we commemorate the fiftieth year of the Universal Declaration of Human Rights, we are fully conscious that extreme forms of violation of the principles expressed therein present the world today with some of the most complex social, political and economic problems. The pace at which consensus evolved to lay down standards for conduct of both the state and society has been overcome by the rapid sequence of events all over the world that have generated conditions causing more grievous violations of human rights than were witnessed during the war which preceded the declaration. The victims of those atrocities are very often the perpetrators of today's violations. Human rights today are hostage to territorial disputes, ideologies based on religious or economic doctrines, and conflicting security interests.

It is because of this adverse environment that emphasis on the universality of human rights has become essential for the protection and promotion of human rights. These values emanate from human experience limited neither to one part of the world nor to a single culture or society. No arguments about regional diversity, cultural specificity and religious differences can be successful in the erosion of the concept of universality. It is not that the concept has not been challenged. Arguments against the concept of universality have sprung from attempts to justify human rights violations by authoritarian regimes, or by non-state forces to legitimise action contrary to human rights norms taken in the name of religion, nationalism or ethnic identity.

As a human rights defender, the most serious challenge to my work has come from attempts at either undermining human rights values or their outright rejection. While declaration of these rights in international instruments have supported the work of defenders, it has been belief in the core values of human rights, independent of their expression in any instrument, that has maintained their legitimacy not only in the social and political debate in the region, but also as the measure for state conduct. Yet this legitimacy remains under attack – which has made it necessary on the one hand to expose the motivation behind these attacks, and on the other to help people to understand that the values proclaimed as "western ideas" are no different from their own aspirations for political, social and economic progress.

Pakistan had signed the Universal Declaration as an independent sovereign state. The prompt support for the principles of this declaration were illustrative of the aspirations of a people who had struggled hard and long to attain the very freedoms that the declaration promised. Who could better recognise the values of human dignity, of freedom from tyranny and oppression, and from want and fear than a population who had experienced a century of colonisation. There is, therefore, nothing more hollow sounding than the argument that the values of human rights are west-oriented, and alien to the culture of people in our part of the world.

The declaration of these principles may have been prompted by events happening in the west. Nevertheless, in the south, people's struggle for the attainment of these ideals preceded their declaration by the international community. The social and political movements in the subcontinent of India bear witness to this reality. There is no contradiction between what are generally proclaimed as "Asian values", or "Islamic human rights", and the universal standards of human rights proclaimed in the Declaration which find further elucidation in subsequent human rights instruments. I would, therefore, insist that the contribution of people's struggles all over the world to the evolution of the international standards be duly recognised. This lacuna of history has to be corrected for the concept of universality to have real meaning.

Human rights activism includes demonstration of the relevance of international human rights to the indigenous movements for rights. Many Asian leaders have challenged the relevance of international human rights to the lives of Asian peoples. Ang San Su Ki is the only such leader who has categorically linked the principles enshrined in the Universal Declaration to the ancient Buddhist traditions. While such statements are important at the political level, it is equally important to use these standards in the legal discourse both in the judicial system, and at the academic level. It is by no means an easy task to achieve where human rights are deliberately de-recognised as a matter of state policy and where violation of rights receives the sanction of the law. Religion, culture and traditional or customary practices have become a political tool for the furtherance of the interests of an élite, which retains a dominance over political power and economic resources. Denial of democratic rights, laws permitting the violation of human rights and autocratic imposition of state authority is given the veneer of legality by the mere act of legislation.

In countries like mine this has affected people's perception of the law, which is seen more as an instrument of control and oppression than that of relief and redress. Consequently, respect for the rule of law has become meaningless in the context of human rights. Assertion of a collective identity in the name of religion or ethnicity has often meant jealous guarding of practices that discriminate against and marginalise disadvantaged sectors of the society. For these sectors the argument for universality is not merely a desirable concept. It has become a practical tool for the attainment of social justice. The denial of women's rights is a case in point.

Islamisation of laws in Pakistan has not only meant an erosion of women's status as equal citizens, but has reduced their human status as well. Legal sanctions to discrimination and bias against women have promoted violence and the undermining of their dignity socially and by the agencies of the state. Constitutional guarantees for protection of fundamental rights are applied to women conditional upon their conformity to social norms which prescribe subservience of women, and which reject their claims to any kind of autonomy. Women's rights to life, liberty and security of person, to the freedom of movement and of expression are systematically denied.

While the legislature panders to the pressure of religious fundamentalists, the judiciary has failed to protect women's human rights. While some judges feel overwhelmed by the militancy of the fundamentalists, and therefore have hesitated to give relief to women, others have openly supported orthodox views which have resulted in reversing any gains that women were able to achieve in the sphere of law. Arguments for liberal or progressive interpretations of religion to afford women any advantage have been unsuccessful, as it is not a religious issue, but one of politics and power. It is in these circumstances that the women's movement in Pakistan has adopted the international standards of human rights as the core values and the standard against which laws must be tested.

States with authoritarian regimes and weak democracies have been the breeding-grounds for fundamentalism and religious militancy. Human rights in such states are violated both by the state and non-state forces who use violence and the tactics of fear to command conformity. History shows that political use of religion has resulted in gross violations of human rights. In Pakistan state policies have allowed fundamentalists to create an atmosphere of intolerance resulting in communal and sectarian violence and in threats to the rights of women and minorities. International politics and the western agenda of the cold war have played a significant role in strengthening the militant Islamic factions in this region. Activities of these militant factions have violated and remain a threat to the security rights of people in this region more than any where else. This threat is not only at the individual level; the whole region has been destabilised by conflict and war.

We therefore fully understand and comprehend the urgency to deal with this phenomenon. Nevertheless the response to fundamentalism has to be political and not military might. Use of terrorist tactics to combat terrorism can never be an acceptable response. Use of such tactics has made even more difficult the work of human rights defenders in the forefront of the struggle against religious fundamentalism and militancy. We cannot afford to give them martyrs. In an unstable environment, with increasing frustration owing to poverty, social injustice and economic inequities, religious extremists find the ideal opportunity for exploiting issues to their advantage and arousing religious passions among the more vulnerable sections of society, especially young people. It gives them yet another opportunity to promote the misconception that they are protecting the values of Islam against invasion by the west, and conceal the reality that their own agenda is the biggest threat to the values of Islam and humanity. It must be understood that terrorism is criminal. It can have no sanction in religion, nor can criminal acts be associated with any one religion. It is imperative that responses to such acts be sensitive, well informed and mature.

The international community must now concentrate on the practical implementation of human rights. We must identify the factors that have become hindrances in the way of the protection and promotion of human rights. International political and economic policies have to be evaluated to assess whether they have been conducive to support for human rights values. In our region we know that the growing political and economic insecurity has raised the potential for human rights violations. The most basic illustration of the interdependence and indivisibility of human rights is the effect of political conditions on economic rights, and the impact of extreme material deprivation on political stability and guarantees for civil and political rights. International policies must, therefore, conform to a standard that not only protects national interests but also does not adversely affect political and economic stability elsewhere.

Verbal support for democracy must be demonstrated in the action of the international community. National and international political economy is now profoundly determined by globalisation. Most countries of the south are experiencing economic crises, worsened by the ever-increasing debt burden. Social sector spending is the first to suffer cuts in this scenario, further diminishing the prospects for economic rights. With policies being dictated by the international financial institutions, people feel shut out of policy-making. The state has surrendered its autonomy to frame economic and social policies to these institutions, and has thereby rendered itself incapable of responding to public demands. Democracy cannot be fostered in these conditions. The limits to globalisation must be determined to ensure the preservation of the capability of decision-making at the local and national level.

Democratic values must be the basis of relations between states. Foreign policy of states must become sensitive to the human rights of people everywhere. National economic or security interests cannot be promoted at the cost of human rights. No one's way of life can be preserved at the cost of others. Use of the Universal Declaration for promoting sensitivity of particularly the politically and economically stronger states in this respect , would be the best form of commemoration of the fiftieth year of the Declaration. Let those committed to the cause of human rights confront global trends that threaten peace, democracy and human rights with unity and solidarity, and fully conscious of the necessity for attitudinal changes if we are to achieve a better record of success in the promotion and protection of human rights.

Jiří Dienstbier

We all know that the Universal Declaration of Human Rights is fifty years old. What we do not always apprehend is the fact that, in the run of human history, fifty years means yesterday.

The very content, level and understanding of human rights is changing with time and development of human civilisation. From this perspective – as well as from many other perspectives – different countries and regions live in a different historical age. And we, in Europe, are happy to be ahead, as the European Convention on Human Rights confirms. But it is also brings the greatest responsibility.

The basic problem of the present world is the growing gap between the situation of people who have some chance of life in dignity and those who live in despair. Only a small percentage of people in despair can change their address by emigration. The majority, mainly young people, may become an easy target of manipulation by the dictators and extremists. Nairobi and Dar-es-Salaam bear witness to it once more.

In these circumstances, social demand brings a supply of demagogues who try to lead the people in despair against the world that they designate as being the cause of their sufferings. The new division would be much more dangerous than the previous bi-polar one. In the old Cold War both sides had a lot to lose, so they monitored not only the other side but themselves too. In the new multi-polar division, existing not only between the countries but inside all societies too, one side would have nothing to lose and, at the same time, it may have at its disposal weapons of mass destruction – like, for instance, in the Tokyo subway. It seems more and more that the new wars would not be the wars between states, not even wars between cultures or civilisations, but wars between groups of terrorists within civil society against culture and civilisation itself. The message is clear: the problems must be solved on the spot, wherever they emerge. People were willing to pay taxes for military growth, rockets with nuclear weapons and possible "star wars". Overcoming the growing human rights gap deserves the same approach internationally and inside our societies. It is a humanitarian question, no doubt. But it is the first of all the strategic security question for all of us. We may even say that the basic strategic question of today is the promotion of human rights in its broadest sense everywhere.

Some autocratic rulers in the world complain that individual human rights are a Western idea, and they refuse them as being a tool of a new form of colonialism. We have no time to discuss these arguments in detail here. So, very briefly: we should accept different cultures in an increasingly multicultural world, but we should not accept these arguments. All people want to live, not to be tortured, and they wish to have a chance of influencing the conditions of their lives. Japan, India or Hong Kong proved that democracy is compatible with their culture. Young Iranian men and women show their discontent towards those who wish to suppress their freedom of choice by imposing their fundamentalist principles. Ultimately, Tienanmen proved that the wall of democracy does not separate cultures, but separates the people from the undemocratic rulers and manipulators of all kinds inside all cultures.

Developments in the states of the former Yugoslavia, the Balkans and Russia, bomb attacks in the Paris Metro, on the Uffici gallery in Florence or in Northern Ireland confirm to us every day that, we, in Europe, should not take it for granted that our "safety belt" of democracy, relative prosperity and respect for human rights is guaranteed. To secure them, we need a lot of instruments and political courage. The Universal Declaration and the pacts on human rights are among those instruments These are not just some documents of moral value; they serve as a practical political tool in our fight for democracy. In 1975 the communist states had to accept in Helsinki the idea that observance of the pacts is no longer an internal affair on the States but one of the preconditions for peace in Europe. We used this window of opportunity. We formed Charter 77, the Committee for the Defence of Workers came into existence in Poland, as well as Helsinki groups in the Soviet Union and other communist countries. Even if we were persecuted, it gave us some legal basis and international standing: the record of violations was discussed at the follow-up conferences of the CSCE. There were 250 original signatories of Charter 77. In November 1989 there were millions of people in the streets. So the declaration and the pacts are valuable instruments not only for the promotion of human rights but for the transition to democracy as well.

As the Special Rapporteur of the United Nations Commission on Human Rights for Yugoslavia, Croatia and Bosnia and Herzegovina, I try to explain to my interlocutors in the region that the implementation of human rights requires permanent attention on the part of both national and international governmental institutions, media, NGOs and the people themselves. It is especially important in the global village where no problem is local anymore.

Criticism should not be seen by governments as an inconvenience, but as a support on the road to democracy. This should be especially understood in the countries in transition from communism to democracy, who have no democratic traditions, where there is a heritage of recent war and hatred, but whose ambition is to join gradually the European mainstream, to be members of the Council of Europe and to become members of the European Union.

Having come myself from a formerly communist state, I am aware of the difficulties in the transition to an open society. Many of the problems afflicting the countries of my mandate are due to the failure to respect the human rights associated with democratic principles.

On the practical level, the basic problem is the return of hundreds of thousands of people belonging to ethnic groups, which are, or have become, minorities in their places of origin. Lack of security and of available housing, lack of respect for property rights, occupation of houses and apartments by refugees from other parts of the region, burning of houses of other ethnic groups, inaction on the part of the administrations, open opposition that prevents the solutions, all this prevents returns. The destruction of the economy and the resulting lack of employment – up to 80% in certain regions – prevents even majority returns. Special problem are created by a failure to respect the religion of the others: for example, the Banja Luka authorities keep refusing the rebuilding of the historical Ferhadija mosque. In July, a large Orthodox cross was destroyed by an explosion during celebrations of a Croatian football victory in Beli Monastir.

The challenge for political leaders is to instil in their communities the meaning of democracy – by encouraging free expression, the rule of law and, above all, understanding of the principle that government's main purpose is not to rule but to serve the freely expressed will of the people. The problem is that a lot of political representatives who believe themselves to be democrats do not understand the meaning of democracy. Consequently, positive decisions are often blocked by the unwillingness to implement them. Some ethnic local authorities take them as having been imposed by the international community against their interests. They are often encouraged to ignore them by highly placed politicians. For example, the Croatian program for Return is a step forward, but it was not easy to get it through the parliament even as a resolution. Its implementation is challenged from below – as I found last month in debates with people in eastern and western Slavonia. The deposed President of the Supreme Court of Croatia was not reinstated despite last April's decision by Constitutional Court that it should be so.

Such an approach also applies to the legal regulation of property. The principle of the independence of the judiciary and the police is not understood. Politicians should not only respect their independence but also refuse their requests for political approval. Moreover, the judges and the police often come to discriminatory decisions because of their political or ethnic prejudices. So the role of state institutions is in teaching them to respect the law only.

Some new laws even worsen the situation: the new criminal code in force since January in Croatia includes the prosecution of journalists and people who insult the president and other state officials. Even if journalists prove the veracity of their reporting they can be sentenced for inflicting "emotional anguish". In the ex-Yugoslav states freedom of the media is officially guaranteed. However, the main electronic media, especially television (the decisive source of information in all three countries) are controlled by the governments or ruling ethnic political parties. Some media promote ethnic hatred. Professional and non-partisan private televisions and radio stations are limited by legal or quasi-legal obstructions and lack of resources. There are courageous newspapers which are harassed in the same way. Under this pressure, many editors and reporters apply self-censorship.

The incredible amount of hatred towards other ethnic groups in all three countries has to be challenged and methods to promote tolerance and reconciliation must be developed as a precondition for sustainable peace and democratic development.

Whatever progress has been achieved, it has been mostly due to the active assistance of, and sometimes to pressure from the international community. Its role is highly appreciated by the elements of civil society which are still weak, but gradually growing. In Sarajevo, young people promise to return home as a minority, or not to emigrate, if the international community remains on the spot for the next twenty years. So the role of the international community is essential in assisting governments to improve their human rights records and in helping people to assure that the past will not be repeated. The international community will be obliged to continue its work in promoting respect for human rights throughout the region as long as development of democracy and civil society is irreversible. This is also the responsibility of the Council of Europe. We are never active enough in promoting human rights, the rule of law, and freedom of the media. The Balkans are Europe and the success of civil society there is essential for all of us.

Adama Dieng

The Universal Declaration of Human Rights began as an instrument of hope before becoming an instrument of progress. It was also the muse of many an NGO, in a sense becoming their founding charter. For fifty years, the Universal Declaration has inspired us, retaining its full credibility through constant adaptation, singing us an ode to progress which we have sought to take up. However, we have come here today not to look back but to pledge to make human rights even more of a priority in future.

A number of battles have already been won, but other fronts have opened up. The canker of racism and exclusion has taken hold in our societies. Minorities are denied the right to be different, and poverty is rampant. Society must have the honesty not to disregard the fate of these minorities, be they social, ethnic or other. To do so would lead us into a dangerous wait-and-see position, or even social regression. The Council of Europe's efforts to establish standards and models in order to stem these ills deserve the highest praise and must be continued. But we have a right to expect even more.

Our role as NGOs is to highlight what we consider intolerable, and yours is to ensure that the response will not be just fear but also action. To do so, your priorities must coincide with ours. In the past, the Council of Europe has often pointed the way in the defence and promotion of human rights. Even today, it is vital for it to assert itself as a model and to guide and support those who work to ensure respect for human rights.

We cannot but salute, at this very moment, the courage of thousands of human rights defenders who have fallen victim to government arbitrariness, including on this continent. Their sole crime was to refuse to remain silent in the face of violations of the Universal Declaration. Let us never forget: silence perpetuates oppression. So it is no surprise that yesterday's NGO Forum here focused its first general recommendation on the fate of human rights defenders. It is a pity that time was not allocated here for the presentation of the recommendations of the forum; but at least the text will be circulated, and I have no doubt that it will serve as a guide for recommendations of your own.

To all my NGO colleagues who have come here from all over Europe I should simply like to say "thank you" – you have done your duty and you have done it well. We now expect all European governments to follow suit, by making every effort to ensure that in December the United Nations General Assembly adopts the draft declaration on human rights defenders. But they must also go further and take every care to enforce the rights of human rights defenders.

What we are suggesting is a partnership for freedom, a partnership for human rights. What we, the NGOs, have to offer is our presence on the ground, our availability, our experience and our enthusiasm. You, as an intergovermental institution, can contribute your political determination, your moral authority, the courage to say that respect for human rights is a priority and above all the readiness to act accordingly.

As a logical extension of catering for individual choice, the law of the market does not allow for any development of a sense of collective responsibility. And yet it is essential for the partnership to include all those whose activities might be prejudicial to the full enjoyment of human rights. The multinationals or international financial organisations, for example, do not have the same social, economic or even moral responsibilities as states, but that does not absolve them – and they certainly must not be absolved – of all obligations. The danger that they pose to human rights requires that human rights enter the market sphere, to which a blind eye has been turned until now, and that it be made clear that power and wealth entail responsibility.

The partnership we are proposing must be one based on all rights – civil, political, economic, social and cultural. These rights are indivisible and all have the same force, so they must have equal legal and judicial protection. We must have the courage to apply the word "violation" to infringement of an economic, social or cultural right. The Additional Protocol to the European Social Charter providing for a System of Collective Complaints, which was adopted in 1995 but did not enter into force until just a few weeks ago, is an important step in this direction. Let us hope that a protocol setting up an individual complaints procedure will soon be added to the International Covenant on Economic, Social and Cultural Rights. That would be tangible proof that states firmly believe economic, social and cultural rights to have the same importance as civil and political rights, for which such a procedure already exists.

But please do not regard my emphasis on the future of economic and social rights as a sign that nothing further needs to be done for civil and political rights, whether at world or Council of Europe level. A protocol to the European Convention on Human Rights on the rights of persons deprived of freedom would be a great step forward but we note with great concern that Council of Europe member states are opposed to adopting one.

Another issue which continues to cause concern is women's human rights, which require effective implementation.

Protection for the rights of asylum-seekers and of migrant workers is also a serious and persistent preoccupation and we would like to see the Council of Europe give it more attention.

The creation of a commissioner for human rights within the Council of Europe would constitute a reaffirmation of your commitment, an expression of your priorities and a promise of progress in the cause of human rights. But let us not be so naïve as to see it as a panacea. A human rights commissioner will not be of any use unless he or she is part of and strengthens the existing Council of Europe machinery and is given the legal and material means to do the job.

Finally, to be useful to all, the partnership we are suggesting must above all be one within which everyone is entitled to his or her distinctiveness and can make his or her unique contribution. So the partnership will have room for national minorities, who will be the better protected for having their rights recognised as legitimate and for being associated with co-existence rather than conflict. Let us express our solidarity with them and acknowledge that "differentness" and diversity are more often an asset than a handicap.

In addition, the partnership must be a firm link leading to closer and constantly growing co-operation between western European countries and the new democracies in eastern Europe, which have shown their determination to build a future that breaks with their past.

Lastly, others will have to learn that it is the ones who divide and exclude who harm society, not those who seek entry to it. And if common sense is not enough, then the law must impose tolerance on those who refuse to learn it and must ultimately achieve the elimination of all forms of discrimination and the affirmation of the principle of equality. Here a protocol to the European Convention on Human Rights extending the scope of Article 14 would be an excellent thing, provided that it can free itself from the praiseworthy but sterile good intentions which have too long predominated. A protocol would be an important step forward and demonstrate that states are truly determined to fight injustice.

The 50th anniversary of the Universal Declaration is a proper occasion to celebrate the progress already made but it should serve above all to acknowledge what remains to be done to attain the "common standard" of which the declaration speaks. We must travel this road together, with courage and perseverance, constantly repeating our commitment to human rights, which we must not just protect in the abstract but defend and promote and above all give tangible form.

To do so, it is essential to step up the war on impunity and corruption, and that presupposes an independent and effective judiciary. It is also important to ensure that all Council of Europe member states ratify the Statute of the International Criminal Court and accept the ICC's universal jurisdiction for war crimes. The Council of Europe for its part can help states amend their law so as to comply with their international legal obligations.

In closing, allow me, on behalf of civil society, to express the hope that this commemoration of the Universal Declaration will see the forty Council of Europe member states make a concrete commitment to taking all necessary measures to help eradicate human rights violations on this continent.

Universal Declaration of Human Rights and the establishment of a European public order in the field of human rights

Statement by the Chairmanship of the Committee of Ministers
Stelios Perrakis
Secretary General for European Affairs
Ministry of Foreign Affairs, Athens (Greece)

I. Introduction

The issue of human rights protection under the international legal system, particularly at the European level, has gradually and laboriously progressed from the stage of ideology, the visionary approach and theological demands and debates to that of effective implementation, supervision and policy: a policy applicable at both the national and the international levels, either as a component of states' regional or global external policy or as the constitutional basis of the new European public order.

Of course the transition from application of the fundamental principle of "non-interference in the internal affairs of states" – which influenced the international attitude to situations of serious violations of human rights throughout the post-war period – to the acceptance of "legitimate interference" and the "legitimate interest" of the international community in the matter, took place as a result of political maturation, legal commitments entered into by governments and, more recently, a combination of historical circumstances that redefined the situation and reversed conceptions in the European environment.

Meanwhile, international human rights law, which is legally based on and inspired by the Universal Declaration of Human Rights, has imposed an impressive set of rules – of varying degrees of general and specific legal value – which have considerably enhanced the human being's status as a subject of law protected by multi-dimensional international safeguards.

This legal situation has taken on extraordinary dimensions in Europe. It has been enriched by political and legal inputs from the activities of the various European institutions and would seem to affirm the existence of a "European public order" in the human rights field, in the broad sense of the term.

II. The 1948 Universal Declaration, the Council of Europe and the emergence of a European public order

The Universal Declaration has had a major impact on international human rights law. Moreover, very many international instruments on human rights explicitly aspire to implementing the Declaration, including the two United Nations covenants on human rights and the three regional conventions, namely the European Convention on Human Rights, the American Convention on Human Rights and the Banjul African Charter of Human and Peoples' Rights.

The global influence of the Universal Declaration is explained by the fact that substantively it is not a mere "lowest common denominator" but, on the contrary, it solemnly proclaims the "common ideal to be attained".

Several features corroborate this influence and reveal the modern-day importance of the historic 1948 text. The Universal Declaration is:

- a complete text – it comprises all individual and collective rights, the principles of universality, indivisibility and interdependence of rights and the concept of individual duties);
- an important text – it is ideological and progressive and enshrines rights which are still not recognised today, such as the right of asylum;
- an ambitious, surprisingly topical text aimed at establishing an international/universal order guaranteeing human values, rights and freedoms.

Fifty years after the adoption of the Universal Declaration, the wording of Article 28 reminds us that the authors of the Declaration did indeed have in mind the idea of an international public order: "Everyone is entitled to a social and international order in which the rights and freedoms set forth in this Declaration can be fully realised."

This politico-legal aspiration has blossomed in Europe, where human rights as a political discourse and a binding legal action have over the years become the foundation of a European public order.

This legal, and above all political exercise was initiated by the Council of Europe, primarily through the European Convention on Human Rights. Even in yesterday's divided Europe, an area of politico-legal divergence and ideological antagonism, based on the limited and partial role of the rights secured by the Convention in Europe, a politically-oriented European public order did manage to emerge leaving legal traces in the famous early case-law of the European Commission of Human Rights. In the 1961 case of *Austria v. Italy* the Commission mentioned a "Community public order of free democracies of Europe", and later moved on the concept of a "European public order" in the cases of *Cyprus v. Turkey* and *Chrysostomos and Others v. Turkey*.

In today's Europe, where the Strasbourg institution now comprises forty member countries, the European public order was recently enshrined in case-law in the

Loizidou judgment, in which the European Court of Human Rights declares the Convention to be a "constitutional instrument of the European public order".

The advent of a "European public order" in the human rights field, as we approach the new century with developments in European construction coming thick and fast, is certainly a major event that is having a significant impact on state's conduct vis-à-vis individuals, on both the national and the international fronts.

This "European public order" requires European governments to respect its content, comply with its values and take positive measures; it outlines the politico-legal framework which European states should adopt if they do not wish to be relegated to the fringes of or even excluded from the European family.

Furthermore, the "European public order" is dynamic and open-ended. It now goes beyond the substantive scope of the Statute of the Council and the European Convention on Human Rights to comprise new legal and political elements (relating to democracy, the rule of law, human rights and the rights of minorities) which are laid down in other legal instruments drawn up by the Council of Europe and other European institutions. These texts develop roles and ambitions similar to those of the Council of Europe, thus enriching the work of the Strasbourg Organisation.

A series of factors have helped create this institutional and politico-legal landscape in Europe:

- the intensive work of the European organisations (Council of Europe, OSCE, European Union, etc.);
- the establishment of a multitude of international judicial and other monitoring procedures for monitoring the commitments entered into by states in this field, and
- the formulation, under a complex standard-setting procedure, of rules on promotion and protection of human rights and international supervision thereof by legal and political means, not to forget the international provisions in favour of persons belong to minorities, which originally came under the "soft law" category.

The issue of the rights of minorities is a major factor in the new European order. It plays two roles, one positive and the other negative. The positive aspect is also one of the fundamental principles of the new Europe, i.e. promotion and protection of human rights and the principles of law. The negative side is that these conditions sometimes cause instability in certain regions. The Document of the Copenhagen Meeting of the Conference on the Human Dimension of the CSCE, incorporated into the texts of the Charter of Paris for a New Europe and the Helsinki Summit on the Challenge of Change, specifies that "[the participating states] further reaffirm that respect for the rights of persons belonging to national minorities as part of universally recognised human rights is an essential factor for peace, justice and democracy in the participating states" (IV, 30.1). The Vienna Declaration adopted at the first Summit of Heads of State and Government of member states of the Council of Europe proclaimed the same set of values.

The European Convention on Human Rights is the principal achievement in this legal and political context of principles and standards. Very recently, the European Union confirmed its impact on democracy and stability in Europe in its statement (Chapter on "Human Rights") before the General Assembly of the United Nations in September 1998.

I would like to go on to provide some food for thought on the dimensions of the European public order in the human rights field, based on the aforementioned legal and political framework. I will begin with the Council of Europe before discussing other European organisations.

III. Construction of a European public order in the Council of Europe framework

A. *The return of the rule of law*

It is well established that the rule of law refers not only to a mechanism for producing legal standards but also to a system of values that all state authorities must respect. Reference to the Constitution highlights the aims and values that are based on a broader consensus and the general interests of a well-defined national society and enables us to counter any authoritarian tendencies on the part of legislative or executive bodies.

Moving on from the national to the European level, human rights, which are safeguarded by the international conventions formulated by the Council of Europe, help enhance the rule of law and constitute a European public order in this field. To paraphrase François Ost, we must transfer human rights from the preserve of states to a European public order, the protection of which is a matter for certain supranational bodies.

The Council of Europe's work to establish a European public order is not always legally binding. In the last few years, in addition to the non-binding instruments, the Organisation's political bodies have also made their contribution to establishing a European public order in the human rights field.

B. *Legal efforts*

The Council of Europe is the cornerstone of the European structure for human rights protection. It is the only Organisation with a long-standing international judicial mechanism for supervising respect for the rights and freedoms set out in the European Convention on Human Rights and its protocols, a system that is unique in the whole international legal system.

The Preamble to the Statute of the Council of Europe stresses "the spiritual and moral values which are the common heritage of their peoples and the true source of individual freedom, political liberty and the rule of law, principles which form the basis of all genuine democracy". One year later, the preamble to the European Convention on Human Rights transformed this common heritage into "a common understanding and observance of ... Human Rights".

But what are the legal components of this common understanding?

a. *Standard-setting texts adopted*

The standard-setting texts adopted in the Council of Europe are aimed at "ensuring collective safeguards for some of the rights set forth in the Universal Declaration".

The European Convention on Human Rights, the mainstay of the Strasbourg system, embodies the democratic ideal, international solidarity and the collective guarantee of international action. The Convention is the most effective instrument in the field of international human rights protection: "the Convention comprises more than mere reciprocal engagements between Contracting States. It creates, over and above a network of mutual, bilateral undertakings, objective obligations which, in the words of the Preamble, benefit from a "collective enforcement" (Ireland v. the United Kingdom judgment of 18 January 1978).

The European Convention on Human Rights came into force in 1953 and is currently binding upon all Council of Europe member states. In fact, its ratification was an absolute precondition for the accession of central and eastern European countries to the Council of Europe. Moreover, when the governments applying for Council membership pledged to ratify the Convention, they also had to promise to accept the optional clauses in Articles 25 and 46.

Now that the status of member state of the Council of Europe is inseparable from that of Party to the European Convention on Human Rights, it is even more likely that the old dream of forging an organic link between both instruments (Statute of the Council of Europe and European Convention on Human Rights) will come true. As a result, the Statute will be the Organisation's Constitutional Charter enshrining the Convention as its declaration of rights.

All States Parties have incorporated the Convention into their domestic legal systems (with one exception), thus facilitating legal harmonisation.

Other Council of Europe instruments cover certain aspects of the European public order:

- The Framework Convention for the Protection of National Minorities. This is the fullest international convention on minorities and the first multilateral and legally binding text on the matter.
- The European Social Charter, a necessary complement to the European Convention on Human Rights. Its revised version comprises all the necessary provisions to protect workers. Moreover, its Protocol laying down a system of collective complaints is a real breakthrough in terms of promoting social rights.
- The Convention for the Prevention of Torture, an instrument aimed at preventing inhuman and degrading treatment, is a useful complement to the European Convention on Human Rights.
- The Convention on Nationality. This is a summary of all the recent developments and the first text on this matter to affirm the principle of non-discrimination and the right to nationality.

These instruments have a number of common points: they are conventions (on minorities, torture and nationality) which are also open to non-member countries of the Council of Europe, and are preventive in character.

b. *The European Convention on Human Rights and developments in case-law on the protection of human rights*

The European judges in Strasbourg are no doubt the main symbols of the legal system set up by the Convention. When they receive applications from states, individuals or NGOs they decide on the conformity of national practices, individual measures, decisions and acts by national courts and national legislation with legal standards which are frequently somewhat vague. In this work they have no simple, one-dimensional legal structure to hide behind. As a result, like the issues which they have to adjudicate, their judgments occasionally give rise to national, and even political controversy.

At the present time the case-law of the organs of the Convention looks impressive: over 900 judgments handed down by the Court and more than 2 800 reports adopted by the Commission.

This has provided the Convention with:

- an objective or dynamic interpretation, the foundations of which date back to the *Golder* case (1975). This approach is illustrated by the example of Article 3. In the *Aydin* judgment (1997) the Court for the first time added rape to the list of crimes falling within the ambit of Article 3. This tallies with the case-law of the Criminal Tribunal for the former Yugoslavia and of the new International Criminal Court.
- an autonomous interpretation: this is a *sine qua non* for the prescriptive force of the Convention and its precedence over national legal systems as it facilitates examination of the conformity of domestic law with the Convention on the basis of concepts formulated by the Court itself. It guarantees unity of interpretation and application of the common regulations and equitable burden-sharing by the Contracting States. Lastly, it facilitates the creation, on the basis of Article 6, of a code of judicial law applicable to all domestic civil, criminal, administrative and constitutional courts and guarantees minimum rights for all citizens.

c. *Reinforcing control mechanisms with a view to greater effectiveness*

i. Within the system of the European Convention on Human Rights

In this field we should stress that thanks to Protocol No. 11 the European Court of Human Rights will now be able to fully standardise its case-law because the Commission and Court will no longer be adopting different approaches to the provisions of the Convention. The scope of Article 9 provides an outstanding example of such divergence (see *Darby*, *Tsirlis and Kouloumpas*, *Kalaç* and the *Canea Catholic Church* judgments). Furthermore, the fact that the Committee of Ministers will no longer be intervening will reinforce the judicial character of the whole system.

ii. The Protocol to the European Social Charter providing for a system of collective complaints

The protocol came into force on 1 July 1998. Under this text, international and national employers' and workers' organisations and certain NGOs can submit complaints of violations of the Charter against States Parties.

iii. The European Committee for the Prevention of Torture and Inhuman or Degrading Treatment or Punishment

The committee is currently successfully increasing the scope of its supervision. It visits not only the usual places of detention but also places of "reception" of refugees (airports, etc.).

iv. The Committee of the Framework Convention for the Protection of National Minorities

Fresh efforts are emerging in a field combining politics and law. The Consultative Committee has just been set up. It will carry out very important work for the future of the Convention's implementation, and the first results are eagerly awaited.

d. The role of the Committee of Ministers

The Committee of Ministers is responsible for enforcing the Court's judgments. This is an eminently political role despite the legal content of the honouring of the states' contractual obligations. Such supervision, which is conducted in pursuance of Article 54, should be directed towards further increasing the efficiency of enforcement of the Court's judgments, within a fuller, stricter functional framework. A time-limit must be set for enforcement of Court decisions, the applicant assigned a specific role during this period, and consideration given to requiring the respondent states to adopt general or specific measures, increasing the participation of the Council of Europe's Directorate of Human Rights.

C. The political dimensions

It is interesting to note that with time the Council of Europe has managed to complement the European Convention on Human Rights system with other non-judicial mechanisms and political procedures in the field of human rights protection, creating a kind of "human rights diplomacy". I am thinking of the Parliamentary Assembly's multidimensional activities. It now plays an enhanced role in promoting and protecting human rights from the political angle, particularly following the institutional confirmation of its place in the procedure for examining applications for membership of the Council and the establishment of the monitoring procedure, comprising fact-finding missions in the field of human and minorities' rights. We should also mention the work of the Venice Commission to improve respect for human rights and the rule of law in the countries in democratic transition in central, eastern and south-eastern Europe. The current plan to introduce a Commissioner on Human Rights is also in line with these aims.

All these activities have a preventive dimension aimed at protecting the European public order.

D. *Shortcomings in the system*

While the Council of Europe's political and legal work in the human rights field can be described as important and successful, the efficiency of protection undoubtedly poses a practical problem. We must consider possible obstacles to implementation of such protection. Examples of such problems are certain obtrusive remnants of national sovereignty, simple implementation of obligations arising out of the system and the negative "politicisation" of interstate applications under the Convention. The Council of Europe's exemplary action in the *Greek* Case (1967-74) failed to obtain the desired results.

Similarly, there is a question mark over the extent to which the Strasbourg Court's judgments actually correct unjust situations.

IV. Parallel construction of a European public order

A. *The emergence of the European Union*

The European Union has also played a major role in parallel, complementary construction of the European public order, particularly in the post-Maastricht era. With the new Amsterdam Treaty, signed on 2 October 1997, the European Union, whose founding treaties betray a considerable institutional and legislative deficit in terms of human rights, is apparently attempting to redress the legal and political balance of the system, exploiting past experience, responding to the day-to-day needs of European citizens and emphasising the legitimate European aspiration to intensifying international action to promote and protect human rights.

The European Union does have solid *acquis* in the human rights field, despite the limited powers of the Court of Justice, which has nonetheless developed human rights case-law principles to bolster Community law, of which the European Convention on Human Rights has been one of the mainstays, and of the European Parliament, which has long been very active in promoting human rights within the Union and encouraging external economic relations. Accordingly, following the 1996-97 Intergovernmental Conference the Union introduced an important prescriptive and institutional system for promoting human rights.

The Amsterdam Treaty, which is currently being ratified by the "Fifteen", lays down a series of provisions on human rights protection under the Union's legal system (horizontal clause on equality between women and men, non-discrimination clause, action against racism, protection of personal data, cultural diversity, regulations on religions and denominations, social rights with explicit reference to the European Social Charter, jurisdiction of the Court of Justice of the European Communities, etc.).

However, three facts are particularly noteworthy:

i. The European Union now has a democratic identity some degree of jurisdiction in the human rights field. It is based on the principles of freedom, justice and respect for human rights and the rule of law. The European Convention on Human Rights has become the fundamental standard-setting reference for the Union system.

The Luxembourg Court can now deal with applications submitted by individuals or legal entities.

ii. All applications for membership of the European Union are subject to the condition of compliance with these principles.

iii. For the first time in the history of the European Union/Community, there is now a system of sanctions against any member state violating the said principles, including possible suspension of Union membership.

In the field of relations with non-member states, whether or not they are applying for membership, the issue of human rights and the rights of minorities has become a political and legal prerequisite. The criteria adopted by the European Council in Copenhagen in 1993, the Stability Pact, the European Union's regional approach in the Balkans and "Agenda 2000 for a Stronger and Wider Europe", a European Commission document of cardinal importance for the future of European integration and human and minorities' rights, are now absolute preconditions for developing economic and political relations with the Union. Such preconditions govern the development of all relations with the Union, to the extent of enabling it to impose sanctions on non-member states.

The process of enlarging the Union, which began in March 1998 on the basis of the conclusions of the European Council in Luxembourg, demonstrates that for the fifteen Union member states the issue of democratic institutions, human rights and the rule of law in applicant countries is a *sine qua non* for accession.

Therefore, all these principles governing Union action is reinforcing the European public order initially aspired to by the Council of Europe, particularly in the environment in which the Council began its work all those years ago.

B. *The new Europe, the minorities issue and the contribution of OSCE*

At the same time, the rights of minorities in a Europe undergoing political and economic change now head the agenda. The issue has political connotations which sometimes involve policies of discrimination and human rights violations, development problems, crisis prevention, armed or unarmed ethnic conflict and humanitarian intervention by armed forces, and has attracted the interest of the European institutions. They have responded by launching international initiatives, setting up bodies and adopting rules, which have usually been of a declaratory nature. Concurrently, the European Organisations would seem to have adopted democratic security as a concept and a policy. It is significant that the European Convention on Human Rights is generally regarded as the main achievement in the field of democracy and stability in Europe.

OSCE has had a vital role to play here in fleshing out the concept of "European minorities law". This Organisation also made the human and minorities' rights issue one of the foundations of the new Europe, the new European public order (Copenhagen Final Document, 1990; Charter of Paris, 1990; Helsinki II Final Act, 1992). OSCE has accordingly set up crisis prevention institutions (High Commissioner on National Minorities, preventive diplomacy, etc).

We should not forget the OSCE's major contribution to assisting and observing national elections and thus to the proper functioning of pluralist parliamentary democracies.

V. Conclusion

While the Universal Declaration of Human Rights is indisputably the source of inspiration for the promotion of human rights in Europe today and its influence on European human rights law is obvious, for Europe in the 21st century there remains the question of a European public order, either as a past achievement or a future challenge. In fact, this is a different version of the question of effective protection of human rights, the subject of our colloquy, because the European public order is merely the sum of all the democratic values, principles and rules governing individual human development, respecting human dignity and guaranteeing human rights. The substance of this order, comprising binding legal rules and political principles to be observed, is the "hard core" of European shared ideals.

The fact that the *Loizidou* judgment enshrined the European public order in the Council of Europe reinforces this achievement, but also challenges the European States Parties to the system to back this *acquis* and work in concert to consolidate it. Human rights, as well as democracy, call for a constant struggle for future expansion. The dangers of deviations and selective and partial approaches are demonstrably still looming.

Back in the 1970s, the eminent Greek lawyer and judge, the late Mr Evrigenis, was arguing that the unification of Europe would involve harmonising the law, particularly through the European Convention on Human Rights, with its power to transform. The Council of Europe has mapped out the way with this convention, which is now being followed with new inputs from other European institutions, harbingers of the advent of the European public order.

This European public order, which will consolidate the union among European States, is a solid legal and political instrument for founding an open, democratic, tolerant and fair national society, and a more coherent, stable, developed and safe European society. This is a challenge for the coming century which we must deliver.

Recommendations of the NGO forum to the colloquy

1 September 1998

A. The NGOs present would like to make the following general recommendations:

- In the light of the 50th anniversary of the Universal Declaration of Human rights, the often dramatic situation of the human rights defenders should not be overlooked.

  The Council of Europe should consider their specific situations when monitoring the countries' compliance with the Council's human rights standards, and contribute actively to their protection;

  The governments present should adopt and actively promote the draft declaration on human rights defenders at the United Nations General Assembly in December this year;

  The participants in this colloquy should mainstream this item and consider it in every working group.

- There is also a concern for women's human rights; the Universal Declaration is the basis for the interpretation of their rights and they again should be mainstreamed into all the working groups' debates;

- "Human rights are universal, indivisible and interdependent and interrelated. The international community must treat human rights globally in a fair and equal manner on the same footing and with the same emphasis." It is of crucial importance that this be reminded and effectively implemented within the Council of Europe and within the member states.

- Therefore, the governments present are called upon to ratify all European human rights instruments including the European Social Charter (Revised) and the 1995 Additional Protocol to the European Social Charter Providing for a System of Collective Complaints, the core United Nations Human Rights treaties, and the additional protocols to them, without reservations.

  They are also called upon to lift any reservations they may have made in order to ensure the full implementation of the treaties' spirit.

- However, it should be reminded that ratifying treaties alone is not enough. The true commitment of a country to comply with human rights can only be measured through its willingness to effectively implement its obligations on the national level.
- When negotiating trade and investment liberalisation and other treaties, the states should ensure that these treaties have no negative repercussions for the implementation of human rights nationally and in other countries.
- In order to ensure effective implementation and monitoring thereof, the Council of Europe should also function according to the criteria of transparency and accountability. The NGOs should be closely associated to the monitoring process.
- Another element is the fight against impunity. This implies an effective and independent judiciary and the fight against corruption.

  Lastly, the NGOs would like to remind the participants that the promotion of human rights in Europe is in the hands of all of us:
- the Council of Europe, not only through its judicial mechanisms, but also through its monitoring bodies, its technical assistance and its political organs. They form part of a whole which should be used creatively and pro-actively to further a human rights culture throughout Europe;
- the states, upon which it is incumbent to guarantee and to respect human rights, and the NGOs, through promoting a spirit of tolerance and dialogue which are the true basis for a democratic society.

B. Concerning the six working groups, the NGOs present would like to make the following specific recommendations:

On *"prevention of and responses to structural or large/scale human rights violations"*

- Once a situation has degenerated into structural or large-scale human rights violations, it is too late for prevention. Prevention starts by eliminating single human rights violations as is done in the individual cases handled by the European court, but also through political will.
- The states present are invited to ratify the statutes of the new International Criminal Court and to accept the universal jurisdiction of the Court on war crimes.

  The Council of Europe could help the states to amend their laws in order for them to be in conformity with their international legal obligations.
- The states present that have not yet done so are invited to ratify the United Nations Covenant on Civil and Political Rights and its Optional Protocol, the United Nations Convention against Torture and Other Cruel, Inhuman or Degrading Treatment or Punishment and the European Convention on Nationality, and to lift any reservations. They are asked to encourage a speedy adoption of the draft optional protocol to the United Nations Convention against Torture and Other Cruel, Inhuman or Degrading Treatment or Punishment, of the draft United Na-

tions Convention on Enforced Disappearances and of the draft protocol No. 12 to the European Convention on Human Rights on the rights of detained people.

- The states present are asked to implement the recommendation contained in the concluding observations of the United Nations human rights treaty bodies, as well as the recommendations of the Committee of Ministers concerning the European Social Charter and the recommendations of the European Committee for the Prevention of Torture. They should not delay the publication of its reports, but make sure that the findings and recommendations are widely made known in order to ensure their implementation. A person within the national hierarchy should be named responsible for overseeing the implementation.
- The intergovernmental organisations working for human rights and on a preventive basis within Europe, such as the Council of Europe, the OSCE, the European Union and the United Nations, should co-ordinate more closely. The Council of Europe could take a more pro-active role by evaluating, by proposing interdisciplinary evaluations of existing human rights field experiences within Europe and by making the results widely known. Its role in early warning systems as well as in the evaluation of rising risk factors could also be enhanced.
- The Council of Europe's preventive role should also be enhanced regarding mediation and confidence-building measures within a national context, in order to help create conditions that foster dialogue between different parties within a given country.
- The new Commissioner for Human Rights should be made into a useful tool for the prevention of large-scale violations, providing he/she has sufficient resources and a co-ordinating position within the Council of Europe.

On "social rights: the challenge of indivisibility and interdependence"

- The Council of Europe should make the ratification of the European Social Charter (Revised) obligatory for all the new member states, as is the case for the European Convention on Human Rights and the European Convention for the Prevention of Torture and Inhuman or Degrading Treatment or Punishment.
- The members of the Council of Europe should all ratify without delay and without reservations the Revised Social Charter and the Additional Protocol on Collective Complaints, as well as making the declaration that would enable the national NGOs to submit collective complaints as well. They should also ratify the ILO Conventions and the United Nations International Covenant on Economic, Social and Cultural Rights, and should work towards the adoption of the Additional Protocol to the Covenant on individual complaints.
- The Council of Europe's monitoring bodies should also take into consideration the implementation of social and economic rights, as well as the degree of respect and protection of the human rights defenders working specifically on these subjects.
- In implementing these rights, the states should bear in mind that they also have the obligations to create infrastructure, such as work, health facilities, etc.

- In order to promote a democratic society, the right to form trade unions should be extended to all sectors of the society.
- The right to education and its access should be guaranteed without discrimination.

On "effective implementation of women's rights"

- In order to mainstream the systematic consideration of the implementation of women's rights, the Council of Europe should promote a gender balance within its monitoring mechanisms.
- Although the state bears the prime responsibility for the physical integrity of every human being, the Council of Europe should be aware of increasing problems for women and domestic violence. These aspects should be integrated in its legal assistance work and within the monitoring bodies.
- The states should ratify and without reservations the United Nations Convention on the Elimination of All Forms of Discrimination against Women (CEDAW), as well as work for the speedy adoption of its optional protocol. Reservations that have been made to CEDAW should be lifted.
- The draft protocol to the European Convention on Human Rights, covering in particular the provisions of Article 14, guaranteeing the principle of equality and the prohibition of discrimination should be adopted without delay.

On "effective action at the national level"

- The Council of Europe can assist states in helping them reform their laws in order to bring them in conformity with international human rights law.
- States should also follow up on the concluding observations of the United Nations treaty bodies.
- The parliamentarians of the states bear a major responsibility when drafting national laws and should endeavour to ensure compliance with the existing international human rights law.
- The judiciary is the prime tool for guaranteeing respect of human rights. The states should give it full independence, also through an independent budget and the necessary resources. The judiciary should remain apolitical and non-partisan.
- In order to ensure impartial justice, there should be no special courts or administration of justice set up under special legislation. Military tribunals should not examine human rights cases and ordinary courts should not employ military staff.
- All actors within the system of administration of justice (judges, prosecutors, lawyers and law-enforcement officials) should receive the necessary resources and training.
- States are encouraged to set up systems of increased civilian oversight and monitoring over law enforcement agencies.
- National institutions (national human rights commissions and ombudsmen) can also be used to monitor the implementation of the states' human rights obligations.

- The judiciary should automatically review cases if their ruling has been overturned by the European Court of Human Rights.
- Translation and dissemination of all European human rights instruments and pertaining case law, as well as the CPT reports and the recommendations of the Committee of Ministers under the European Social Charter, are vital tools for an effective implementation. This is the prime responsibility of the states; however, the Council of Europe can provide technical assistance.
- States are encouraged to draw up national plans of action on how to implement human rights together with the NGOs.

On "effective action at the international level"

- In order to enhance the effectiveness of the European Convention and the European Court of Human Rights, all states should ratify the European Agreement relating to persons participating in Proceedings of the European Court of Human Rights of 1996.
- The human rights mechanisms that are active in the countries of the Council of Europe should co-ordinate their actions. They should be mutually informed of their findings and conclusions.
- The NGOs should be closely associated to the drawing up of the Council of Europe Human Rights Commissioner's mandate and plan of action.
- The Council of Europe bodies should take care not to backtrack on already existing rights.
- The NGOs should be more closely associated with the Council of Europe's monitoring processes, due to their specific expertise and knowledge of the field.
- The special mechanism of the Committee of Ministers to monitor the imposition of the death penalty and to intervene in such cases, which has already been approved by the Parliamentary Assembly, should be put into effect.
- The monitoring mechanism of the implementation of human rights should also consider if the CPT recommendations have been followed.
- The CPT should have the necessary means to ensure that its recommendations are implemented.

On "promotion of human rights: information, education and training"

- The Council of Europe should facilitate the creation of adequate training material for all sectors of society.
- States, together with NGOs, should draw up and implement national plans of action for human rights education.
- Human rights training should be undertaken for judges, police, prison staff, lawyers, prosecutors, etc. It should also be included in higher education in universities.

- National and international NGOs can work together in training national NGOs in the necessary human rights fields. National NGOs should also receive professional training in human rights law and monitoring.
- Publicity about and around human rights is an important tool for awareness raising. A public opinion cell should be specifically created, either on its own or in conjunction with the High Commissioner, in order to raise public awareness.

C. The NGOs present point out that the following issues should also be addressed during the colloquy and regret that there is no forum for their discussion:

Protection and promotion of minorities' rights

All member states should ratify without delay or reservation the Framework Convention on the Protection of National Minorities and the European Convention on Regional and Minority Languages.

On discrimination and equality

The Council of Europe should reinforce on the European level the international protection of victims of discrimination rather than fall short of contemporary international standards. To this purpose, the member states of the Council of Europe should adopt without delay an additional protocol to the European Convention on Human Rights concerning its Article 14.

Effective protection can only occur if non-discrimination, together with *de jure* and *de facto* equality, which constitute fundamental principles in the protection of human rights, are secured through the adoption of a binding legal instrument and through a mechanism which will ensure full justiciability of these principles.

Discrimination on any ground such as class, sex, race, sexual orientation, physical or mental disability, colour, language, religion, political or other opinion, national or social origin, association with a national minority, property, birth or other status should be prohibited.

On refugees and asylum seekers

The member states of the Council of Europe should fully comply with Article 14 of the Universal Declaration on Human Rights according to which "Everyone has the right to seek and to enjoy in other countries asylum from persecution". Those member states which have not yet ratified the Geneva Convention relating to the Status of Refugees (1951), and its New York Protocol (1967) should do so without delay nor reservations. The Rule of the Procedures of the European Commission of Human Rights and of the European Court of Human Rights concerning interim measures (such as the suspension of deportation orders) should be made mandatory.

On co-operation between the Council of Europe and the NGOs

The NGOs recommend that the recommendations adopted during the seminar organised by the Council of Europe in Budapest (16-18 April 1998) on the "Role of NGOs in the transition to a democratic society – Ways of co-operation with the Council of Europe", be implemented by the Council of Europe and the NGO Liaison Committee, as well as the NGOs.

Second session – Current challenges

Theme 1: Prevention of and responses to structural or large-scale human rights violations

Rapporteur: Vojin Dimitrijević

The main part of the Council of Europe system for the protection of human rights, that based on the European Convention on Human Rights, is predicated on the assumption that Europe is a region where the general ideal of human rights was attained and remains only to be implemented in full detail. This area was believed to be covered by the territories of similar, like-minded states, accepting in their constitutions and political habits the principles of individualism, liberalism, democracy, separation of powers, etc. The drafters of the Convention and the architects of its protection mechanism assumed that governments were committed to human rights and willing to co-operate in order to ensure and protect these rights. Ever since the early 1950s violations of human rights have been considered an anomaly. The role of the organs of the Council of Europe has been to assist *bona fide* state agencies in doing what they would have been doing anyhow: in finding out inconsistencies in essentially similar legislative provisions of member states and in their interpretation.

The protection of human rights envisaged by the Convention was essentially the same as the one that had pre-existed in most member states of the Council of Europe. It was the conventional legal reaction triggered by the victim of the alleged violation. Its novelty, heralded at the time as revolutionary, was only dramatic in terms of international law and its concept of sovereignty, which could not conceive of individual complainants as equal partners in the proceedings with the state. Otherwise, the mechanism has been passive, as are such procedures, linked to "justiciable" rights, in most states: an individual has a limited *locus standi*, class action is not available and structural deficiencies cannot as a rule be addressed through complaints of individual victims. Its success has also depended on the resoluteness and ability of individuals to initiate proceedings.

To be sure, the effects of the decisions of the European Court and the European Commission (and the fact that the proceedings took place at all) have not been minimal and reduced only to remedying individual wrongs, without questioning the circumstances which made the wrong possible. In some cases the organs of the Convention have determined that the violation was not an accident caused by fallacious interpretation of national law, but that the latter was not in accordance with the provisions of the Convention or of international law in general. In such instances the European Court has assumed the role of a constitutional court, limited by the circumstance that complaints *in abstracto* about legislation and practices are not allowed to individual petitioners.

However, if the violations have not been due to bad law but to systematic misapplication and disregard of it, the system has remained all but powerless. This disappointment might have been avoided had the member states used more frequently and more energetically the avenue open to them in Article 24 of the Convention to refer to the Commission alleged breaches of the Convention by other contracting parties, and had the Commission, the Court and the Committee of Ministers been less guided by political considerations. The reluctance of states to initiate proceedings on human rights violations against other states before judicial and quasi-judicial bodies is, however, not limited to the "friendly" relationships in the European family: for that matter, the Human Rights Committee has so far not received a single communication of a state claiming that another state party of the International Covenant on Civil and Political Rights was not fulfilling its obligations. This reticence has contrasted sharply with the accusations regularly exchanged between United Nations members at meetings of the United Nations Commission on Human Rights. This also reflects the true concern that courts would lose their standing and image if expected too frequently to decide on political issues. In many legal systems they can refer to the executive.

Having now touched on the different climate in a regional setting, such as the Council of Europe, and a universal arena of the United Nations, let us return to the beginning. The idyllic picture of a consistent, human rights friendly and democratic Europe was in fact a projection of western Europe after World War II. Europe is now a whole and the Council encompasses almost all European states. It is now much more probable that Europe and its organisations will face unfavourable human rights situations of the gravity and range considered hitherto to be "non-European".

The Council of Europe had a foretaste of things to come dealing with some geographically non-western states that were added to its membership due to their pronounced adherence to western ideals, inspired also by fears of communism and by strategic considerations. It is no wonder that all interstate complaints, except that against the United Kingdom (the only one that reached the Court), were directed against Turkey and Greece. This has also been felt in proceedings initiated by individuals. The Court has been recently forced to tread on unknown ground when dealing with circumstances that have not been the usual background of violations in most cases it had to consider and which show that the violation has structural origins and that its scale is possibly wider than manifested by the fate of individual complainants. In at least three cases concerning Turkey (*Aksoy, Akdivar and Others,* both 1996, *Mentes and Others,* 1997) the Court has determined that in some parts of this country legal remedies were not available and effective, based on a "realistic account of the general legal and political context in which the remedies operate" (para. 58 of the *Mentes* judgment). In the same case, the Court has even absolved the applicants from attempting to approach Turkish courts, because it was "not satisfied that remedies before the administrative and civil courts were adequate and sufficient in respect of the applicants' complaint ..." (para. 60). In spite of the protests of the Court that its "ruling is confined to the exceptional circumstances of the present case and is not to be interpreted as a general statement that remedies are ineffective in this area of Turkey" (para. 61), the determination by the Court that remedies were futile had not originated only from the facts of the case, but also from previous experience and information from other sources. This is a harsh judgment indeed, even by non-European, United Nations criteria. The Human Rights Committee, which had to deal with very unsavoury situations, was reluctant to admit communications if the author had not tested the availability and effectiveness of remedies in his/her own case. Exceptions were made only when notorious violators were involved and where there was abundant proof, implied in the statements of the responding state, that remedies were "either inapplicable *de jure* or *de facto*" and did "not constitute an effective remedy" (*Dermit Barbato v. Uruguay*, 1982, para. 9.4).

The other concern related to the realisation that lower executive echelons were not up to the highest expectations and not easily controlled by judicial bodies. As very often, the paradigm of such violations was torture. The reaction of the Council of Europe was in the form of the innovative European Convention for the Prevention of Torture and Inhuman or Degrading Treatment or Punishment of 26 November 1987. The mandate of the Committee established by this convention is an example of preventive work done by a non-judiciary body of independent experts.

After 1989 the European continent was "reinstated" in its integrity and the Council of Europe enlarged by new members: most of them are still in "transition" toward the free market, democracy and rule of law. This common orientation cannot conceal the fact that among them, and in comparison with most original members of the Council, they have different cultural and political traditions and are in social situations that western Europe has not lived with for almost half a century.

It is almost unanimously recognised that low development, social inequality, lack of democracy, ethnic differences and armed conflicts are among the principal causes of gross violations of human rights. In various degrees such circumstances are present in at least some of the members of the new European family. This of course does not mean that the existence of one or more of these factors will inevitably result in such phenomena, but it is reasonable to assume that the likelihood of large-scale violations within the Council of Europe has increased since its enlargement. The former Yugoslavia (Socialist Federal Republic of) was an indicative case: back in 1989 it was considered to be the prime candidate among the "communist" countries for admission to European institutions, because of its milder version of "really existing socialism" and a relatively better human rights record. The ensuing events showed that this façade had hidden deadly potential, which materialised due to the simultaneous presence of the above-mentioned factors and the readiness of political forces to exploit them for their purposes.

If one does not believe in uncontrolled determinism, then the presence of this potentially dangerous mix of factors should not be allowed to develop into "gross" human rights violations in terms of their systematic character, gravity, frequency and range. (This more or less covers the general meaning of "structural and large-scale human rights violations" or a "consistent pattern of gross violations" in the language used by the United Nations.) After receiving "early warnings" international organisations must be equipped to act to prevent violations in good time. This is a formidable task, better suited to non-governmental fora that operate on the basis of information and opinions of independent researchers, and not to agencies which act when there is political agreement achieved by governments, which in turn rely on traditional diplomatic information and advice. It is therefore important to discern what international organisations can realistically do at such early stages.

The true prophylactic would have to start even before there are any signs that the presence of negative factors would result in gross violations. This means that mechanisms would have to be triggered by situations that do not fall easily under the rubric of human rights, but are considered to be conducive to large-scale violations. This has been realised by European institutions, such as the Council of Europe, the Organisation (Conference) on Security and Co-operation in Europe (OSCE/CSCE), and the European Union (Community) and resulted in their efforts to promote economic change, democratic institutions and the rule of law in countries in transition. It has also been an opportunity for intergovernmental organisations to co-operate closely with international and national non-governmental organisations (NGOs) in the creation and restitution of the civil society, which is an important barrier to the worst kind of violations, those that occur with the support and consent of a major part of the population. In the context of extreme nationalism, this means violations of minority rights supported by the majority, but also the "sacrifice" of the rights of individual members of the ethnic majority in the name of higher national interests and of the attainment of collective rights of the majority group.

Possibly the first decision where the term "early warning" was used was the Helsinki 1992 Document *The Challenges of Change*, which contained the mandate of the then established CSCE High Commissioner on National Minorities. He was to "provide 'early warning' and, as appropriate, 'early action' at the earliest possible stage in regard to tensions involving national minority issues which have not yet developed beyond an early warning stage, but ... have the potential to develop into a conflict within the CSCE area ...". The Commissioner's mandate belongs to the traditional early detection of international conflicts, as confirmed by the concern of this document, which goes on to mention peace and stability of relations between states; it is quite clear that the aim was also to prevent human rights violations in the context of ethnic differences. In some areas the very presence and activity of the High Commissioner have probably prevented minority tensions from aggravating, but not in others, especially when he was not allowed entry into the state concerned. The dependence of such procedures and actions, including OSCE (CSCE) missions, on the consent of governments and on international bodies composed of representatives of governments have presented familiar impediments to timely action.

"Action" is the word intended to indicate the need to react to a threatening situation. This refers to prevention in the narrower sense. International organisations are then faced with acute dangers of gross violations in situations where the accumulations of harmful factors can easily be translated into actions of violators, state or non-state. For some organisations this is already familiar ground. If the Council of Europe has to learn from the United Nations, the following experiences can be quoted and adapted:

Non-conventional responses to allegations of gross violations of human rights and fundamental freedoms

These are procedures controlled by the United Nations Commission on Human Rights, based on the ECOSOC resolutions 1235 (XLII) of 1967 and 1503 (XLVIII) of 1970. Without entering into details, the advantage of such procedures are that they rely on the United Nations Charter and the Universal Declaration of Human Rights and do not depend on prior contractual consent of the territorial state, do not hinge on individual applications, that the Resolution 1503 procedure is initiated without the consent of bodies composed of government representatives, and that the overall situation can be gauged, irrespective of the "justiciable" or non-justiciable" nature of the rights.

Non-conventional United Nations procedures have been, sometimes fiercely, resisted as too intrusive by most governments affected. Such sensitivity has been met by the confidentiality of procedures; the Commission has also tended to replace country working groups, rapporteurs and experts by corresponding bodies and individuals dealing with certain types of gross violations believed to exist in several countries ("thematic" rapporteurs, etc.). In spite of such concessions, the end results have tended to be disappointing: the Commission has not been able to muster political consent to terminate any procedure by a clear statement that there was a violation. However, the very fact that a country was submitted to such scrutiny has affected the human rights situation and some compromises ("friendly dialogues") with governments have resulted in improvements. The fact that governments have attempted to be removed from the lists of potential violators by all available means testifies that these procedures, no matter how "toothless", have their impacts. They should not only be measured by the compliance of national powers-to-be with minimal human rights standards, but by the boost local democratic forces receive from the support of international institutions in their efforts to remove oppressive regimes. However, the truth that sometimes only radical political change can terminate gross violations cannot be publicly recognised in international organisations: frustrations related to the non-conventional procedures have therefore been caused by the need of government representatives in the Commission on Human Rights and other United Nations organs to find ways to deal with the offending governments without totally alienating them and, what is more important, burdened with aims and interests unrelated to human rights.

In some respects the monitoring procedure of the Council of Europe's Committee of Ministers, established by its declarations of 10 November 1994 and 20 April 1995, resembles the United Nations procedures just described. It refers to all commitments Council of Europe members have undertaken in the realms of democracy, human rights and the rule of law, and not only to those covered by the European Convention on Human Rights. There is however no independent body of experts to initiate proceedings, as is the case with the Sub-Commission of the United Nations Commission on Human Rights (if this role is not to be played by the Parliamentary Assembly). Other parties empowered to refer "questions" to the Committee of Ministers are member states and the Secretary General. Such an arrangement keeps NGOs outside the process, unless they find channels via member states or the Secretariat. The likelihood that the Committee of Ministers will tend to behave as the United Nations Commission or as the Committee itself did in some Convention cases still remains. The exclusive use of the "thematic" approach and the absence of any action so far under Article 4 of the 1994 Declaration directed towards specific situations in a member state can mean either that there have not been any concerns or that there has been hesitance to test the sensitivities of governments.

When aimed at pure prevention and not implying that systemic problems were at stake, independent bodies have been easier to establish, as was the case of the European Committee for the Prevention of Torture and Inhuman or Degrading Treatment or Punishment.

Periodic reports to independent "treaty bodies"

The basic obligation of the signatories of the treaties for the respect and protection of human rights, adopted under the auspices of the United Nations, is to submit initial and later periodic reports on the measures parties have undertaken to implement the relevant treaty. Reports are submitted to "treaty bodies" provided for in the relevant instrument and consisting of independent experts. The system has evolved from the mere study of the report and "constructive dialogue" with the representatives of governments to more thorough examination allowing treaty bodies to pronounce comments on the human rights situation in the reporting state; they can now even disregard periodicity and demand reports when deeming that there are dangerous situations. Reporting procedure has been particularly suited to detect structural problems, especially in the legislation and administrative practices, and possible violations resulting therefrom, otherwise not clearly cognisable in proceedings dealing with individual complaints. Unfortunately, treaty bodies are overburdened, understaffed and left alone to cope with states parties that default in their reporting obligations.

European human rights treaties rely on classical methods of monitoring. The logic of the European arrangement is related to the nature of human rights guaranteed and protected by the European Convention. It deals mainly with the cluster of human rights referred to as civil and political and presumed to be enforceable before courts. It is then held that, in this respect, the ratification of the Convention should have immediate internal effects and that there is no excuse whatsoever for a right contained therein not to be enjoyed in its full scope. Non-compliance can therefore be detected through individual and interstate complaints. It is then understandable that the only reporting obligation of the signatories of the European Convention, contained in Article 57, refers to information as to how their "internal law ensures the effective implementation of any of the provisions of the Convention". These explanations can be requested by the Council of Europe's Secretary General, who cannot pronounce any judgment as to whether internal arrangements described by the state party do in fact ensure effective implementation.

A confirmation of such reasoning can be found in the European Social Charter and its Additional Protocol, which deal with the cluster of rights called economic and social. These rights are generally not judicially enforceable and the states parties undertake only to treat them as goals to be attained by various means, with a minimum (to be determined by each state party) they consider to be valid immediately (Article 20). It follows then that there is need for the signatory states to report on their corresponding decisions and to record progress made toward the goals determined in the Charter. These reports are examined by a series of bodies and organs of the Council of Europe, who can issue relevant views and recommendations (Articles 21-29 of the Social Charter and Article 6 of the protocol). In this case the nature of the international obligation, which heavily depends on circumstances, has dictated the nature of supervision. The Charter and the Additional Protocol do not even envisage the possibility of violation and consequently do not contain provisions on the settlement of disputes between states parties. The prevailing western idea of social and related human rights seems to be that international norms pertaining thereto are "soft law" and that reporting procedures are adequate only where information, consultation and advice is needed on how states will gradually, reasonably and *bona fide* fulfil their "soft" obligations. On the other hand, "hard" obligations relating to civil and political rights are viewed as immediate and unconditional so that their fulfilment can only be tested in judicial or quasi-judicial proceedings, there being no need to report on any "progress", which is logically unthinkable for absolute and present obligations. As we have tried to demonstrate, this is a method that cannot properly and timely identify gross violations and cope with them. With the entry into force of the 1995 Additional Protocol to the European Social Charter Providing for a System of Collective Complaints, the existing supervisory system of the European Social Charter will not depend only on government initiatives and reports: non-governmental organisations will be able to address complaints to the Committee of Independent Experts. The 1996 revised version of the Social Charter also refers to such complaints.

This approach appears to be confirmed by the 1995 Framework Convention for the Protection of National Minorities. Provisions of that treaty are "soft" indeed, especially when compared to the pre-existing obligations of European states under universal and regional treaties. They are in fact guiding principles and only "giving effect" to these principles is a matter to be studied in the reporting procedure envisaged in Section IV of the Framework Convention. Unlike with United Nations procedures, the supervision is not done by an organ of independent experts but by a political body, although assisted by an advisory committee (Article 26).

The possibility, at the regional European level, of appraising the human rights situation in a country through the study of the reports of its government by independent bodies would contribute to the rounding of the protection mechanisms and to adequate detection of structural problems. As reflected in the compromise in the Framework Convention, dilemmas remain regarding the nature of the supervisory body: if it is to be quasi-judicial in terms of the personal independence and apolitical qualities of its members, the danger remains that it would be overawed when facing political problems of greater dimensions, that it would be perceived as morally pompous but unrealistic and impotent, that its findings would be disregarded and its members exposed to excessive pressure eventually leading to suspicions and loss of authority. Even if supervisory bodies would be mandated only to carefully review national legislation for its consistency with human rights obligations, they could perform useful preventing functions.

Field operations

In the recent experience of the United Nations and some other organisations, fact finding, contacts and arrangements with governments can be realised by *ad hoc* or sedentary missions residing in the territory where gross violations are taking place or are considered a present possibility. In fact, field operations are a derivative and refinement of the work of special country rapporteurs. Such operations have as a rule been a part of a wider effort to end conflicts resulting in gross violations of human rights and are not truly preventive in nature. However, they have been an important response to such violations and have been emulated to a certain extent by OSCE missions of different duration. Experiences gained so far have been dependant to a large extent on the given country, the nature of the conflict and the scope of the international reaction. At present it is difficult to make generalisations and to relate them to the Council of Europe.

Theme 1: Prevention of and responses to structural or large-scale human rights violations

Written contribution by Peter Jambrek

Individual complaints v. structural violence; reactive and proactive role of the Strasbourg court of law

Introduction

The notion of "structural violence" was borrowed from H.J. Geiger,[1] and applied from health research on racial discrimination to broader issues of gross, structural, or large-scale human rights violations. As such, structural violence does not refer only to violence as the use of physical force by individuals to cause injury, but also to pervasive personal and institutional actions and policies, which, by intent or omission, result in predictable harm to, and violation of human rights and fundamental freedoms of large populations. Structural violence is entrenched in social fabrics, political economy, and government structure. It is manifest in a wide variety of social policies and legislative actions. The attribute of "structural" points to aetiology, and large-scale to phenomenology of violence/violation. The presence of determinants of systematic violation as a rule results in massive, repetitive and persistent injuries to individual human rights. The attribute of "gross", however, denotes another dimension of violation: its seriousness in terms of the degree of human suffering inflicted. There are tragic instances where both dimensions concur. These are practices of torture, summary, arbitrary and unlawful killings or executions, genocide, slavery-like practices (forced labour, concentration camps), disappearances, arbitrary and prolonged detention, destruction of homes, property and villages ("ethnic cleansing", forced evictions of populations), mass rapes, and systematic discrimination in the enjoyment of fundamental political rights. Such gross, structural and large-scale violations may be termed humanitarian catastrophes, disasters and emergencies. They are concomitant to non-international and international armed conflict, and to ethnopolitical, intergroup or intercommunal strife. Human rights crises are especially aggravated and prolonged where they occur within an authoritarian political culture.

---

1 H. Jack Geiger, "Inequity as Violence: Race, Health and Human Rights in the United States", *Health and Human Rights* (Harvard School of Public Health), Vol. 2, No. 3.

Studies of structural human rights violations do not fail to address the issue of the capacity of the Strasbourg and other international mechanisms of dealing with individual complaints to respond to this kind of violation. In this respect, a court of law and its judges may aptly be compared to doctors in a health clinic. To use the medical analogy, those in the human rights judicial systems act "for the most part like doctors in the emergency room, waiting for the next victims to be wheeled in and then doing the best we can to prevent these patients from dying".[1] Solving individual cases is increasingly seen as "too little" and "too late" as effective crisis response to human rights disasters on a large-scale. In addition to the re-active, the pro-active role of the European Court of Human Rights is therefore increasingly salient.

I. Distinctions between structural and individual violations

1. *Persistence, scale, and seriousness of violations*

Structural, large-scale and gross violations of human rights are not phenomena of the same kind. Human rights abuses, and the respective events, situations and claims, which are embedded in social fabric, in political economy and government practices, are implemented by social policies and legislative action, or are determined by major forms of group discrimination, might be termed "structural" or "systematic". The quantity of structural violation, counted in the number of respective claims, cases, or Court-found breaches, results in "scale", or proportion of actual harm inflicted. Although structural violation tends to be large in scale, there is no conceptual identity between the two dimensions. The category of "gross" violation is equally distinct. It denotes situations of major, absolute, uniquely disproportional, serious, aggravated, excessive, or particularly offensive acts against protected human rights. Gross violations may also vary in scale, i.e. it may occur in rare cases, or be persistent. It may be produced by structural factors, or it may represent a chance and isolated event.

There are tragic situations, where social determinants generate gross violations on a large-scale, giving rise to human rights emergency. Even emergencies may be persistent, as experienced in cases of the three twentieth century systems of total control and repression of individual freedom and human dignity, i.e. by Nazism, communism, and apartheid, all three equally approaching the notion of the absolute evil. Another kind of modern human rights disasters represent crimes against peace and security of mankind.[2]

---

1 Morton Winston, "The Prevention of Institutionalized Intergroup Violence", *Health and Human Rights* (Harvard School of Public Health), Vol. 2, No. 3, p. 16.

2 These kinds of case were already heard by the Nuremberg and Tokyo War Tribunals, by the International War Crimes Tribunal for the Former Yugoslavia and for Rwanda. See also the Code of Crimes against Peace and Security of Mankind proposed by the International Law Commission. There, crimes of aggression, the war of aggression, genocide, crimes against humanity committed in a systematic manner or on a large-scale, political crimes, terrorism, organised violence, institutionalised discrimination, forced disappearance of persons, rape, enforced prostitution, and war crimes are treated. For a discussion of the proposed code see also Christian Tomuschat, *"Das*

2. *Dimensions and typology of abuses*

The three main dimensions of persistence (structural, systematic violations), scale (numbers) and seriousness (gross) might be further split into more specific indicators, while concrete cases are to be found on different ranks of the suggested continua. In this respect distinctions are noteworthy between individual versus large-scale, isolated versus institutional, spontaneous versus intentional, instantaneous versus persistent, incipient versus emergency situation, relative versus gross, specific versus structural, and partial versus total.

Constitutional and international adjudication of individual cases as a rule relates to large numbers of similar cases in similar legal positions. **Large-scale** is thus hardly an exceptional characteristic of a case heard by the Strasbourg Court when Convention standards are applied to domestic legislative and administrative practices or to constitutional adjudication. Institutional are not only cases produced by official policies, but also by the *Drittwirkung* of non-governmental associations. Some of the harm-inflicting practices represent chance-effects of **spontaneous** action in distinction to the intentional, public, and planned official actions. In between both kinds of violation might be placed intentional and persistent, albeit **covert official practices**, such as torture, disappearances and systematic discrimination. Structural determinants produce repetitive, continuous, persistent violations. Their occurrence depends upon the dynamics of the producer and proceeds from the incipient event to the full outbreak of a human rights catastrophe; like the health epidemic, the evolution of a humanitarian emergency may also be best controlled at the very beginning. Obvious candidates for the category of gross violations are breaches of absolute rights and of other rights highly placed on the hierarchy of the Convention-protected human values. Structural and massive violations may be partial, limited to a distinct sector or region, or total and nation-wide. Communism, for example, achieved its goal of total control by mass intimidation, institutional repression, and indoctrination. In its more developed stage it demonstrated the evolution "from mass killings to mass surveillance",[1] and in its fully fledged form of an unchallenged power of party bureaucrats it even engaged in the hypocrisy of a formal domestic recognition of international human rights.

II. Reactive role of the European Court of Human Rights

1. *Effects of individual case adjudication*

Liberal reformers try to reduce injustice by responding to individual claims, while the other strategy is to help individuals by reducing injustice. The European Court of Human Rights is empowered to deal with individual cases only, and is to that

---

Strafgesetzbuch der Verbrechen gegen den Frieden und die Sicherheit der Menschheit", EuGRZ, 25. Jg., Heft 1-4 (1998).

1 "Human rights abuses in state-party systems in more recent years took the form of mass surveillance, instead of mass killing...", in Gabor Halmai, Laszlo Majtenyi, and Kim Lane Scheppele, "Who is an Agent and what can a Constitutional State do with him?" *East European Human Rights Review* (Den Bosch, the Netherlands), Vol. 1, No. 1 (1995), p. 115.

extent embedded into the liberal paradigm. It is therefore vulnerable to the same kind of criticisms. It was suggested, that it responded disappointingly to gross and system violations, and the question was asked whether the use of an individual petition mechanism is at all suited to addressing an ethnopolitical conflict, such as the one taking place in south-eastern Turkey. I am arguing, on the other side, that the reasoning and the implementation of a judgment, although responding to an individual claim only, bear effects which often transcend specific circumstances of the case. Whenever the breach was produced by an established official practice, execution of the judgment as a rule has general effects.

European Convention provisions call in the first place for the *restitutio in integrum*, next for reparation, and if the internal law allows only partial reparation to be made for the consequences of the measure taken by a legal authority in conflict with the Convention, the Court is empowered to afford just satisfaction to the victim.

Thus, when an individual application arose from a structural context, restitution of an individual's rights is necessarily possible only by means of the legal reform, or the change of the official practice. Redress of an individual violation triggers change of the wider pattern or context, although the concrete judgment may lack an explicit *erga omnes* effect. In addition, the Commission and the Court recognised the importance of the context in which an individual has suffered a violation, in order to address the proper nature of a structural violation,[1] termed also "an aggravated violation" where there is "repetition of acts and official tolerance". If the examination and adjudication of an individual case must be performed "within the context", then an analogous consideration must also be granted to its execution, raising special responsibilities of both national authorities and European supervision in case of structural violation. Pierre-Henri Imbert in this context pointed to genuine difficulties in carrying out judgments where governments may be expected to display a certain lack of goodwill, "particularly when structural or highly political problems arise".

2. *Preliminary objections to the hearing of an individual case of structural or large-scale violation*

In my dissenting opinion to the *Loizidou* judgment (merits) of 18 December 1996 I suggested an examination of whether the case is focused in a monocentric way and is ripe for decision, or whether it is not overly moot and political. Robin C.A. White discussed these issues raised by the same judgment under the heading of "justiciability" and summed up the Court's dilemma of "the priority to the effectiveness of the remedies the Convention offers over judicial restraint in the face of issues which might better be addressed in a political forum".[2] In the *Loizidou* judgments on the preliminary objections and on the merits, these kind of issues

---

1 See the Commission's reports and the Court's decisions in the Irish, Cyprus and the Turkish inter-state cases.

2 Robin C.A. White, "Tackling Political Disputes Through Individual Applications", *European Human Rights Law Review* (Sweet and Maxwell Ltd), Issue 1 (1998), p. 72.

were discussed while taking stands on *exceptio ratione temporis*. In several recent Turkish cases they were related to reasoning over exhaustion of domestic remedies. In *Mentes and Others v. Turkey* judgment of 28 November 1997, I discussed in the partly dissenting opinion justiciability of the case in the terms of the division of roles between the domestic authorities and the Strasbourg institutions: difficulties in securing probative evidence, and administrative enquiries, on which such remedies depend, affect not only domestic legal proceedings, but also, and maybe even more so, the international judge's ability to establish and evaluate the facts of the case.

The Court has no discretion to consider explicitly procedural obstacles related to the "political question doctrine" or "justiciability" (as distinct from the United States Supreme Court, where such formulae evolved). Several dissenting judges nevertheless considered such issues under the veil of other preliminary issues. Nonetheless, it must be clearly assessed that the recently established case-law of the European Commission and the Court firmly sided with the opposite view of irrelevance of one or the other facet of the "justiciability doctrine". It therefore even invites comments as to the special appropriateness of the judicial treatment of structural violations: "the more serious the allegations, the more this judicial role is needed, because such cases are much more vigorously contested than allegations of unintentional, technical breaches".[1]

In my dissenting opinion to the *Loizidou* judgment (merits) I discussed the "political nature" of the case from the point of view of the place of the courts in general, and of the Strasbourg mechanism in particular, in the scheme of the division and separation of powers. There, the courts have a different role to play than, e.g. the legislative and executive bodies. Courts are adjudicating in individual and in concrete cases according to prescribed legal standards. They are ill-equipped to deal with large-scale and complex issues which as a rule call for normative and legal reform. There are two weak points to the above argument. First, the overriding task of a human rights court, on domestic and the international level alike, is the protection of human rights, while both legislative and executive bodies have other responsibilities to consider. It may be assumed that on the international plane, parliamentary and executive bodies may show even less concern for human rights issues in view of their orientation to the interests of sovereign member States, and to their common inter-state interests. Therefore, the courts must accept their responsibility for protection of human rights, and maybe even more so, if they happen to be structural, large-scale or gross.

3. *Procedural obstacles and limitations*

There are three main obstacles which limit the efficiency of the European Court's response to applications alleging structural or large-scale violations. Non-collaboration of domestic authorities may be assumed more frequent where covert, intentional

1 Menno T. Kamminga, "Is the European Convention on Human Rights sufficiently equipped to cope with gross and systematic violations?", *Netherlands Quarterly of Human Rights*, Vol. 12, No. 2 (1994).

policies are pursued in contradiction with the Convention standards. Instances were already observed of official interferences with the right to individual complaint. In this respect attempts at intimidation of the actual or potential applicants are most devious. Thirdly, obstacles and limits of domestic and international fact-finding are to be expected where domestic remedies are deficient, ineffective, or even non-existent. Here, reference must be made to the Commission's and the Court's frequent complaint of difficulties in securing and assessing documentary evidence. Both Strasbourg bodies are confronted with inconsistencies and weaknesses in the evidence, difficulties attached to assessing evidence orally through interpreters, or lack of precision and credibility of the testimony.

III. Proactive role of the European Court of Human Rights

1. *The European Court of Human Rights as a constitutional court*

Rolv Ryssdal on several occasions promoted the idea of the European Court of Human Rights as the European Constitutional Court. My concurring opinion in the *Fischer v. Austria* judgment of 26 April 1995 followed the same line. Accordingly, the European Court should not confine itself to ascertaining whether, in the circumstances of the case, the requirements of the Convention's provisions were satisfied or not. It should not hesitate also to couch its findings in more general terms. It would thereby contribute better to the quality of the Court's case-law in the service of the Convention as a living constitutional instrument of European public order. Judge Martens referred to this quality of the Court's case-law in terms of its duty to see to it "that this case-law meets the very same standards of clarity, precision and foreseeability by which the Court usually measures laws of member states in the field of fundamental rights and freedoms". More recently Pierre-Henri Imbert also stressed the need to set European Court's judgments in the wider process of reforms at European level by means of establishing the broad underlying principles that should regulate the member states' legal systems. The role of a constitutional court would obviously facilitate response of the Strasbourg mechanism to the structural and large-scale violations.

2. *Preventative function of the Court's precedents*

Continuity and consistency of the European case-law strengthens its role of a standard-setting judicial body, transcending its sheer function of case by case adjudication. The more predictable, precise and foreseeable the prospective judgments of the Court are in view of its established case-law, the more general and preventative are effects of its precedents. Prospective perpetrators of the firmly set human rights standards might thus be discouraged from repeating the same kind of offences.

3. *Hidden and unintended functions of dealing with individual complaints*

Non-legal consequences of settling and redressing individual cases are probably underestimated by the legal practitioners. Early warning, detection in intervention functions of incipient cases of large-scale or structural violations might stall further development of a human rights epidemic, or prevent the outbreak of a human rights disaster. European judgment in an individual case nevertheless facilitates international and domestic public exposure of deviant official practices, policies and legislation. Independent judicial examination and hearing of a case might intimidate domestic authorities in view of the forthcoming international sanctions. The finding of an individual violation de-legitimates domestic official tolerance of structural violation and its official tolerance and justification. Adjudication of a concrete case may lead to international pressure and the respective requests to reform social determinants of systematic violations.

Final remarks

Large-scale or structural human rights violations are endemic also in the established western democracies. The large-scale and enduring cases of violations of the reasonable time requirement of Article 6 of the Convention, massive complaints about dangers of water, soil, and air pollution by chemical factories, maritime port waste disposals, or the alleged risks for life and health of residents close to a nuclear power station, official responsibility for infections of haemophilia patients with the HIV virus, or isolated Article 2 complaints against domestic government are examples which prove the point.

Complaints about the particularly gross and large-scale structural violations nevertheless originate from those European regions where ethnopolitical conflict prevails, e.g. in Cyprus, Northern Ireland, and south-eastern Turkey. There, repressive official practices add to the spread of human rights disasters. New European regions of intercommunal conflict may be expected to enter the list, e.g. Bosnia and Herzegovina, Kosovo, or Chechnya.

Another issue of great concern represents totalitarian heritage of the European communist regimes. The European Court's task in this respect involves elimination of the remaining institutional determinants of past structural human rights abuses, provision of remedies for victims of large-scale human rights abuses perpetrated under the communist rule, and assessment of responsibility versus impunity for gross and large-scale human rights violation of former communist officials.

In conclusion, I would recommend the following main judicial and extra-judicial strategies to deal with large-scale or structural violations on the European level:

- Continued adherence to the doctrine of subsidiarity in view of the exhaustion of effective domestic remedies only;
- Irrelevance of the "political question doctrine" in responding to and redressing human rights abuses;
- Strengthened constitutional method of adjudication for the European Court of Human Rights;
- Recognition and articulation of the still hidden and unintended preventative and general functions of individual cases adjudication; and,
- Global approach in solving structural issues, relying upon links and bridges of the European Court to the other "supporting" Council of Europe mechanisms.

Theme 1: Prevention of and responses to structural or large-scale human rights violations

Report on Discussion Group 1: Vojin Dimitrijević

The discussion was marked by a broad consensus among participants on the proven usefulness of existing instruments and procedures at European level in preventing structural or large-scale human rights violations. However, procedures based on individual applications have their limits, both legal and political, in responding to structural problems. Therefore, most contributions referred to the need for improvements in the Council of Europe's armoury for the defence of human rights throughout the continent, even beyond the boundaries of its forty member states, using a variety of judicial and extra-judicial means. The gradual development of international and inter-governmental structures within the Council of Europe over five decades has given rise to a solid *acquis* upon which to base future activities in this domain and to face ever-present threats to human life, freedom, welfare and dignity.

The discussion initially centred on the nature and scope of prevention. United Nations High Commissioner Mary Robinson had spoken during the opening session of a continuum in the prevention of human rights violations on a wide scale. This idea was echoed by a number of speakers who developed the theme that remedial action forms part of prevention. Even where human rights have already suffered gross infringement, the intervention of human rights or humanitarian agencies serves to prevent recurrence or a worsening in a situation which is already critical and unstable.

Speakers emphasised the importance of detecting factors which may lead to gross violations of human rights. Practical examples were given from the experience of both international bodies and NGOs. Examples were also given by participants of cases in which the failure to detect such factors or to take action at an early stage led to catastrophic results, among them Rwanda and Kosovo.

The contribution of NGOs to the prevention of structural human rights violations was raised in many contributions, which underlined the inestimable value of their vigilance and their potential to act as catalysts of changes in public opinion. NGOs have a proven record in highlighting the unacceptability and illegality of situations which constitute a negation of the rights of groups of citizens. The need to support the adoption of the United Nations draft declaration on the protection of human rights defenders was underlined. As the rapporteur had observed in his written report, the expansion of the Council of Europe eastwards brought it into contact with states of markedly different legal and civil cultures and traditions, not always supportive of the standards and mechanisms of human rights supervision. NGOs have a crucial role in bringing about a human rights culture, although the efforts of all sectors of society and government are needed in the long term to achieve this objective.

Similarly, the Council of Europe's co-operation programmes with new member states play an important role in promoting an effective national framework for the protection of human rights, full democracy, the rule of law, economic development and a strong civil society. Many participants considered that in the absence of active human rights groups at the domestic level, any international initiatives or action in defence of human rights would not have full effect. NGO representatives at the discussion were supported in their request for readier access to the various Council of Europe organs responsible for various aspects of human rights protection and a better flow of information between both sides.

Within the existing framework of the Council of Europe, the preventive role of the Committee for the Prevention of Torture, described as providing "risk assessment" to states and the Council of Europe, was considered. The discussion acknowledged the success of the Committee in carrying out its mandate and alerting states to the dangers of torture, inhuman or degrading treatment occurring in places of detention. However, examples were also given of failure to follow up on the Committee's recommendations, effectively undermining the value of its role as an organ of prevention. In order to overcome this problem, the necessity of publicising human rights violations and the means available to redress them was stressed.

The importance of deterrents, including criminal prosecution of violators, was discussed, with appeals to all member states of the Council of Europe to ratify the statute of the International Criminal Court rapidly, and to clearly demonstrate their support for the work of the Hague Tribunal on the Former Yugoslavia. Existing judicial procedures do have certain inhibitive effects, but they seem not to deter potential perpetrators of large-scale human rights violations Impunity for gross violations of human rights should not be tolerated.

States were urged to demonstrate their adherence to the cause of human rights protection by ratifying all relevant international treaties. They should also ensure that other international agreements, e.g. trade agreements, do not contradict this objective by supporting policies likely to result in situations conducive to large-scale violations of human rights.

Participants agreed that attention should be focussed on improving existing mechanisms and procedures for detecting and preventing human rights abuses rather than creating new ones.

The only exception considered was the proposed Commissioner for Human Rights. However, some participants warned that the functions of the European Commissioner remain vague and ill-defined and that there was a danger that his/her activity would duplicate that of the United Nations High Commissioner.

Other speakers supported the establishment of the new office, provided it does not simply replace the outgoing Commission but deals with matters related to prevention, the provision of information and the making available of advice and good offices. The new Commissioner should be allowed to develop the capacity of the Council of Europe to receive advance warning of grave threats to human rights and to take appropriate action. There were suggestions, nevertheless, that these functions could be carried out by the Secretary General under the existing terms of his office.

The need for cohesion between the various Council of Europe human rights bodies was affirmed by speakers. Specifically, this could take the form of regular meetings of chairpersons of such bodies, the permanent exchange of information and expertise, the streamlining and co-ordination of the various procedures to gain more transparency, avoiding wasted efforts and time.

With reference to the European Convention on Human Rights, the imminent entry into force of the Eleventh Protocol was welcomed. There was agreement that more effort is required in supervising the implementation of Court decisions, especially where the case raises issues of broader application within the state concerned. In this way, the individual decision can have beneficial repercussions on a broader group of people. The Committee of Ministers should ensure that, in accordance with its role under Article 54 of the Convention, states take all appropriate steps to comply with decisions, including structural changes. Judge Jambrek's argument that the doctrine of political question had no place in the reasoning of an international court was supported on condition that the Court not be expected to perform the task of the political organs of the Council of Europe.

The value of reporting systems was debated. Although the flaws of this method of supervision are widely known, valuable examples were given of how United Nations bodies have refined the basic reporting system so as to overcome the problems of incompleteness, lateness and lack of transparency. Again, the input of NGOs was recognised as being of the utmost importance. The Additional Protocol to the European Social Charter providing for a System of Collective Complaints was welcomed as a significant improvement in the supervisory mechanism of the Charter, hitherto dependent on national reports. A speaker from the European Commission against Racism and Intolerance informed the discussion of his Committee's progress in improving its method of gathering information and liaising with other sources of information. The Committee for the Protection of National Minorities' potential to establish itself as a truly independent body was raised. Participants were assured of its intention to do so. It was suggested that it could strengthen its contribution by publicising its findings in advance of the final decision of the Committee of Ministers, bringing transparency to the procedure.

There was a strong feeling that the existing monitoring procedures of the Committee of Ministers and the Parliamentary Assembly need to be substantially strengthened and made more transparent. Other strategies such as the appointment of country or thematic rapporteurs were recommended.

The importance was stressed of ensuring that all international interventions in defence of peace and security incorporate human rights protection and include human rights experts. Experience gained from United Nations and CSCE field operations should be carefully studied in order to secure a strong human rights element in all efforts at conflict prevention and resolution.

Finally, emphasis was placed on closer co-operation between the Council of Europe and other organisations such as the European Union and the OSCE when confronted with situations which contain the potential to erupt into massive, widespread human rights violations. These organisations should already exchange information and ensure regular consultation with one another. Participants welcomed the existing co-operation in this field, but could only call for renewed efforts especially with respect to preventive measures.

Theme 2: Social rights: the challenge of indivisibility and interdependence

Rapporteur: Aalt Willem Heringa

1. Introduction

Human rights are universal, indivisible and interdependent and interrelated. Civil rights and liberties have found an increasingly effective protection within (the Council of) Europe. Social rights protection does exist, but these rights seem somehow to lack a similarly effective and widely accepted recognition. Amazing in this respect is the Council of Europe's "double approach": on the one hand underlining the indivisibility of human rights; "relaunching" and strengthening the European Social Charter and drafting the European Social Charter (Revised), while at the same time allowing states to become a member of the Council of Europe without being a party to the Charter. In that respect the European Convention on Human Rights enjoys a preferential treatment as compared to the Charter. Bearing this in mind, it would be important to link accession to the Council of Europe with a commitment to ratify the Charter as well. Such an approach would also be an important signal for those member states that as yet have not ratified the Charter.

In this paper I will focus on the question of how to improve this situation and how to give hands and feet to the need to protect vulnerable groups, to prevent and end social exclusion and to further state obligations in various important areas such as education and health.

In recent years many attempts have been made to "relaunch" the European Social Charter and to improve its record of effective implementation. New protocols have been added: adding new rights (1988); revising the supervision procedure (1991); adding a system for collective complaints (1995); even a European Social Charter (Revised) has been adopted (1996). Although these efforts are important, much still remains to be hoped for. For instance:

- many more states signing and ratifying the Charter and its protocols;
- more attention to be paid to the Charter and the results of the supervision procedures specifically in the national (legal) order;
- a greater awareness of the links between liberties and social rights.

It is also interesting to note that only recently the first east European state (Poland) ratified the European Social Charter. In my opinion the Charter has, unjustly, been perceived as a costly threat to the development of a new society and a new economy. This perception, however, missed the point that liberties are also expensive (e.g. under Article 6 of the European Convention on Human Rights), and that social rights create a balance in society.

In my opinion it is important to draw our inspiration in this respect from the strength of civil rights and liberties and their systems of protection. This approach, however, should not lead us to close our eyes to the fact that social rights protection occasionally needs a different setting. I will, however, try to underline that social rights can profit from an open mind as to a new *modus operandi*.

2. The strength of civil liberties

In order to be able to transplant "libertarian approaches" to the area of social rights one has to identify the strengths of the protection of civil rights. Basically they are the following:

- Their *enforceability in courts*: it is easier for a court to prohibit censorship than it is to determine how many police may be necessary in order to protect a specific demonstration. However, even in this area courts managed to work out various instruments and tests, for instance: was the refusal to provide police protection reasonable, proportionate or not arbitrary?
- The reliance on *concrete, individual cases*. It is far easier to balance the situation of an individual citizen *vis-à-vis* the state than it is to balance the interests of groups (or even of abstract concepts, such as a "clean environment") and the state. But also in these areas courts have managed to develop criteria to do so.
- The increasing reliance on abstract *aides of interpretation* in establishing and gradually developing human rights instruments: rights must be effective and not illusory; rights are based on principles and the determination of the relevant principle can help in distilling even other rights and further principles.
- The reliance on *remedies* in order to allow individuals to invoke their claims and have them enforced.
- The necessity in this respect of *open deliberative democratic procedures* through which interests, rights and counter-interests can be challenged and processed; the recognition of transparency, debate and consultation is specifically relevant.
- In this respect non-governmental organisations, trade unions etc. are important. The 1995 Protocol to the Charter is also proof of this. Their role is, in any society, important in the protection of liberties and of social rights.
- The need to judge specific situations from the point of view of whether the individual had an *effective access* to the civil liberty: a specific state might have an excellent court system, but if an individual is in practice prevented from having access to it, that right can be considered to be infringed. Therefore, one can some-

times discuss issues of legal rights in terms of access to the (protective) institutions whose existence is also part of the guarantee itself.

These aspects can be noticed in the case-law of the European Court of Human Rights as well as in constitutional case-law in various European countries.

3. Using these findings in the area of social rights

Evidently, social rights are rights with a different background and focus than civil liberties. Their primary aim is to promote and stimulate state action; they see the individual in its relations with other individuals; they are partly related to the prosperity and economic situation in a given society. The absence of censorship can be claimed irrespective to economic circumstances, whereas the level of social benefits is closely related to the welfare-level. However: it has to be noted that even a relatively straightforward right, as is the right to be free from censorship, is related to the situation in society, be it not the economic state of affairs but the public order. Under Article 10 (2) of the European Convention on Human Rights even censorship can be justifiable if necessary in a democratic society.

Bearing this in mind I suggest the following proposals; they have the common aim of improving awareness and possibly the effectiveness of social rights by more explicitly connecting them to civil liberties.

1. *Enforceability*

One of the essential features of civil liberties is their enforceability: they are formulated as directly enforceable rights: this means that one option would be to gradually try to formulate social rights whenever and wherever possible as such rights. For instance: instead of only formulating a right to good working conditions, it would be feasible also to draft, as part of a general claim to proper working conditions, a right not to be confronted with unsafe, unhealthy, dangerous or risky working conditions.

2. *Social rights advice*

Another aspect of civil liberties concerns the procedural aspect: the necessity of having an open and transparent discussion as to the restrictions of civil liberties and as to the implementation of social rights. This implies, evidently, debates and decision-making by the proper public authorities and, ultimately, by national legislatures and parliaments. Such a transparent reasoned decision-making process presumes the availability of data, processed also from the social rights perspective and not only from an economic perspective. In many countries decision-making in the area of social rights is based upon reports and findings drafted by organs with budgetary and accounting responsibilities. My proposal in this respect would be to install an organ/commission/departmental department, which has the explicit task of reviewing and discussing governmental proposals, bills, budgets, etc. from the perspective of their consequences to social rights. Such advice, together with a response from the competent government authority (for instance in a "social rights paragraph" in the explanatory memorandum), would definitely lead to a greater awareness of the content of social rights. It would also improve debate and the search for creative solutions, whilst recognising the primary responsibility of the competent legislature and political authorities.

This function of criticising and debating with national authorities their social rights record is at present a very important task of the supervisory organs under the European Social Charter. Their role could be strengthened if they could rely on an equivalent national organ; the existence and functioning of national advisory bodies (or a similar institution) would definitively improve and facilitate the supervision by the Council of Europe. Such a national institution would enable States to set things straight before an international organ pronounces on a state's performance as to the implementation of treaty obligations. Such an advisory body could e.g. comment on the report the state has to submit under the Charter; it could have its comments annexed to this report so as to provide invaluable information to the Committee of Independent Experts; it could monitor the implementation of suggestions and recommendations of the supervisory organs, etc. It also seems a good step to include non-governmental organisations in the composition of these bodies. That would also strengthen civil society and signal a recognition of the important role in society of non-governmental organisations.

3. *Right of access*

Under Article 6 of the European Convention on Human Rights the Court has formulated a right to have access to courts; an effective access occasionally also requires the obligation to provide effective legal aid and legal assistance by a lawyer. To put it differently: a right of access to the institution "courts" and to the institution "legal aid" and "legal assistance". Aspects of social rights could also be perceived in similar terms: for instance the right to access to hospitals or to schools. As in the field of access to the courts, an individual could claim an effective right of access to social rights' institutions.

4. *Concrete cases*

The case-law of the European Court of Human Rights, particularly with respect to "positive obligations", has gradually been developed. This development took place on the basis of concrete cases. This enabled the Court to slowly shape the contours of this obligation: what is the scope of this obligation in the context of a fair trial (Article 6) and what is the context of Article 8 (private life and family life)? The advantage of this approach has been that the Court was not tempted to come up with general statements and the formulation of abstract obligations: they were very concrete and linked to the specific circumstances of the cases in hand. Even so, looking back on the various cases dealing with different aspects of the positive obligations doctrine of the Court one can see the emergence of general criteria.

The European Court's case law with respect to positive obligations is, considered from the social rights perspective, not at all perfect. The Court could certainly draw more inspiration from the Charter in its attempts to formulate specific positive obligations. If we consider (social) exclusion of minorities, the indigent or the handicapped to be one of the evils of modern society, the European Social Charter (Revised) explicitly addresses this issue. The European Court might take this

Charter more explicitly into account in formulating positive obligations, linking them to the European Convention as well as to the Charter.

The feature of gradual development is not an uncommon one in national legal systems: the development of the law in relatively new areas takes place gradually. This aspect has been neglected in legal thinking and the codification of social rights. They have been written down as abstract principles, sometimes not even as clearly enforceable rights, without a clear link to the way legal orders operate. In order to change this situation, it is imperative to enable individuals to resort to social rights in legal proceedings. This can be done directly, in the sense that one claims a right to a social benefit, or indirectly: utilising social rights arguments as supporting arguments for instance in claiming the absence of due process: one's interests have not been balanced properly.

On the international level this approach implies the need to have an international complaints procedure under treaties such as the International Covenant on Economic, Social and Cultural Rights and the European Social Charter. An interesting first step is the signing and entering into force of the 1995 Additional Protocol to the European Social Charter Providing for a System of Collective Complaints. This protocol is in my opinion an essential step forward; and so is a generous recognition of non-governmental organisations which will be qualified to lodge a complaint under this protocol. But, apart from that, such a procedure must be considered only as a first step: the requirements attached to it still imply that social rights issues can only be addressed in the abstract. A next step would be in my opinion to set up a European court of social rights, that in the long term could gradually merge with the European Court of Human Rights, possibly through an intermediate structure of one court with two chambers. In order to prepare for such a social rights court, the Charter has to be strengthened through the increase of ratifications and of its weight in national (legal) opinion. I do not consider it a good option to transfer individual rights from the Charter to the European Convention. This approach ignores the fact that liberties and social rights are mutually dependent and also the fact that social rights have many aspects which cannot be treated in isolation. In general I am convinced that the long-term future goal has to be that the European Convention and the Social Charter will have to merge: this will also do justice to the fact that these rights have many features in common.

4. Principles and rights common to both social rights and civil liberties

Basically social rights and civil liberties have a common denominator and goal: *respect for the individual human being*. This implies, since this finding is valid for all human beings, the necessity of equal respect. Acceptance as a human being implies: the rights to be educated, to speak out, to have access to all parts of social and economic life, etc..

Another common principle seems to be *the principle of personhood*: the principle that each individual has the right to personality and personal development. This principle has two aspects: (1) to be free from interference = the right to privacy in its libertarian sense, and (2) the right to have the possibility to develop one's personality, to develop relations with other human beings, etc.: this aspect can lead to the establishment of positive obligations for the national authorities to effectively enable the individual citizen to enjoy his personhood. This second aspect is in my opinion presently "under construction" in the case-law of the European Court of Human Rights.

A third common element is the *equality principle*: liberties and rights are rights of all individuals: this simple recognition presumes the attachment of these rights to the notion of non-discrimination and equality. Subsequently the question arises what meaning has to be attached to the notion of equality in this respect: only the notion of non-discrimination, that is the absence of arbitrary distinctions. Or, also including the aspect of equal opportunities and the realisation of *de facto* equality, in the sense that the enjoyment of the rights guaranteed must be accessible effectively and equally, so as not to create illusory rights. The second interpretation can lead to positive obligations for the national authorities, because it will be for them to ensure this equality in the enjoyment of social rights.

Thus, whenever a state sets up a specific system and level of benefits of some kind, the equality principle implies that no arbitrary distinctions are made. And when the right to decent housing is concerned the consequences will be that no discrimination exists in the allocation of houses, or that housing programmes in general are balanced such as to meet the demands of various house-seekers. The equality principle also plays an important role in the *Conclusions* of the Committee of Independent Experts; it seems to consider the absence of discrimination to be an inherent feature of the Charter's social rights. The European Court's case-law with respect to Article 14 also conforms this trend. Very important in the context of social rights protection, however, will also be the coming about of a non-discrimination/equality protocol to the European Convention. Such a protocol could and should ensure that social rights will have to be guaranteed and implemented in a non-discriminatory manner.

Fourthly, social rights are based upon the effective existence of liberties and liberties are based on the realisation of social rights: *the principle of mutual dependence*. The right to respect of private life is related to "old-fashioned" infringements such as searches and seizures by the police, but also to modern-day invasions of privacy through noise, pollution and contamination of one's private sphere. A transparent public debate about the implementation of social rights requires, among others, freedom of speech, the existence of political parties and trade unions. The development in the case-law of the European Court of Human Rights of so-called "positive obligations" is illustrative in this respect; and so is the attention paid in the European Social Charter to liberties as the freedom of association, and in the restriction clause, to the necessity in a democratic society.

5. Using these common fundamentals for social rights

It is interesting to note that many of the aspects described in the preceding paragraph are in fact principles that introduce in the area of liberties "social rights elements", that is, elements that impose obligations on the states. It seems to me that under the case law of the European Court the freedoms laid down in the European Convention of Human Rights are opening up for social rights. The fear of many that social rights might lead to the abolition of freedom and of liberties is unfounded: the provisions in the Convention seem to prosper because of the generous case-law of the Court with respect to its reliance on positive obligations.

The advantages of such a combined approach are also visible vice versa: liberties, such as the freedom of trade unions, also strengthen the effects and impact of social rights. In this respect I have also touched upon the increasing relevance in the area of social rights of Article 8 (private life) of the European Convention. One can also add in this respect Article 3 of the European Convention, in the sense that social exclusion can attain such a level so as to constitute a form of degrading treatment. Finally, Article 6 of the European Convention is a good example of the relevance of judicial proceedings also in social rights disputes (when they qualify as civil rights). The right to employment and specifically the accompanying right to be protected against unfair dismissal benefits from adequate legal remedies and an effective access to a court.

Another important matter relates to the development of a right which protects against intrusions in the widest possible sense: intrusions in one's home and privacy; noise; pollution; effects on one's health; the need to be informed (and consulted) on possible (likely) effects on health and private life; the right to be able to develop relations with others etc: the notion of the right to personhood. This right is an important basis for strengthening social rights through an individual approach. An employee can invoke this right in order to be informed about important relevant decisions that affect his work and his job; or to invoke adequate protection with regard to dangerous working conditions; or to initiate claims when his health has been severely damaged by labour conditions. Claims and individual rights like these will inevitably lead to in general better procedures of consultation and better working conditions.

6. Concluding remarks

We have seen the emergence of many elements common to all human rights:

1. *Access* to institutional human rights guarantees. This access can only be limited on the basis of necessary and proportional restrictions. Restrictions are not *per se* unacceptable, but what is, is a lack of an effective access, or a discriminatory or arbitrary or structural denial.

2. *Democratic procedures* that ensure that human rights are taken into account and that can help a state to fully act in conformity with treaty obligations and will help the contracting states to improve their respective levels of achievement. A national advisory body and the introduction of explanatory "social rights" paragraphs could be helpful in this respect. In line with the finding that human rights are interrelated, it might even be better to install a general national human rights commission/body and general human rights paragraphs.

3. Attention for the existence of *liberties in social rights* (freedom of trade unions) and of *social rights in liberties* ("positive obligations"). It is already the practice in

the case-law of the European Court to pay attention to factual possibilities to fully participate in legal and social life.

4. The recognition of the role of *non-governmental organisations* and their importance in mediation, consultation and voicing individual demands; the recognition of their involvement in national implementation and monitoring procedures.
5. The existence of *common denominators* such as the right to personhood and the equality-principle. These rights are in fact mixed rights: liberty as well as social right. In my opinion, they are powerful tools in combining liberty and social right approaches and in strengthening liberties as well as social rights.
6. Emphasis on the notions of effective enjoyment. In that respect one has to bear in mind the undisputed aim to seek to adequately respect all human beings as equals.
7. The importance not only to focus on abstract policies and goals, but also on individual concrete cases. The step forward we can and have to make in the area of social rights is by recognising that this focus is also possible in the field of social rights.
8. In reviewing the states' performances under the European Social Charter the Committee of Experts ought to continue and expand its approach with respect to drawing inspiration from liberties as those guaranteed in the European Convention. Also it appears to be useful to try to distinguish the various elements and layers of rights and obligations contained in the provisions in the Charter.

   Mutatis mutandis the development by the European Court of Human Rights of the doctrine of "positive obligations" has to be applauded. In this respect it seems useful to have regard to the rights and obligations in the Social Charter. The Charter could also be referred to when giving content to the right to "personhood" under Article 8; or when interpreting the notion of "degrading treatment" in Article 3.

   In the case-law of both supervisory organs the roots of such a mutually inspired course are visible. It is a promising course. It shows that the European system of protection of human rights is a dynamic one and is open to further development and progress. It is also a course of small steps and gradual evolution. But precisely these characteristics will prove to be the strength of the system.
9. The recognition of the (Revised) European Social Charter as a treaty with a status equal to that of the European Convention of Human Rights, as a document which has to be accepted by all the Council of Europe's member states.

Theme 2: Social rights: the challenge of indivisibility and interdependence

Written contribution by Giorgio Filibeck

Towards a right to the satisfaction of basic material human needs

"Fraternity was invented to resolve the contradictions between freedom and equality. Solidarity has attenuated the class war. But social citizenship has yet to be invented."

A. Madec/N. Murard, *Citoyenneté et politiques sociales*

If there is one challenge to the indivisibility and interdependence of human rights, it is certainly the fact that there are people in every European country, although in varying proportions, who find themselves without clothing, shelter, food and medical care, to the extent that their lives are in danger.

At the inter-university colloquy held in Fribourg in 1983 on the indivisibility of human rights, M. Borghi made the point that, ultimately, human rights cannot be divided for the simple reason that they are a response to the individual's basic needs: one cannot, for instance, draw a distinction between the need to express one's opinion and the need for food and shelter.

Clearly, the needs mentioned above are basic needs: if they are not met, the very concept of human dignity shrivels; it is, as it were, truncated and becomes an outright caricature.

Moreover, these are needs that defy assignment to a category. It would be wrong to limit them to the "social" sphere, since they are part of what can only be defined as the specifically human sphere and therefore have two dimensions: individual and collective.

As Patrice Meyer-Bisch pointed out at the Fribourg colloquy mentioned above, whether we like it or not the indivisibility of human rights necessitates an individually and community based form of anthropology, which forsakes the two abstract entities constituted by the individual and the community in favour of a specific concept of the human being, as an irreducible social entity.

In fact, to talk of the right to the satisfaction of basic material human needs is tantamount not only to asserting a fundamental human right but also to reaching out to every human being in distress.

Various aspects of such a right are recognised at European level by certain provisions of the European Social Charter and at national level by constitutions, legislation or case-law.

In particular, a Swiss Federal Court judgment of 27 October 1995 asserted that this right could be enforced by the courts. Accordingly, at the Holy See delegation's suggestion, the Council of Europe Steering Committee for Human Rights (CDDH) saw fit to embark on a study of the matter. Initially, it raised the issue at the Conference on Human Dignity and Social Exclusion (Helsinki, 18-20 May 1998). Its contribution to the proceedings was taken into account, and one of the proposals for action that emerged from the conference concerns the role that a new human rights approach can play in combating social exclusion.

For its part, the CDDH decided to continue its research by appointing an ad hoc working group to examine the conference action plan and suggest follow-up measures.

This is a major challenge, since the work could lead to the inclusion of the right to the satisfaction of basic material human needs in the machinery of the European Convention on Human Rights (ECHR), by means of an additional protocol. Its inclusion would be exemplary in demonstrating that the false dichotomy between human rights and social rights can and must be transcended.

It is worth noting that at the start of its work on the subject, the CDDH talked of the right to minimum subsistence conditions. But as it delved further into the matter, it became apparent that this expression could not only be interpreted as aiming at a "minimalist" approach to what is, after all, a crucial issue, but also be confused with systems providing for a minimum wage.

It was therefore thought preferable to use different terminology and refer to the concept of basic material human needs, which has the additional advantage of making it clear from the outset that there are also basic spiritual human needs, which are, moreover, already covered by the ECHR.

In any event, it is important to make the point that setting out such a right in no way undermines a state's obligations in the social field. Measures taken at national level to ensure that this right is observed can on no account replace existing social security and family support systems.

If the right to the satisfaction of basic material human needs is to be properly recognised, current efforts to promote it need to be protected both from unduly enthusiastic advocates and from over-critical opponents. The former hamper progress with somewhat naïve enthusiasm, underestimating the various ramifications, while the latter overestimate the difficulties and sometimes tend to put obstacles in its path, fearing that the European Court of Human Rights will have too much power to supervise national policy in the social field, or that such a right would cost too much.

Yet it is possible to formulate such a right in a balanced fashion that should neither disappoint the enthusiasts nor frighten the sceptics. The constitutions and legislation of certain European countries already recognise, to a greater or lesser extent, the existence of such a right and provide for means of enforcing it at national or local level.

It is time to be clear-sighted and to give the right to the satisfaction of basic material human needs the protection it deserves – that which is consistent with human dignity – by proclaiming this right as a human right.

Allow me to remind you of the verse in the Gospel where Jesus says, "The poor always ye have with you." These words are sometimes somewhat cynically misused in the world of globalisation in which we live, subject to seemingly unchanging economic laws.

But the poverty resulting from limited resources is one thing; the poverty of someone who is shivering with cold, has no roof over his or her head, is underfed, needs medical care and is wasting away is quite another. Let us not forget the simple but haunting message of Father Joseph Wrensinski, whose name is justifiably displayed on the forecourt of the Palais de l'Europe: "Slavery has been abolished; poverty can be abolished too."

Theme 2: Social rights: the challenge of indivisibility and interdependence

Written contribution by Evelyn Messner

1. Introduction

In the field of the legal protection of human rights the emphasis is still laid on the protection of civil rights and liberties. In other words, the predominating role is played by these "classic" human rights. The problem of social rights seems to have been regarded as less important and there seems to be a lack of awareness that social rights form an indivisible part of human rights and do need special, and above all effective, legal protection.

In my opinion it is clear that many more states should ratify the European Social Charter and its protocols in order to strengthen the legal basis of social rights as an inevitable basis for the effective protection of these rights. But in order to attain this objective one must work to further the general consciousness and acceptance of social rights. In what follows I shall try to point out the special problems affecting the legal protection of social rights and their acceptance as an indispensable part of universal human rights.

2. The role of the prevailing economic doctrine of neoliberalism

The exercise of social rights, such as the right to work, is closely connected with and dependent on the economic situation and the economic standards in the individual state. According to the prevailing doctrine of neoliberalism the state should generally restrict its activities to the creation of a stable framework which provides for the unrestricted development of the mechanisms of free markets. The effective protection of "classic" civil rights, such as the right to property and the freedom of gainful activity, has to be regarded as one essential part of this framework. According to liberal philosophy the generally free development of market mechanisms is supposed to lead to a just allocation of goods and the creation of welfare. In the light of these considerations one could conclude that the effective protection of civil rights and liberties by state institutions or by international authorities or courts more or less automatically implies the effective exercise of social rights. So in the light of such a doctrine the special protection of social rights as such does not seem to be necessary.

Against that background the economic doctrine of neoliberalism as described above must be seen as one essential factor – which makes it so difficult to understand and accept that a specific and effective legal protection is essential not only as far as civil rights are concerned but also in the field of social rights.

3. The problem of having full scope in economic policy

Whereas civil rights and liberties primarily aim at the protection of the individual against state action and hence are to curtail state intervention, social rights are generally intended to promote state activities. Against this background it is often stated that social rights could involve considerable costs, that is, expense to the state.

So the undertaking of legally binding obligations to guarantee and to protect the exercise of social rights implies two problems: on the one hand, states may be afraid of losing their autonomy to decide on measures concerning their economic policy. For example, an attained level of social security or economic and social protection of families must be kept, even in times of poor economic situations – a consideration which more or less determines actions and reactions in the field of economic policy. On the other hand, the question arises whether under the present conditions of globalisation and internationalisation a single state in fact still has the possibilities and power to take effective measures in order to finance social rights. In other word, one can ask the question: does competition between states for international investors leave room enough for fiscal and other measures covering the protection of social human rights.

Considering these circumstances I am of the opinion that it would be necessary to make greater efforts to convince people of the fact that guaranteed social rights and hence social freedom do create a positive climate for a prosperous and steady development of economic activities and welfare. One has to realise that the protection of social rights does not only imply costs. We have to be conscious of the fact that social rights can also be profitable in an economic sense.

The challenge of avoiding "social dumping" in the context of globalisation must be met by a more intensive co-operation between states in social matters. Uncoordinated legal measures on a national basis cannot be successful in this context. On the other hand, one must be aware of the fact that there are also problems on the national level that can hinder the effective protection of human rights.

4. The problem of enforceability under national law in Austria

The problem of enforceability is a direct consequence of the fact that social rights generally necessitate state action. It has been the subject of intense discussions in Austrian jurisprudence.

The Austrian Constitution places the protection of the "classic" civil rights and freedoms in the hands of the Austrian Constitutional Court, which is entitled and obliged to reverse decisions of the authorities and to repeal legal provisions that infringe human rights. The Constitutional Court, however, has no right to oblige the parliament to pass special legal provisions; in other words, it has no power to determine directly the contents of legal provisions.

Against this background the effective enforceability of social rights would require a fundamental change in the competences and functions of the Austrian Constitutional Court. This aspect has often been emphasised in discussions on human rights in Austria. The mere power to reverse decisions and to repeal legal provisions is not sufficient to enforce social rights. I should like to illustrate that by giving an example.

With a view to ensuring the effective exercise of the right to benefit from social welfare services, a state has to promote or to provide services which, by using methods of social work, contribute to the welfare and development of both individuals and groups in the community, and to their adjustment to the social environment. The effective enforcement of this right in the form of asserting a claim before a court would require the court to be empowered to oblige the state – that is, specific state authorities – to establish adequate services or to procure, for instance, subsidies promoting private institutions. The whole situation is similar as regards the right to education. Considering the present scope of competence of the Austrian Constitutional Court, such necessary reforms would represent an enormous legal change which is not likely to be accepted in the near future.

In my opinion it would be more realistic to incorporate social rights into the Austrian Constitutional law as general targets and as guidelines covering the exercise of competences of state authorities. Considering that important changes generally take their time, such a measure could be regarded as a first step in paving the way for a universal reform of the protection of social rights.

5. Conclusion

The effectiveness of social rights protection seems to be curtailed by a lack of awareness of the importance and the possible beneficial economic effects of social rights, by global economic conditions and by a lack of adequate instruments in national laws. An improvement in effectiveness would require both national and international measures.

Theme 2: Social rights: the challenge of indivisibility and interdependence

Written contribution by Patrice Meyer-Bisch

The application of the "indivisibility" principle

1. Paradoxically, it is perhaps in Europe more than Asia or the Middle East that the universality of human rights is most contested. In Europe human rights do not all enjoy the same regard, i.e. their enforceability is not identical, and so indivisibility, the logical foundation of universality, remains an exclusively moral concern. I agree fully with Aalt Willem Heringa when, in his introductory report, he addresses the Council of Europe's "two-tier" approach. At the United Nations, indivisibility has been proclaimed, but has scarcely been analysed or given tangible form. At the Council of Europe, we suffer from an insufficient theoretical framework in this area.

A two-tier approach

2. None of the supposedly inherent distinctions between the accepted categories of human rights justifies the persistence of a two-tier approach, which is a reflection of legal and political cultures that have now proved inadequate. If there is no ethical difference between death from torture and the pain of parents whose child dies because they have no electricity in their slum dwelling, then there should not be any legal or political difference either. For us, this is of the essence, especially as – to pursue this example – this aspect of a right to an adequate living standard can be secured by setting a mandatory energy supply level which can be claimed in court. Such a line of reasoning holds for all economic, social and cultural rights.

3. It is too simple to say that our theory is good but that we are unable to apply it everywhere. In actual fact, it has certain shortcomings; a theory is no use unless it provides for ways of putting it into practice. Today, for each right, we can imagine a corresponding legal and political structure.

4. This is not to suggest that all human rights are identical. On the contrary, their variety is essential, for it is an invaluable approach to the many facets of human dignity. *This is why indivisibility does not mean an all-embracing approach.*

   The *indivisibility* of human rights can be understood as the need to define, interpret and ensure respect for all rights equally, while taking into account both interaction and logical differences.

Interdependence is a consequence of indivisibility. It means that the interpretation and enforcement of any right must allow for the interpretation and enforcement of all other rights. This in no way detracts from the principle that each right is of priority importance and that its enforcement cannot await the enforcement of another. Interdependence has often masked this ambiguity.

5. It follows from the above that a failure to recognise economic and social rights is not only serious for these rights but also implies a failure to recognise the economic and social dimensions of all human rights.

6. *This also holds for cultural rights*, which are still virtually ignored and, apart from the right to education, have sunk into oblivion as a result of the two-tier European approach. Persons who belong to minorities are not the only ones with identity problems, since extreme poverty makes a mockery of the identity of entire segments of the population.

Problems of logic

7. Taking a human right as it relates to three defined terms, namely subject, object and guarantor, we can refer briefly to the value of social and economic rights in understanding all human rights as a function of these three aspects of the legal relation.

8. **The subject**: The human being is the subject of all rights – the individual who exercises his or her status as a subject alone or in a group; this is unconditional. The temptation to assume that social rights are collective – or more collective – is without foundation; it is the result of an erroneous line of reasoning, namely transference from the subject to the object. It is the object which is of a social and systemic nature, not the subject.

9. **The object**: Consequently, the object poses much more interesting questions, because it is based on a continuous and systemic logic. The object of an economic right is not a good (food or lodging), but a dignified relation which permits the subject to acquire the goods needed for his or her dignity (food and lodging). The legal relation should be included in the ethics of an economic relation. Lastly, to make matters more complicated, the economic relation is only possible in a system of relations (a market).

   This is not limited to economic rights, however, because freedoms are only conceivable in a unified logical structure: a freedom is a dignified relation which is part of a system of freedoms (a public domain).

   Moreover, the complexity of the object on no account does away with the possibility of setting limits for everyone, beyond which the right loses its substance – limits of respect which are binding on *us* because *we are all concerned*.

10. **The guarantor**: For many, the state is the primary guarantor of human rights. But it is only the primary guarantor (in the logical sense, which does not automatically mean the first to enforce). Human rights are a matter for all protagonists in a democratic society, and they have the duty and power to respect and enforce them as well as to turn them fully to account. The public authorities are the guarantors of this system.

In the case of social rights, the state's limits seem more obvious, the welfare state's weaknesses having been amply noted. But here again, a two-tier approach is a simplification:

- the public authorities continue to have full responsibility at all levels, domestic and international, as far as limits are concerned, notably for all populations living in extreme poverty, and there can be no question of endorsing a reduction in the responsibilities that the authorities have;
- the same applies to classic freedoms, which clearly are exercised in an interplay between private companies, associations and public authorities. It is in this interaction that individual freedoms can unfold.

11. All human rights are enforceable. In institutional terms, this entails close interaction, subject to democratic scrutiny, between companies, associations and public authorities. The logical problem of indivisibility is matched by the political problem of the complementarity of protagonists in a democratic society. It is time for the NGOs and the IGOs to be fully cognisant of the scope of enforceability.

The useful distinction cuts across all human rights

12. It would be more sensible to undertake a systematic analysis of the limits of the object of each right. It can be seen that the most important line of distinction, assuming there is one, is not an ideological division between liberal and social rights, but a distinction between rights whose object is indivisible (prohibition of torture, respect for an adequate standard of living) and those whose object, although it has a coherent limit (beyond which the right loses its substance), has infinite scope (all freedoms, whether civil, political, cultural or economic). This tallies in part with the distinction between rights and freedoms.

13. If our colloquy can show that this two-tier approach is a thing of the past, then the fifty years since the Universal Declaration will not have been in vain. I subscribe unreservedly to Mr Heringa's proposal that accession to the Council of Europe be dependent on a commitment to ratify its Charter as well. In the meantime, it is important to expunge all traces of this two-tier approach from the Council's programmes, and this calls for an active policy of research and partnership.

Theme 2: Social rights: the challenge of indivisibility and interdependence

Report on Discussion Group 2 by Aalt Willem Heringa

A. General comments

1. The general starting point was the recognition of the indivisibility and interdependence of civil and political rights on one hand, and of economic, social and cultural rights on the other hand. This starting point however needs to have the necessary legal and practical implications. It means for one thing the recognition that there are rights and elements of rights in common between the various relevant treaties. There are overlaps between the International Covenant on Civil and Political Rights and the International Covenant on Economic, Social and Cultural Rights and between the European Convention on Human Rights and the European Social Charter. One example is the right concerning freedom of association and the other is Article 8 of the European Convention on Human Rights that also incorporates social rights elements.

2. This first point implies that on one hand, these two sets of rights can strengthen each other and that on the other hand, potential conflicts between rights exist. We should not ignore these potential conflicts between rights (that is the case within civil and political rights, within economic and social rights, as well as between civil and political rights on the one hand and economic and social rights on the other hand). This aspect, however, should not be used as an argument against indivisibility. On the contrary, the recognition of the existence of these conflicts between fundamental rights and interests will allow us to look for better solutions once we are fully aware of which rights and interests have to be balanced.

3. The acknowledgement of overlaps and possible conflicts also leads, in my opinion, to the necessity of having co-ordination between the various existing human rights mechanisms and monitoring bodies on the European level, global level and between the two.

   One should even ponder to what extent human rights mechanisms on the European level should merge. Similarly at the global level.

4. The effective implementation of economic and social rights can be enhanced through various means:

- The reporting system should be improved through greater involvement of national Human Rights commissions and Ombudsmen;
- Greater transparency in the operation of supervisory and monitoring bodies, including full dissemination of the outcome of their activities;
- Better follow up should be ensured after the adoption of concluding observations and recommendations of supervisory bodies.

5. The indivisibility of human rights as well as an analysis of social rights should lead to the recognition of the 'optimal justiciability of these rights. This is not the same as saying that all social rights are fully and completely justiciable and that courts are fully free to unbalance national budgets. However, having said that, it still remains possible to define minimum standards, core obligations, that have to be met. No forced labour; a minimum level of subsistence; are relevant examples. These rights can and should be enforced in the courts if necessary. What should be done therefore, in order to enhance and facilitate justiciability? Clear indicators must be defined as to what the core obligations are and what constitutes a violation. Social rights include justiciable rights, as well as a more general obligation on the part of the States to improve the level of protection.

   We should be clear about the content of social rights, their core, the minimum levels of protection and those areas and aspects where national means and conflicting policies do play a role. It is imperative to carefully identify the different components of social rights.

6. Within the context of social rights, one of the aspects often raised is the question of their so-called "affordability". It ought to be stressed that the question of cost concerns equally some civil and political rights and some economic and social rights. For instance, the costs of eradicating torture and ensuring fair trial is considerable, whereas the cost of ensuring freedom of association for trade unions is non existent for the state. In considering the cost of social and economic rights, one should bear in mind the benefits of their implementation and consider this cost not as a loss but as an investment for the future. One should also bear in mind the cost, often higher, of the non-implementation of these rights.

7. Whilst recognising the need for optimal justiciability of economic and social rights, the efforts of national legislatures and other public agencies to further implementation of economic and social rights are essential too.

8. Private actors, such as representatives of civil society (NGOs), as well as national and transnational entities (e.g. private employers) also have their share of responsibility in the promotion and implementation of economic and social rights.

9. Obviously, a greater dialogue among all the above mentioned actors (national and international supervisory and judicial bodies, legislatures, executive, national Human Rights Commissions and Ombudsmen, NGOs, etc.) is indispensable for the full and effective implementation of economic and social rights.

10. In order to make the respective duties of legislatures, courts, executives, civil society as clear as possible for everybody, large-scale awareness campaigns must be

carried out, aimed at the general public and at the various private, semi-public and public institutions involved in the implementation of economic and social rights. In this respect, a greater use could and should be made of the Internet and other forms of information technology.

11. Finally, a new point that has been raised concerned the desirability to include human rights clauses in international trade and investment liberalisation agreements. Because of the increasing globalisation of world trade we have to make sure that human rights remain effectively guaranteed even in this world of globalisation. In this respect it was pointed out that there is a need for an assessment of the negative impact which the activities of the international financial institutions may have on human rights.

B. European level

Where does the above lead us at the level of the Council of Europe? In this respect I would like to make eight points which, however, must be interpreted in connection with the tasks incumbent upon the states. If I may put it this way: the Council should strive to become superfluous, in the sense that the Council of Europe mechanisms are secondary and that the states fully implement rights to the maximum, with no lacunae and on their own initiative. Since we are all human beings and even guards have to be guarded, this is not realistic but this approach leads to the important recognition of the importance, even necessity, of state-action.

1. First of all, without being complacent, it is important to recognise the achievements with respect to the re-launch of the European Social Charter. Reporting procedures have been streamlined and been made more transparent. Also, the entering into force of the Collective Complaints Protocol is a great achievement.

2. The number of states having signed the Charter is increasing and so is the number of States which have ratified (parts of) the Charter. In this respect, the Parliamentary Assembly carries out a sustained campaign to encourage Member States to ratify the Social Charter. We should strive for the ratification of the Revised Charter and the Collective Complaints Protocol by all the Member states of the Council of Europe. The recognition of the indivisibility of human rights implies that the new Member States of the Council of Europe should be under the obligation to sign and ratify the Charter and its Protocols, as they are currently under the obligation of signing the European Convention on Human Rights within a year from their entry into the Council of Europe. In this respect the 'á la carte' approach which enables states to ratify only specific parts of the Charter is certainly an interesting feature which enables this approach. As has been pointed out during our meetings, this aspects lowers the threshold and it can induce states to enter the Charter family. This will certainly be beneficial, in particular when such a partial ratification concerns amongst others the articles 5 and 6, relating to the freedom to organise. One should not forget that a partial ratification ought to lead to a full ratification, at a later stage.

3. In line with a previous finding to co-ordination between human rights mechanisms it seems self-evident that such a co-ordination will take place between the European Court and the Committee of Experts. Taking this as a long-term perspective, a beginning could be made with co-ordination meetings, exchange of views, etc.

4. In line with our general recommendation as to awareness campaigns, work of the Council of Europe should be continued and intensified to make the Social Charter and its precise very elaborate contents better known: accessibility is important in this respect. Although we should acknowledge the efforts already made in this respect it is "never enough", to quote the Secretary General in his speech on the first day of our colloquy.

5. The Council of Europe has an important task in facilitating the work of national institutions that have a task in national human rights policies. In this respect I wish to draw the attention to the Recommendation of the Committee of Ministers (R (97) 14) and Resolution (97) 11, calling for a Council of Europe platform for national Human Rights Commissions and for the institution of national Human Rights Commissions with a pluralist composition.

6. During the discussion, the crucial importance of the principle of equality and the fight against discrimination appeared as a recurrent theme in connection with the implementation of all human rights. The Revised Social Charter explicitly recognises the equality/non-discrimination principle in a substantive provision, while, the European Convention still lacks such an essential substantive guarantee. Therefore, the adoption of a Protocol to the European Convention on Human Rights on equality and non-discrimination is an essential step forward.

7. Recently, the new collective complaints protocol to the European Social Charter entered into force: we not only urge for ratification of this protocol, but also invite the Council of Europe to monitor closely the effectiveness of this new procedure and to propose changes to the mechanism whenever they appear necessary in order to enhance its accessibility, its effect and to continuously promote its existence and its use. In this respect there is also a duty incumbent upon civil society: the non-governmental organisations. Their activities are essential to make a success out of this new procedure. It is their responsibility to come forward with claims that are well motivated and well argued. This is an essential precondition to make full use of the new protocol and to enable the Committee of Experts to interpret the Charter creatively. The Council of Europe should therefore, endeavour to allocate appropriate means to facilitate the Committee of Independent Experts to achieve this goal.

8. Finally, we should briefly look into the future. What else is there to wish in the area of standard setting and reform of procedures? Two proposals have been put forward during the meeting of the working group.

- The first was to continue work at a clause making the right, to have basic human needs met, part of the European Convention. On one hand, this is an appealing thought because it makes this right subject to the jurisdiction of the Court, which will show that social rights can be justiciable. On the other hand, it seems good to point out that the inclusion of this right in the European Convention could create the impression that only this right is a justiciable right. Apart from that, isn't the right to subsistence a part of Article 2 or 3 of the Convention? It surely affects the quality of life and it is an inhuman treatment. Such an approach, incorporating this right in Article 2 or 3 could be as effective and also show the indivisibility of all human rights. This incorporation proposal does lead me to propose that at least a recommendation be passed urging for the interpretation of Article 2 or 3 as mentioned above.

- Secondly, within the Council of Europe we have to continue the thinking about possible mergers of supervising and monitoring mechanisms. Isn't it a good long-term perspective to have one court for all the Council of Europe human rights treaties? This court should deal with individual complaints, collective complaints and inter-state complaints. These procedures could be used with varying intensity depending on the treaty or the provision of a treaty, as compared to another.

C. National level

1. The importance of the national domestic level cannot be emphasised enough. Lawmaking in particular is indispensable to have social rights successfully implemented. Legislative procedures do also enable public discussion to take place with regard to social goals and priorities within the society.

   This central importance of national legislation and the debates it can generate within a given society brings along the need to be as explicit in legislation about the human rights consequences and effects as possible. In that connection it might be helpful to insert human rights paragraphs in explanatory memoranda, explaining the human rights choices that have been made and why.

2. It was our opinion that the establishment of national Human Rights Commission's amongst others furthers a national debate and a thorough analysis. I referred to this issue before. This proposal is made whilst recognising the importance of existing national institutions such as the Ombudsman offices in many countries. But in this connection I wish to repeat the Secretary-General's motto: Never enough.

3. We urge the states to help in making the supervising mechanisms under the Charter work effectively. In the first place by recognising the national NGOs as qualified to lodge complaints under the new Collective Complaints Protocol. Finland is the first country to have deposited such a declaration under Article 2 of the Collective Complaints Protocol. It is hoped that other countries will follow this positive example.

   Our second suggestion in this connection is to involve NGOs more directly in the process of drawing up the national reports. A suggestion made in this respect is to even have their comments annexed to the national reports.

   In addition, the Ombudsmen offices should have a role in informing the Council of Europe on national practices in their countries, which affect or impede the full implementation of the social charter.

4. This point further elaborates the issue of the importance of national legislation and constitutional law. Without denying the importance of the Charter within the domestic legal order, it is still the case that also national constitutions and laws do play an enormously important role in the effective guaranteeing of human rights. Adding social rights in the national constitution and in national laws would implicitly add to the level of social rights protection. National legislation is also imperative in the sense that it can help making social rights justiciable. Courts are helped enormously when there is legislation in a specific social rights area; they are prepared to fill lacunae, but their task becomes tremendously difficult, if not impossible, when a social rights claim is about making new laws. So it really is a combined effort: lawmakers and courts and supervisory organs. One activity makes it easier for the other to take another step and vice versa.

5. It is imperative that campaigns be continued and set up to educate the public, lawyers, courts, lawmakers and officials about the Social Charter. We know much has already been done. In this respect it is worth mentioning Samuel's book about the Charter and the monographs set up by the secretariat.

D. Universal level

In connection with the universal level I can be relatively brief. Most what has been said as general remarks and with respect to European action and national activities applies *mutatis mutandis* to the universal level.

The most obvious aspects are:

1. To support the proposal for a new individual complaints protocol to be attached to the International Covenant on Economic, Social and Cultural Rights.

2. To investigate the feasibility of a collective complaints procedure under the same treaty, in particular when this new procedure under the Charter turns out to be effective and successful. And I have no doubt that it will.

3. To lift reservations with regard to the International Covenant on Economic, Social and Cultural Rights and to strive for a full ratification of this treaty and the new Individual Complaints Protocol. This applies *mutatis mutandis* to conventions of the International Labour Organization.

4. To further coherence and co-ordination between the Human Rights Committee and the Committee on economic and social and cultural rights.

5. To further the exchange of information and ideas between these two organs and the European Court and the Committee of Experts.

E. New challenges

1. More and more one can witness the international regulation of previous national issues. This increasing internationalisation ought not to be a means, or have as its effect, that specific areas of the law escape from the supervision of the human rights organs of the Council of Europe. Simply because they are no longer the

primary responsibility of a state, but have been transferred to an international legal entity which as such is not a party to the Convention or the Charter.

2. Bearing in mind the increasing competence of the European Union in the area of economic, social and cultural rights (inclusion of the Social Chapter in the Treaty on European Union through the Amsterdam Treaty) it is of utmost importance to achieve greater co-ordination between the European union and the Council of Europe. The main purpose of this co-ordination ought to be to ensure that no conflicting Union and the Council of Europe endeavour to co-ordinate their interpretation of the law. What has to prevail is the highest level of protection in case of conflict between two instruments.

Theme 3: Effective implementation of women's rights

Rapporteur: Katarina Tomaševski

The historical heritage of lesser rights for women was transformed during the past five decades from an accepted rule into an unacceptable exception. Women's equal rights have become the rule, but this rule is still defied by exceptions. Progress is reflected in exposing and opposing discrimination as the first step towards its elimination. The ability to eliminate discrimination requires its recognition as discrimination, as a departure from the postulate of equal rights for all.

The postulate that all people have equal rights necessitates redressing unequal power, reflected in the notion of women's empowerment. Elimination of discrimination therefore spans political and economic rights, individual and collective rights, public and private sphere, individual as well as structural level. Governmental obligations to eliminate discrimination include the formal recognition of equal rights as well as equalising opportunities for the enjoyment of the nominally equal rights. The initial definition of human rights as safeguards against the abuse of power by the state resulted in the marginalisation of abuses of power in the private sphere, within the marriage, family or household, or else within the labour market. That bias was exposed though the global mobilisation around violence against women and the revived interest for the elimination of obstacles to women's equal labour participation and professional advancement. The shift from sex to gender discrimination revealed multiple layers of discrimination impeding gender equality.

Our global discriminatory heritage was identified as the culprit for the states' previous acquiescence in violence against women. The marginalisation of economic and social rights for women could not be blamed solely on the discriminatory heritage, however, because it was exacerbated by the redefined role of the state in the economy and the corollary absence of safeguards against abuse of economic power. Combating discrimination is a permanent process, where the interplay between discriminatory heritage and newly created discrimination requires constant monitoring and corrective interventions.

Retrospective overview

During the early post-war decades, generic rather than gender-specific approach prevailed in international human rights law, including European regional law.

Gender-specific approach was impossible because gender did not exist as a term at the time. Sex had been included in the prohibited grounds of discrimination, but it was discovered much later that both women and men could be victims of discrimination on the ground of sex. In these earlier decades, women had been mentioned in international human rights instruments as childbearers and child-rearers through the protection of motherhood. Again, it was discovered much later that protection of motherhood jeopardised women's equal rights because its objective was to protect children rather than the woman.

When the Universal Declaration of Human Rights was adopted in 1948, no more than a simple prohibition of discrimination was included in the final text. An initial draft proposing an affirmation that "all men are brothers" had been successfully challenged; discrimination on the ground of sex was prohibited and an effort made to affirm that all people had all rights. This did not encompass the whole text, however. The protection of *his* privacy and family did not encompass also *hers*; only *his* property was protected against arbitrary deprivation; only his right to remuneration to support *his* family was affirmed while not *hers*. These omissions of *her* rights in the final text of the Universal Declaration of Human Rights were neither a coincidence nor were they confined to the language. *Her* privacy or property, or *her* role of breadwinner for *her* family, attained a legal recognition three or four decades after the Universal Declaration had been adopted.

The change of terminology from sex to gender aimed at capturing the historically constructed inferior role for women in public and private life, in politics, in the family, in the community, in society. Women's reproductive role was reflected, in the worst case scenario, in treating women as instruments for childbearing and childrearing. Different from women, men cannot bear children, but can rear them. The terminological change from maternity leave to parental leave accompanied the discovery of the difference between sex and gender. The introduction of terms such as *workers with family responsibilities* by the International Labour Organization or *parental leave* in the European Community law were signposts on the road to differentiating between sex and gender.

Such terminological changes would not have accomplished much were they not accompanied by the liberation of women from traditional family functions, especially from caring for dependant family members. Comprehensive social rights and the corresponding obligations of the state relocated the burden of family obligations. The corollary was the disappearance of *marriage* as a basis for childbearing from countries in the northern part of Europe and the *family* was remoulded into single-parent or single-person households. The single parent is still regularly the mother, however.

Before the human rights strategy urged scrutiny of the status of each person within the family, relations within the family had been beyond governmental powers. Family autonomy was strengthened by the prohibition of arbitrary interference by the state. Marriage routinely entailed lesser rights for married – as compared with unmarried – women. Law routinely recognised the marital power of the husband over his wife; a wife's power over her husband did not exist in any language, let alone in law. The husband's marital power was reinforced by the notion of the head of the family, placing the wife in a dependent relationship towards her husband, father, or even her own son. Demands upon the state to interfere and equalise the status of women and girls with that of men and boys overruled family autonomy, domestically and internationally. International litigation often preceded domestic changes and validated the reliance of human rights upon the rule of law rather than democracy. Where legal reform did not take place through domestic political processes, it was mandated by decisions of international human rights bodies.

Freedom from discrimination

The Human Rights Committee of the United Nations has declared equal and effective protection against discrimination to be an autonomous right and extended justiciability to all human rights – civil, political, economic, social and cultural – when discrimination is at issue. A similar broadening of freedom from discrimination is anticipated within the Council of Europe. The Parliamentary Assembly of the Council of Europe recommended in 1994 an additional protocol to the European Convention on Human Rights to embody the right to freedom from discrimination as an independent and enforceable right, and preparatory work for an additional protocol – long overdue – is approaching completion.

In a series of cases, the Human Rights Committee applied prohibition of discrimination to unemployment benefits or social security, broadening the reach of the International Covenant on Civil and Political Rights to social and economic rights and bringing them into the realm of justiciability. A typical problem which the Committee encountered was that a married woman had not been assumed to be a breadwinner but had to furnish evidence that she was not economically dependent upon her husband. The Committee found such assumptions both discriminatory and outdated. Indeed they have become outdated in the meantime and testify to the fact that gender roles *do* change.

Legal responses to changing gender roles differ a great deal. Law can be an obstacle to change when is legalises lesser rights for women. It can be an engine for change when it enhances gender equality.

Domestic laws differentiate between the two sexes by imposing compulsory military service upon men or prescribing younger age for marriage for women. The former has created a great deal of controversy because it was deemed to constitute discrimination against either sex. The latter was challenged by the Committee on the Rights of the Child as a form of discrimination against girls. Although lower minimum age for girls is part of our global heritage, the Committee insists that the minimum age for marriage should be equal for both sexes. Most countries in the world should accordingly change their legislation, few have done so. Much as with other human rights issues, the process of change begins with the articulation of the human rights approach to prompt reconsideration of discriminatory attitudes into which we have all been socialised.

Gender-neutral legislation apparently does not differentiate between women and men but can be discriminatory when failing to address the obstacles faced by women. Governmental human rights obligations therefore encompass identification and elimination of such obstacles. By definition, this process cannot be either fast or easy. Corrective legislation is often necessary to give women preferential treatment in order to redress the consequences of our universal discriminatory heritage.

Gender-neutral laws, such as regulations pertaining to part-time work, were challenged and changed by the European Court of Justice. Because the majority of part-time workers were – and are – women, non-existent or diminished labour rights affect women disproportionately and were thus outlawed as a form of gender discrimination. The difference between sex- and gender-based discrimination was confirmed by data on the implementation of equal-pay guarantees. Differences between the earnings of single women approached those of men, but the earnings of married women lagged behind. Single women's earnings were in the western part of Germany higher than men's (103%) but for married women they were only 57% of the men's. Similarly, in Norway and Sweden, single women earned 94% of men's salary but married women only 72%. An important reason for the persistent gap in earnings is the (married) woman's need to reconcile out-of-house work with family responsibilities. Because of necessity rather than choice, many women still opt for part-time work. It is possible that the right to rest and leisure, thus far marginalised in international human rights law, represents a key to understanding gender differences. The women's proverbial double burden of in- and out-of-house work indeed impedes not only rest and leisure, but often also women's political or social or cultural activism. Time-constraints are added to all well-known obstacles to women's equal political representation. Indeed, women's political rights may be nominally equal to men's but result in women's minuscule political representation. Europe remains heterogeneous and this is reflected in the regional bodies. Within the Parliamentary Assembly of the Council of Europe, nine parliamentary delegations had no women delegates as late as 1995.

The process of distinguishing between women with and without family obligations, single and married women, able-bodied and disabled women, has deepened the analysis of differences in the enjoyment of rights among women, moving beyond comparisons between women and men. Nevertheless, access to citizenship demonstrates the continued importance of differences between men and women. Access to citizenship still follows the head-of-family approach and denies equal rights to women. Women migrants often derive their right to residence and/or citizenship from that of their husband. The pre-1973 pattern of labour migration to western Europe had been driven by the demand for "foreign labour" (understood as male manual workers) and most women migrated subsequently on the basis of family reunification. Admitted as dependant family members, the position of wives cumulates legal with economic dependence upon their husbands. After immigration had become legally impossible, a vast and diverse – if clandestine – market was created. A new crime of alien smuggling was created and offences of trafficking in human beings re-defined. Both emphasise the vulnerability of victims of smuggling and/or trafficking to victimisation. By no coincidence, women tend to be victimised more than men, but women's fate is routinely cloaked behind the sexless category of "migrants" or "illegal aliens".

Safeguards against abuse of physical power: violence against women

A concerted international action to expose and oppose violence against women was possible only after equality for women had been accepted as the yardstick for scrutinising the phenomenon of violence. Because abuse of power is a structural problem, structural remedies are necessary. The purpose of human rights safeguards is to prevent abuse of power, to alter those structural variables that make women – but not men – vulnerable to abuse.

As long as the thrust of human rights was to protect individuals against abuses of power by the state, gender-based violence was beyond the reach of human rights law, domestic or international. Precedent-setting cases in international human rights jurisprudence affirmed in the 1980s that states were obliged to prevent human rights violations as well as to protect individuals against abuses by other individuals. A state can therefore violate women's rights when it fails to enact and enforce legislation guaranteeing women equal protection against violence.

Elimination of discrimination is an integral part of combating violence against women. Addressing consequences rather than tackling causes, much as with any other issue, are not likely to result in a sustainable improvement. Projects assisting battered wives do not reach beyond alleviating consequences when they disregard the crucial importance of the wives' legal and financial dependence upon their husbands. The wives' legal rights concerning housing, family property, child custody and maintenance, should – but often do not – inform projects aiming to combat violence against women. When wives are non-citizens, their paucity of legal rights extends to residence and citizenship; escape from an abusive relationship routinely entails return to the country of origin. The conflict between a desire to facilitate the wives' acquisition of legal rights and a wish to decrease the number of resident non-citizens regularly produces self-contradictory legal responses. The nature and scope of governmental human rights obligations is therefore subjected to a constant re-examination.

An assertion that violence against women is a violation of human rights has been a frequently used slogan and has contributed much more heat than light to the on-going debates about governmental human rights obligations. Misconceptions about what human rights are – and are not – proliferated with regard to the difference between torture against persons in custody of the state and physical abuse of wives by their husbands. The United Nations Expert group on the development of guidelines for gender integration into human rights programme criticised "the interpretation of the right to freedom from torture [because it] has failed to encompass violence in the family". That "failure" is a reflection of differentiated governmental human rights obligations. Governments have the obligation to eliminate torture because they have the monopoly of legally detaining and imprisoning people and are responsible for people in their custody; rape in custody was subsumed under torture by the European Court of Human Rights (*Aydin v. Turkey*, judgment of 25.9.97). Governmental obligations concerning violence in the family and society are obligations of conduct, rather than result as is the case with obligations relating to torture. The necessary measures to prevent, suppress and penalise violence include safeguards against abuse of power. In the case of *X and Y v. the Netherlands* (judgment of 26.3.85), the European Court of Human Rights clarified the distinction between different types of governmental human rights obligations. The Court refused to subsume safeguards against sexual abuse of a girl in a private home for mentally handicapped children under the prohibition of torture. Rather, it subsumed protection of individual's physical and moral integrity under the states' obligation to protect private life, which encompasses "the sphere of the relations of individuals between themselves". The Court found the Netherlands in breach of Article 8 of the European Convention on Human Rights because the then legal gap made it impossible to bring criminal charges for such sexual abuse, and endorsed the view of the Commission that the government could not be held responsible under Article 3.

The global mobilisation around violence against women as the symptom of unequal power between men and women has intensified and the European Parliament called for 1999 to be designated the European year against violence against women. From the human rights perspective, this focus on physical abuse as the most visible consequence of the absence of human rights protection can be usefully complemented by a complementary emphasis on the abuse of economic power.

Safeguards against abuse of economic power?

The World Bank holds that public policies should "compensate for market failures in the area of gender equality" because investment in women has a high social – but not economic – return. Women's unequal status spans inequalities in intra-household allocation of resources and reaches further to the labour market, ultimately also encompassing economic governance at the global level. The burden of women's unpaid work within the household hampers their economic productivity. In the labour market employers discriminate against women because of their lower productivity, stemming from their family and/or household responsibilities. The main institutions of global economic governance exclude women's representation and the absence of women's input is routinely reflected in the output that has a negative impact on women.

International law had included protection of maternity long before human rights were introduced into it. Early international labour law discriminated against women by protecting their reproductive role at the expense of their productive role, namely women's equal right to work and equal rights in work. Pregnant women and mothers with dependant children were – and are – accorded special protection because childbearing and childrearing necessitates social and economic support. The aim of human rights is, however, to accord everyone equal opportunities for free and full development; hence the methods of eliminating discrimination included challenging overprotective labour legislation, as the Committee for the Elimination of All Forms of Discrimination against Women did in 1996, when it observed that "protective labour laws had the sole effect of restricting women's economic opportunities". A balance between women's and men's productive and reproductive role obviously remains a challenge for the international human rights law of the future. The shift from maternity to parental leave signifies the political and legal commitment to equalise parental and family responsibilities. The role of the state in sharing some of these responsibilities has, however, become unclear with the diminished revenue-raising capacity of the state and the corresponding decrease of the state's ability to finance and provide social services that include child-care.

The affirmation of internationally enforceable social and economic rights has lagged far behind civil and political rights. The European Social Charter was amended in 1988, ten years ago, to introduce women's equal opportunities and treatment in employment and occupation, but that additional protocol was ratified by only eight states (the four Nordic countries – Denmark, Finland, Norway and Sweden – as well as Greece, Italy, the Netherlands and Slovakia). The European Social Charter (Revised), promising comprehensive protection, has received only one ratification so far (by Sweden). The necessity for public policies to safeguard women against economic exploitation, as emphasised by the World Bank, thus needs to find a powerful human-rights constituency, even within Europe which has the longest social-rights tradition.

The means for attaining gender equality

No country in the world has – as yet – attained gender equality. The term has been in use less than a decade, while specific national policies to redress inequalities between women and men emerged in the 1960s. Exposing and opposing gender discrimination is a process which begins with a commitment to non-discrimination. Translating that commitment into practice necessitates the creation of data which previously did not exist. Data on women's political participation and representation are today available, but not yet data on women's ownership of property. In the human rights work, the absence of data signifies that the problem has not yet been addressed rather than the absence of the problem.

International human rights bodies started systematically addressing human rights of women only in the 1990s. An overview of violations of the human rights of women still necessitates sifting through mountains of documents produced by various global and regional human rights bodies; mainstreaming has yet to be accomplished in the area of human rights. Attempts at stock-taking are compounded by the parallel existence of specialised women's bodies, which increasingly include women's rights into their work. These two parallel tracks exist within inter- and non-governmental organisations and embody a promise of merging different perspectives and strengthening the women's-rights approach, but also a risk of the repetition of the experience from previous decades when women's rights issues fell into the crack in-between these two parallel tracks.

The Vienna Declaration and Programme of Action achieved a veritable precedent in elevating women's rights from a brief mention somewhere at the bottom of the agenda into the core of the final document. The language introduced in the final documents of subsequent United Nations-sponsored global conferences departed from human rights terminology, however. The terms equality and equity were used interchangeably, thus re-opening the debate about the very purpose of agreed international action. Radhika Coomaraswamy, the United Nations Special Rapporteur on Violence against Women, warned against the shift from equality to equity. She pointed out that equity was a flexible replacement for equality, allowing departures from the principle of formal equality and diminishing women's rights.

The diversity of objectives embodied in gender perspectives – equity, equality, balance, or parity – reveals differences from the human rights approach. Gender equity is not an appropriate objective from the human rights viewpoint because it might entail perpetuation of discrimination. The absence of safeguards against gender discrimination in the labour market is routinely reflected in denials of women's equal rights. On the other hand, the principle of gender *parity* goes further than international human rights law. For example, the Committee for the Elimination of All Forms of Discrimination against Women objected to Denmark's failure to reach gender parity in women's political representation, while the European Court of Justice found Germany's attempt to reach gender parity in public employment to constitute a breach of European Community law. The Court found women's absolute and unconditional priority for appointment or promotion to constitute a breach of the postulate of equal opportunity and treatment (*Kalanke* judgment of 17.10.95). The Court subsequently ruled in favour of preferential treatment for women if opportunities had to be equalised, while the requirement of parity remained outlawed (*Marschall* judgment of 11.11.97).

The risk that women's rights may be diminished rather than enlarged is always present. It is reflected in varying definitions of equality as the goal, with the obvious implications for gender equality. Governmental obligations to eliminate gender discrimination span multiple and compounded grounds of discrimination (direct and indirect, public and private, legal and *de facto*) and governments are obliged to ensure elimination of all forms of discrimination in all areas. Corrective and compensatory policies in favour of those categories that were subjected to discrimination as well as those that remain vulnerable to it have been subsumed under governmental human rights obligations. The Human Rights Committee has held that governments have an obligation to undertake affirmative action designed to ensure equal enjoyment of rights. A formal recognition of equal rights for women is thus only the first step on the road to *de facto* equality. From securing that rights for women become equal to those granted to men, international human rights standards evolved further because "women" do not constitute a homogeneous group. Some categories are often deprived of their basic rights (victims of trafficking for prostitution or pornography) and others are particularly susceptible to human rights violations (domestic servants or foreign women migrant workers). Attainment of *de facto* equality necessitates elimination of obstacles faced by different categories of women some of who – such as domestic servants – may lack even the recognition of their legal personality.

Theme 3: Effective implementation of women's rights

Report on Discussion Group 3: Katarina Tomaševski

Summary

Thematic Group 3 on women's rights had a wide-ranging discussion, which covered many theoretical and practical issues. It is impossible to indicate whether the majority of participants were men or women; and this constitutes a sign of success, a genuine success, when people get involved in human rights issues because these are important, and not because they are personally concerned. And indeed, there was no substantive difference between "male" and "female" contributions.

The discussion covered all levels, from theoretical controversies about the meaning of equality, the use of human rights language and its implications, to specific projects that different organisations were involved in.

The discussion about the meaning of human rights and women's human rights achieved a wide consensus. There was no dissent from the conclusion that the issue at hand was not biological differences between women and men. Moreover, there was no dissent from the conclusion that the objectives of any policy or programme which aims to achieve parity ought to be reviewed if not compatible with what human rights stand for, namely substantive equality rather than parity.

Regarding language, participants brought up a number of interesting examples of linguistic differences. Some inter-language differences are well known, such as those between English, German and French, for example. Others illustrate how much more thought is necessary to define what specifically we are trying to achieve. One illustrative example was "positive" and "negative" discrimination, which continues creating controversies. Terms such as "empowerment" or "mainstreaming" have not and perhaps cannot be translated from English. The emphasis had to be on **effectiveness**, which the participants identified as the keyword of this meeting. The ideas and proposals developed had to take account of their potential for effective implementation.

There was full support for the development of an additional protocol on non-discrimination to the European Convention on Human Rights, developing Article 14 of the Convention, as well as for the protocol to the Convention on the Elimination of All Forms of Discrimination against Women. These were seen as another step towards making women's right to freedom from discrimination enforceable.

Moreover, participants emphasised the need to integrate women's rights throughout the different activities carried out by the Council of Europe in the human rights field. It was underlined that instruments such as the Bioethics Convention or the Framework Convention for the Protection of National Minorities fail to take into account the fact that biomedical issues or minority status affect women differently, thus making human rights problems and solutions different.

Detailed report

A. General assessment of the situation

The participants unanimously agreed that equality and non-discrimination between women and men is a fundamental prerequisite to the existence of a genuine democracy. In this respect, it was recalled that Article 2 of the Universal Declaration on Human Rights provides that everyone can enjoy the rights and freedoms proclaimed in the Declaration without any distinction based, in particular, on sex.

It was acknowledged that, since the adoption of the Declaration, a number of positive steps have been taken at both national and international levels towards these objectives. Reference was made, for example, to the United Nations Convention on the Elimination of all Forms of Discrimination against Women.

However, it was also noted that, including in the member states of the Council of Europe, women are still subject to unacceptable treatment and discrimination, sometimes on a massive scale. The participants unanimously condemned in particular such phenomena as trafficking in and violence against women, which all member States of the Council of Europe should combat. Although less serious, it was stressed that discrimination in the working place should no longer be accepted. No traditions – be they cultural, religious or other – should be considered as an excuse for the violation of women's rights, nor as a reason for refraining from taking action against such violations.

Against this background it was agreed that further steps should be taken in order to allow women to enjoy the fundamental rights and freedoms enshrined in the Universal Declaration on a day-to-day basis. This should take place at home, in their working environment as well as in the public sphere, in particular in the political field. Those steps are absolutely necessary to make equality between women and men a reality.

B. Approach to be taken

The group discussed whether it would be more appropriate to address the problems faced by women in the enjoyment of their rights and freedoms exclusively from a gender perspective or whether, on the contrary, it would be preferable to adopt an inclusive approach, given the fact that these problems might also affect other groups of people such as children or men. Several participants were of the opinion that the point of departure of any strategy or action should be the rights and freedoms of human beings in general, with a specific gender sensitivity.

Although the definition of common lines of action applicable at the global level might be desirable, it was stressed that any action should be adapted to the specific economic, social, cultural, religious and other circumstances of each country if it were to have an effective impact. At the same time, the universality and indivisibility of human rights should be constantly borne in mind as a fundamental requirement for the effective protection and promotion of these rights, including those of women.

Both international organisations such as the Council of Europe and governments have specific duties in this respect. It was underlined that non-governmental organisations are vital sources of information for governments and international organisations for detecting cases of violations of the rights of women, and should be involved in any strategy aimed at combating these violations and promoting women's rights.

C. *Action in the legal field*

The establishment of an appropriate legal framework at both the national and international levels is absolutely necessary to allow women to fully exercise their rights and freedoms, as embodied in the Universal Declaration. Support was expressed for the on-going work within the Council of Europe on the preparation of a protocol on non-discrimination to the European Convention on Human Rights.

Similarly, the initiative to work out a protocol to the Convention on the Elimination of all forms of Discrimination against Women was praised and welcomed. At the same time, it was noted that the complaints mechanism to be established under this Protocol should not replace similar existing mechanisms which have demonstrated their efficiency.

The participants expressed the firm hope that these two texts would be rapidly finalised and that they would enter into force as soon as possible. In a similar vein, it was underlined that all states, in particular the member states of the Council of Europe, should ratify without reservation the above Convention and withdraw any reservations which they might have made in regard to this instrument.

Over and above the preparation of new international instruments, the need was felt to implement existing human rights instruments, including those prepared within the framework of the Council of Europe, in a more effective way. The Council of Europe bodies responsible for supervising the implementation of instruments such as the European Convention on Human Rights, the European Social Charter and the European Convention on the Protection against Torture should be more sensitive to the gender perspective in their work.

In this respect, the recent entry into force of the Additional Protocol to the European Social Charter Providing for a System of Collective Complaints was welcomed, given its relevance from a gender perspective. The preparation of a protocol to the United Nations International Covenant on Economic, Social and Cultural Rights which would provide for a similar complaints mechanism was advocated.

It was also suggested that guidelines adopted at the international level for the interpretation and application of international instruments of relevance to the issue of women's rights should be reviewed to assess their effectiveness. In addition, the Council of Europe could examine the advisability of preparing such guidelines at the European level.

Finally, it was recommended that the procedures undertaken by both the Committee of Ministers and the Parliamentary Assembly of the Council of Europe to monitor compliance with the commitments to be met by applicant states as well as member states should pay particular attention to the question of women's rights, on the basis of Article 14 of the European Convention on Human Rights.

In a similar vein, it was suggested that national commissions on human rights should supervise the implementation of relevant international instruments and standards, over and above domestic laws and regulations. These commissions should, in addition, develop further contacts with international intergovernmental organisations so as to report on any deficiencies identified in their respective countries. Such contacts could take the form of regular meetings for the exchange of information and experience on solutions possibly developed to remedy such deficiencies. In order to carry out their activities in a proper way, these committees should be equipped with adequate expertise on gender issues.

As regards the national level, states should review their domestic legislation and policies to assess to what extent they address in an efficient and effective way the problems encountered by women in the enjoyment of their rights and freedoms. In particular, states should examine the appropriateness of adopting specific legislation to combat violence against women, over and above the general laws which might be of relevance to this problem.

Furthermore, the Council of Europe and other international intergovernmental organisations could usefully assist those European and non-European countries where gender issues are less familiar and not addressed properly under domestic law in drafting new laws which take account of the gender perspective and provide a framework for the full enjoyment of their rights and freedoms by women.

D. Action in the field of education and training

Although the legal framework is important, it is not sufficient, however, to achieve a genuine equality between women and men. It was stressed that education is an essential element of any strategy towards the empowerment of women in society and could have a significant contribution in eradicating violence against women. It was underlined that educational activities should be directed at both women and men. Accordingly, member States should encourage the development of educational programmes and material, as well as promote the wide availability and accessibility of these programmes and material.

Furthermore, it was recommended that states should develop specific training activities for law enforcement officials who are responsible for dealing with cases of violence against women, so as to make public action more effective in the fight against violence.

Finally, it was suggested that the awareness-raising, information and educational activities carried out by the Council of Europe in the human rights field should integrate the gender sensitivity referred to above.

E. *Action in the family, economic and political spheres*

It was acknowledged that concrete action on the economic and family environment is essential if women's rights are to be fully implemented. Specific awareness-raising and training activities should be targeted at those national administrations and public officials responsible for supervising the effective implementation of laws and regulations concerning equality in the working place, as well as at employers themselves.

Governments should design and promote new initiatives so that women and men share on a more equal footing parental responsibilities and duties, thus allowing women to play a more active role in the economic and political fields. Some participants advocated parity between women and men in public positions, although other participants expressed reservations in this respect.

In addition, it was noted that positive measures should, where appropriate, be examined and developed where such measures are the only means of remedying inequalities between women and men. These measures should only be of a transitional nature, until mentalities and society make them unnecessary, and should not be based on the assumption that biological differences exist between genders.

In this context the participants discussed the advisability of introducing quotas aimed at fostering the participation of women in public life, in their domestic law and policy systems. Some participants were of the opinion that quotas should only be a measure of last resort and underlined that quotas cannot solve all the problems faced by women.

Finally, the group discussed the question of free choice by women in matters of reproduction and lifestyles. The participants were informed about the work conducted by the Council of Europe's Steering Committee for Equality between Women and Men in this respect.

F. *Action in situations of conflict and tension*

Several participants underlined the fact that women are often more in danger than others in war time or in situations of tension. Therefore, particular attention should be paid to such circumstances. It was acknowledged that the protection afforded by international human rights instruments, although useful, has proven to be insufficient, and even sometimes ineffective. Accordingly, both international organisations and States should review these instruments so as to determine whether they should be amended or supplemented to remedy their shortcomings.

It was noted that one way of ensuring the effective protection of individuals, in particular women, in war time or situations of tension would be to encourage recourse to field missions to monitor the situation and possibly prevent conflicts from blowing up. Specific training activities should be organised for persons involved in such missions so as to make them aware of the specific problems and dangers to which women can be exposed in war time.

It was underlined that human rights law and humanitarian law are closely related in war time. Accordingly, it was suggested that the Council of Europe should supplement the initiatives undertaken by organisations such as the Red Cross to carry out awareness-raising and training activities on humanitarian law. Such action should be undertaken not only where a conflict has already occurred but also as far as possible before, so as to prevent such conflicts.

Finally, given the fact that refugee women represent a particular vulnerable group and face particular hazards, the Council of Europe should encourage its member states to adopt an approach which is sensitive to gender-related concerns and which ensures that women whose claims are based upon a well-founded fear of persecution, including persecution through sexual violence or other gender-related persecution, are recognised as refugees.

Third session – Effective action to protect and promote human rights

Theme 4: Protection: effective action at the national level

Rapporteur: Régis de Gouttes

Five years ago, in January 1993, shortly before the World Conference on Human Rights, the Council of Europe organised an interregional meeting on human rights at the dawn of the 21st century.

Perhaps the discussion should have addressed human rights not just at the "dawn" of the 21st century, but also at the "twilight" of the 20th century: there are lessons that might have been learnt from the failures and lapses of the late 20th century, which will not leave an exemplary account of itself in the human rights field – quite the reverse.

Nevertheless, by taking stock of the disturbing human rights situation across the world and attempting to sketch out some lines for future discussion and action, the interregional meeting drew a number of conclusions. I will consider three of them, which were emphasised in particular by Catherine Lalumière, then Secretary General of the Council of Europe.

1. Firstly, without wishing to belittle or denigrate the efforts made since 1945 and the progress achieved particularly within the Council of Europe, through the European Convention on Human Rights, the 1993 meeting noted that an assessment of respect for human rights could not but be critical. There was no room for self-congratulation, even in the last few years, when, in the words of Catherine Lalumière, "the great surge of hope [created by the end of the East-West confrontation] has largely subsided and given way [too often] to disillusion or resignation".
2. Secondly, after so many proclamations, declarations and conventions on human rights, the essential point now, it was stated in 1993, was effective implementation of these rights, making them an everyday reality instead of a forever unkept promise.
3. Thirdly, effective implementation ought to start, said the 1993 meeting, at the national level, since effective human rights protection began and ended domestically; the primary responsibility for the observance of human rights was vested in each state, and international machinery had at most a subsidiary role.

I think that we should draw on these conclusions of the 1993 interregional meeting to reconsider today, in 1998, as the 50th anniversary of the Universal Declaration of Human Rights approaches, what has been done and what remains to be done at the national level by seeking to identify what agencies or institutions are needed nationally if human rights protection is to be truly effective.

In this sphere, each of our states doubtless has its own experience, history and culture, and we are bound to respect these distinctive national features. Some of our countries recently have had to rebuild, in some cases to build, their democracy and their system for human rights protection, and their situation is quite different from that of the older democracies.

However, over and above these national differences we have to try to define and identify the minimum institutional basis – without which there is no real rule of law – for effective domestic human rights protection.

When we attempt to define this minimum basis, we should start from the assumption that human rights invariably need promoting and protecting as a counterweight not only to authority, that of the state first and foremost, but also to power generally, whether political, economic, social, military, media-based, scientific, technological or other. As Catherine Lalumière wrote in 1993, in a world where power centres are shifting, our concern for human rights should encourage us to be constantly on the lookout for incipient power expansions.

Any exercise of power is accompanied by the temptation to abuse it. Human rights are designed precisely to limit power, whatever its nature, to signpost its scope and to attenuate any force it exerts.

How then should this power, or these powers, be checked at the national level to protect human rights? That is the question. In looking for an answer, the first part of this report, will consider what national machinery for supervising or protecting human rights is essential within the state apparatus itself. The concern here is state actors. The state's internal checking mechanisms are not enough, however, and in the second part we will turn to the protection mechanisms outside and independent of the state, which act as counterpoises and are no less essential for effective protection of human rights.

First part: state actors for the protection of human rights

The prime responsibility for observance of human rights lies with the State apparatus in each country.

The duties on the state in this connection have considerably increased in modern society: the state no longer merely has obligations to refrain – a duty not to interfere with individual liberties (as, initially, in the case of civil and political rights). It also has "positive" obligations to take various measures, chiefly in the economic and social fields, so as to ensure that certain rights are fully enjoyed and observed, even in transactions between private individuals (this effect of rights is termed "horizontal" – "*Drittwirkung*" in German).

But the state, like Janus, has two faces: it can be the protector of human rights or, if it becomes an instrument of oppression, their most ruthless enemy. Contemporary experience shows us however, that the absence or collapse of the state may present just as great a risk for human rights as an authoritarian and intrusive state ...

That said, within the apparatus of the state itself there is a whole set of bodies and institutions which need to be involved in the chain of human rights protection or supervision, from the legislature to the judiciary and the executive.

It is clearly impossible to analyse this entire machinery here. I will restrict myself to the three pillars we can consider to be essential or fundamental to any genuine state governed by the rule of law.

First pillar: an independent and effective judicial system

In a state governed by the rule of law, the prime responsibility for protecting human rights is vested in the judicial power. (Article 66 of the French Constitution states, for example, that the courts are the "guardian" of individual liberty.)

Provided the people who operate the judicial system are genuinely and thoroughly human-rights-minded (see Theme 6 of our colloquy), no other institution, however evolved it might be, would appear capable of assuming the role traditionally performed by the judicial system. And I mean the term in its broadest sense, encompassing ordinary, administrative and specialised courts as well as constitutional courts or constitutional councils (which, in verifying the constitutionality of laws, can examine whether texts submitted to them comply with human rights requirements).

For protection by the judicial system to be effective, there are a number of requirements, that come under 4 main headings:

1. *Access to justice for all*

We must ensure, first and foremost, that our national judicial systems guarantee everyone genuine access to a court , as defined in the case law of the European Court of Human Rights, which sanctions material hindrances to access to justice such as exorbitant procedural costs or unavailability of effective free legal aid (cf. *Airey v. Ireland* judgment of 9 October 1979, *Artico v. Italy* judgment of 13 May 1980, and *Pakelli v. Germany* judgment of 25 April 1983) no less than legal ones.

a. Access to justice means, first of all, that victims of human rights infringements, especially the most underprivileged of them, are helped to obtain access to the law, legal advice, information and counselling, as advocated, for instance, by Recommendation No. R (93) 1 of the Council of Europe on effective access to the law and to justice for the very poor.

Much remains to be done in each of our countries to promote the work of organisations which assist disadvantaged victims and litigants, and to develop the role of justice centres, neighbourhood associations, "legal-aid shops" and in-community centres for legal advice set up and run voluntarily by lawyers or legal specialists keen to bring the justice system closer to the people.

b. Access to justice then presupposes actual legal aid, available on as wide a basis as possible so that the less well off seeking legal redress can have their costs covered in any court.

   It must be acknowledged that progress has been accomplished in this area, by virtue of the recent laws in several states (e.g. French law of 10 July 1991). But further efforts are needed, for instance to boost the funding of legal aid programmes and make the conditions governing eligibility more flexible, particularly with regard to the requirement of habitual residence in the country concerned.

c. Access to justice also requires, under Article 6 (3) of the European Convention on Human Rights, that anyone charged with a criminal offence be given legal assistance free if they do not have sufficient means to pay for it, along with the services of an interpreter free of charge if they do not speak the language used in court.

d. Lastly, access to justice, in the broadest sense of the term, also entails readier access, whenever necessary, to parajudicial forms of dispute settlement such as mediation or conciliation, with the assistance, if required, of voluntary organisations.

2. *Independent and impartial justice*

   a. The case-law of the European Court of Human Rights is useful in clarifying the criteria and scope of independence and impartiality of tribunals as required by Article 6 (1) of the European Convention on Human Rights.

      Judging from the considerable number of violations found on this score by the European Court, not one of our countries is safe from the Court's censure: we all still have a great deal of progress to make.

      Independence and impartiality of justice must be understood as a safeguard the citizen is entitled to rather than a corporatist means of self-protection for judges. The reason why the independence of the judge has to be above reproach is, as the European Court has pointed out, to ensure that people have the confidence in the system that is basic to respect for the law, without which no democratic society can exist.

      As we know, independence and impartiality are appraised, as the European Court has stated, both "subjectively", in terms of a judge's personal impartiality, and "objectively" or "organically", which includes the "appearances" aspect – the visibility of independence necessary to banish any legitimate doubt from the public mind.

      These requirements, finally, assume not only independence in relation to the executive but also impartiality in respect of litigants or any other authority (cf. judgments in *Hauschild v. Denmark* of 24 May 1989, *Fey v. Austria* of 24 February 1993, *Saraiva de Carvalho v. Portugal* of 22 April 1994, and *Beaumartin v. France* of 24 November 1994, etc).

   b. In concrete terms, there cannot be proper independence and impartiality of judges in any of our countries unless a basis is provided by rules governing judicial office and infrastructure or institutions that protect judges:

- the rules governing judicial office must specifically guarantee: impartiality of entry to and training for the judicial profession; independence and irremovability of the judiciary and quasi-judicial status for state counsel and public prosecutors; adequate material and financial provision to ensure proper professional standards;
- institutions to protect judges, which must include an appropriate training body, such as France's *École nationale de la magistrature*, and an independent high authority with the task of supervising appointments and any disciplinary proceedings against judges (the *Conseil supérieur de la magistrature* established by the French Constitution is one possible model).

c. It is noteworthy that, over and above these national safeguards, new European rules on judges are beginning to emerge by virtue of the case-law of the European Court of Human Rights. As a result the judiciary will no longer be a matter for the individual sovereign state alone, but will be protected by international standards and, above all, by the European Convention on Human Rights.

As noted by Professor Jean-Claude Soyer, a member of the European Commission of Human Rights, judicial independence is increasingly coming under international conventions and the supervision of international courts, from which each state will find it more and more politically difficult to break away. This will provide increased protection in the future against arbitrary interference.

3. *A justice system that protects human rights*

Attitudes are the key here: it is vital that those who operate the judicial system draw, in their daily practice, on a genuine human rights culture (see Theme 6 of our colloquy on information, education and training).

Specifically, in all our European countries, a justice system protective of human rights is one as close as possible to the model of and based on independent and impartial courts and fair trial that results from the case-law of the European Court of Human Rights.

a. It is now important therefore that, in all our states, judges should have a very firm grasp indeed of European standards so as to be able to translate them into their domestic decisions.

The judge must no longer make do with "awareness" of the human rights issue. He must henceforth be a true specialist in human rights law and thoroughly acquainted with the Strasbourg case-law (and that of the Court of Justice of the European Communities), together with the practice of the United Nations convention committees on human rights.

The many judgments of the European Court of Human Rights which have found violations of Article 6 of the European Convention and the principle of fair trial show that there is still much work to be done in this area.

b. At the same time there is room at national level for improved enforcement of judgments delivered by the European Court of Human Rights.

Care needs taking that states comply fully with the judgments of the Strasbourg Court by not only paying victims of violations any sum due in just satisfaction but also taking specific steps to put a stop to the violation (among other things this raises the issue of whether to review or reopen the national case after a finding of violation), and even, where appropriate, adopting general measures to bring domestic law into line with the European Convention.

Once again, national courts can play a decisive role in this connection by remaining heedful of the European Court's case-law, and by drawing on it to adapt or modify their national case-law where appropriate.

4. *Effective justice*

Two important requirements still remain to be met if victims of human rights infringements are to feel properly protected by the judicial system.

a. Firstly, before the courts they need effective remedies available without discrimination, fair judgments delivered within a reasonable time, and fair and appropriate compensation for any harm they have suffered. That would also include, to my mind, being able to apply to reopen criminal proceedings and to apply for compensation following unwarranted detention on remand.

Yet in all our countries there are many hindrances: backlogs in the courts, excessive length of proceedings, dilatoriness on the part of the prosecuting authorities, discontinuance of cases, judicial lack of attention to human rights aspects of some cases, etc.

It is worth pointing out the key role which may be played in this connection by procedures such as allowing human rights organisations to bring actions or allowing public prosecutor's offices to institute proceedings on their own initiative.

b. Once the courts have found in their favour, victims of human rights offences must also be able to have the judgment enforced.

Once again, as we all know, there is no shortage of problems: in civil cases, injured parties often have difficulty in getting judgments in their favour enforced, especially when police action is required; even in criminal cases, court backlogs and the overcrowded prisons may mean that sentences for human rights infringements are executed late or only partially.

We are dealing here with a familiar problem and one which faces almost all our countries: that of under-resourcing the judicial system. Protection of human rights is one of the things that suffer.

Second pillar: a democratic and protective legislature

The legislature has a key role to play as the anchor in the chain of human rights protection. For parliament to perform its legislative task to the full, of course, it must in the first place have resulted from free and democratic elections, organised within a politically pluralistic system and in a lawful and supervised manner. That is a prerequisite for the rule of law. In their attitudes and practice, members of parliament must also be inspired by the human rights "culture" to which we have already alluded (see Theme 6 of our colloquy).

If it meets these requirements, parliament can then be said to have a twofold role to play in the protection of human rights.

- As the people's representative, parliament must legislate in keeping with people's aspirations as regards protection of their most fundamental rights. Accordingly, all parliaments' legislative activity is extensively concerned with individual liberties and human rights.

  Independently of government initiative, it is usually possible for members of parliament to table private members' bills. We can only encourage them to exercise that option in the field of human rights protection.

- It is also the duty of parliament to ensure that domestic law complies with international and constitutional law on human rights.

  All legislative action must consequently have regard to the requirements of the European Convention on Human Rights right from the drafting stage.

  In several countries, members of parliament and the authorities are already showing an increasingly marked awareness of the European Convention and a growing keenness that new legislation conform to its requirements.

  In some cases, domestic legislation refers explicitly to the European Convention (e.g. on the subject of refusal of entry and deportation, Article 27 *bis* of France's law of 24 August 1993 amending the Order of 2 November 1945 on the entry and circulation of aliens) referred explicitly to Article 3 of the European Convention on Human Rights. In other cases (such as the Netherlands), there is even a systematic prior screening procedure to ensure that all draft legislation complies with the European Convention on Human Rights.

  In addition, whenever existing legislation proves to be at variance or not to comply with European standards, it is for parliament to amend or replace it.

  There are many examples of amendments of this kind.

  In France, for instance, besides the law of 10 July 1991 on telephone tapping (adopted following the European Court judgment of 24 April 1990 against France in the *Kruslin and Huvig* case), there have been the law of 10 July 1991 on legal aid, and laws of 4 January 1993, 24 August 1993 and 30 December 1996 concerning access to a lawyer during police custody, limitation of remand, prisoners' rights, safeguards in disciplinary proceedings and streamlining of criminal proceedings.

Third pillar: accessible administrative authorities which are subject to control

In a state governed by the rule of law, it is essential that administrative departments, constituting the executive power, be accessible, aware of human rights issues and subject to control.

A great deal of work still remains to be done in making administrative authority "accessible" to the public, despite the many programmes set up for that purpose.

Administrative human rights "awareness" is highly dependent on public servants' attitudes. For that reason it is very important that proper human rights training and education are provided for public servants, especially those directly involved in applying the law, such as police, *gendarmerie*, prison staff and staff in psychiatric hospitals. These are in the "front line" – in direct contact with people in difficulty, working in situations where human rights violations may occur.

Effective "control" of observance of human rights by the public service calls for at least two things:

- Internal or hierarchical control: it is necessary for all public servants to know that in performing their duties they are answerable to an authority or superior and that disciplinary sanctions may be taken against them for any misconduct. Incidentally, before having to resort to the courts, private individuals ought to be able to apply to the administrative authorities to reconsider contested decisions.
- External control: anyone who is the victim of a human rights infringement by a public servant or administrative department must be able to apply to a tribunal for compensation for injury suffered and annulment of the prejudicial measure or decision or action. Depending on the country, this may involve the ordinary courts or, as in France, the administrative courts: the essential point is that the remedy be effective and before an independent tribunal.

Second part: human rights protection actors independent of the state

Alongside bodies coming directly under the state, there are many bodies in each country working independently to monitor and promote human rights; as such they act as necessary counterweights.

They are the voice of what is generally known as civil society. They encompass a wide variety of entities, from national human rights institutions and ombudsmen, to the press and media, to non-governmental organisations.

They should never be considered a replacement for state human rights protection machinery, as whose main component the judicial system must continue to perform its vital traditional role. They should be seen, in fact, as a "complementary" machinery for supervising and protecting human rights.

1. *National institutions for the promotion and protection of human rights*

a. In Recommendation No. R (97) 14 of 30 September 1997, the Committee of Ministers of the Council of Europe called on member states to set up independent national institutions for the protection and promotion of human rights, such as human rights commissions with a pluralist membership, ombudsmen (or mediators) or similar institutions.

In an accompanying resolution (Resolution No. (97) 11), the Committee of Ministers agreed to develop co-operation between such institutions and the Council of Europe, in particular by means of regular meetings.

This recommendation and resolution supplement Recommendation No. R (85) 13 of the Council of Europe on the institution of the Ombudsman, and followed several United Nations resolutions promoting such institutions, especially Resolution 48/134 of the General Assembly of the United Nations of 20 December 1993, setting out what are known as the Paris principles on the role and composition of independent national institutions.

b. The fact that the United Nations, the Council of Europe and other international organisations have fostered the setting up of independent bodies of this kind, and that such bodies have already emerged in numerous states in Europe and across the world, testifies that they respond to three marked needs in our societies:

Firstly, poised between the state and "civil society", they bring together the state's representatives on one side and representatives of human rights associations, non-governmental organisations, trade unions and various societal trends on the other. By virtue of their pluralist membership, they provide opportunities to compare government thinking and the thinking of human rights activists, helping the two sides find common ground and thereby playing a part in the preservation of social harmony, so often threatened in contemporary societies. The basis of all these institutions is the conviction that ignorance, neglect or blatant disregard of human rights can be lastingly reduced only by constantly narrowing the gap between institutional action, whether of the executive, legislature or judiciary, and what the various players in society actually do.

Secondly, independent national institutions for human rights protection, especially the national human rights commissions, perform monitoring, preventive, information-sharing and advisory functions and instigate legislative change. They are active before government action, when bills, regulations, international instruments, policies and programmes are being prepared; and afterwards, in seeing how effectively observance of human rights is translated into administrative practice.

Thirdly, some of these independent national institutions, principally the "ombudsmen" or mediators, may also be empowered to deal out of court with individual complaints or disputes between individuals and the authorities in human rights matters and to make recommendations to the authorities.

The round tables at which the European ombudsmen periodically meet have provided an opportunity for very worthwhile exchange of information and experience regarding ombudsman intervention.

c. In line with the recent recommendations of the Council of Europe and the United Nations, our regional colloquy could therefore remind governments of the case for setting up and developing independent national institutions to protect human rights, emphasising the safeguards which would need building into such institutions' statutes and the standards of independence and impartiality they would have to meet, both in their functioning and composition, in order to be fully recognised as effective.

2. *Non-governmental human rights organisations*

Both internationally and nationally, the role and number of NGOs defending human rights has continually grown over the last few years. This applies equally to those with a general remit and those defending particular spheres of interest. The Council of Europe itself allows them considerable prominence.

No doubt the growing success of the NGOs will encourage them to target their action, co-ordinate with each other, make practical proposals, check the objectivity of their information sources, in short avoid giving any impression of disorganisation. At all events the NGOs are irreplaceable, being a direct and concrete expression of the population's needs and troubles.

There is no need to dwell here on the various aspects of their work, which are generally well known: providing information and education in human rights, whistleblowing on human rights violations, challenging the authorities, lobbying, mustering public opinion, assistance and, of course, legal aid.

The state has a duty to treat the voluntary sector and NGOs with respect, not to hinder their lawful activities, and indeed to help and encourage them in their action, which may very well complement the State action to forestall social unrest and ensure smoothly functioning democracy.

Of all the various things which states should do to promote the work of human rights NGOs, I would select two in particular: the first is to enable them to genuinely influence governmental human rights policy and action through the independent national institutions or commissions for human rights protection; the second is to allow them to take legal action on behalf of victims of human rights violations, a role already recognised by legislation in many countries (cf Articles 2 (1) to 2 (15) of the French Code of Criminal Procedure, recognising the right of various associations to sue for damages in criminal proceedings).

3. *Press and media*

Any discussion of national infrastructure for the protection of human rights must – to conclude – refer to the role of the press and other media.

I will allude to this topic only briefly, since it will be addressed as part of Theme 6 of our interregional colloquy; it has also been the subject of many conferences and studies at the Council of Europe.

As has often been said, the media are a potent force, whether for good or ill. They may promote human rights or cause infringements of them; they can spread the truth or spread lies. Article 10 of the European Convention accordingly points out that exercise of the right to freedom of expression carries with it "duties and responsibilities".

I believe that we should stress two essential points when discussing the responsibilities of the press and media in human rights protection.

Firstly, the media deserve utmost support not just in their role of informing about and raising awareness of human rights issues, but also as publicisers of human rights abuses. This encompasses what the European Court of Human Rights has called the press's crucial "watchdog" role. This function obviously requires that journalists themselves and other media people make the effort to acquire in-depth knowledge of human rights.

Secondly, the media should take the initiative in guarding themselves against the dangers inherent in their work and the human rights infringements they may cause. To that end, it would be desirable if they developed professional ethics through proper codes of conduct for the press and broadcasting.

This is entirely in their own interest. Otherwise, it is government or the courts that are liable to set about tackling abuses of media power. Invasion of privacy and violation of human dignity are obvious examples, as is propagation of racism, xenophobia, intolerance, fanaticism, violence or sexual exploitation.

There have been some self-scrutiny and a few positive self-regulatory moves by a number of newspapers and broadcasting companies. Such experiments should be encouraged in the future.

Conclusion

In conclusion, given this constellation of national institutions capable of a human rights role, we may wonder whether, when all is said and done, the individual emerges better protected.

The answer was touched on at the January 1993 regional colloquy: no single one of these institutions is able to safeguard human rights on its own; rather it is the "interaction" between them and their combined vigilance which is able to establish the optimum conditions for effective human rights protection. The "interactivity" between ombudsmen and national human rights commissions on the one hand and administrative authorities or parliament on the other, between the press and the judicial system, or between NGOs and government is a prime example.

Theme 4: Protection: effective action at the national level

Report on Discussion Group 4 by Régis de Gouttes

Participants in the Discussion Group on Theme 4, "Protection: effective action at the national level", pointed out that human rights protection both started and finished at national level.

As the introductory report emphasised, those involved in human rights protection at national level either depended on the state or were independent of it.

Where those who were tied to the state were concerned, the three pillars identified by the report were an independent and effective judicial system, a democratic and protective legislature, and accessible administrative authorities which are subject to control.

Generally speaking, it was appropriate to foster and improve interaction and dialogue among the various parties involved in the protection of human rights, at both national and international level.

1. Persons responsible for the protection of human rights at national level dependent on the state

At the outset, several speakers said that other players who were dependent on the state were very important to the protection of human rights at domestic level: the police, prison staff, the staff of psychiatric hospitals ... Human rights training for these various categories of staff was quite fundamental. The same applied to the government staff responsible for defending their governments before the European Court of Human Rights. These government servants should also receive training and enjoy the assistance of competent staff. In any case, the list of actors dependent on the state should be lengthened.

a. Participants drew attention to their attachment to *impartial justice*: if justice were to be truly independent, states would have to give it the necessary resources. It would have to remain apolitical and non-partisan. It was also important to avoid having exceptional courts, such as courts martial.

In order to ensure that the various parties involved in the judicial system were independent, it was vital for these individuals (judges, prosecutors, lawyers, representatives of the law and staff of the authorities responsible for public order) to be given all the necessary funds, as well as appropriate training in human rights.

Furthermore, the *translation of Strasbourg's international texts and case-law* into the languages of the various countries concerned, particularly those of central and eastern Europe, was absolutely essential. The reports drawn up by the European Committee for the Prevention of Torture and Inhuman or Degrading Treatment or Punishment, and the recommendations of the Committee of Ministers drawn up under the European Social Charter were also instruments which ought to be translated.

Several participants expressed the view that it would be necessary to increase the pace of the *reform of judicial and prison systems* in those countries where these did not yet meet the European standards, reinforcing the role in this context of national human rights protection institutions, ombudsmen and non-governmental organisations, and also providing for the findings of the Committee of Ministers of the Council of Europe during the monitoring procedure to be made public.

Some participants emphasised the fact that the *rights of foreigners* before the courts deserved particular protection because of these people's vulnerability. Particular emphasis should be laid on the interpretation from which they should benefit during proceedings and on the training of judges, who should be made aware of the cultural conflicts likely to exist when foreigners were the subject of court proceedings.

As far as the European Convention on Human Rights was concerned, its self-executing nature was quite fundamental, and those states which had not yet done so had been recommended to *incorporate the Convention into their domestic law*.

It was also important for states to make more frequent use of the possibility of *intervening during proceedings in the European Court of Human Rights in cases concerning other states*. This system, very frequently used in the Court of Justice of the European Communities in Luxembourg, was not sufficiently used in the European Court of Human Rights. Intervention of this kind would enable a state to make its viewpoint known, even if no application had been made against it.

More use should be made of the scope available to the Court to give *advisory opinions*.

Machinery enabling the *reopening of domestic proceedings* following a judgment of the European Court of Human Rights should also be set up.

b. Where the legislative authority was concerned, and within the framework of parliamentary procedures, methods of systematically examining the *compatibility of draft legislation* with the European Convention on Human Rights should be used. Several states had set up machinery to make sure that new laws were compatible with the European Convention on Human Rights. Such practices should be encouraged. The idea of attaching explanatory reports to draft legislation covering the compatibility of the law concerned with the European Convention on Human Rights was put forward.

The Council of Europe itself should help states to reform their legislation so as to bring it into line with international human rights legislation and case-law.

Several participants felt that the different states' reports on social rights submitted to the United Nations committees should be widely distributed and that parliaments should be involved in the drafting of these reports, and in their follow-up.

Generally speaking, the comment was made that *states should act more fully* on the points made in the observations of the organs and committees set up under the United Nations conventions in the human rights sphere. A check-list should be drawn up after each report to these organs, covering the following points:

- check whether domestic legislation is in conformity with the United Nations treaties;
- improve dialogue between the government and the international bodies on the report concerned;
- inform decentralised authorities and municipalities about the obligations deriving from the international treaties;
- include the international treaties in civil servants' training;
- promote human rights teaching in educational establishments;
- improve the collection of data enabling human rights protection to be put into practice (statistics, etc.);
- examine the budgetary impact of human rights protection.

2. Persons responsible for the protection of human rights at national level independent of the state

With reference to the players not tied to the state, the emphasis was placed on the importance of the *training of lawyers*, whose role was vital to human rights protection, and of certain *interest groups* (NGOs, trade unions, etc.). These interest groups could play an important part in the defence of victims of human rights violations.

Some participants took the view that the states should set up systems enabling **NGOs** to monitor public institutions to a greater extent, and that they should also draw up national action plans in conjunction with these NGOs.

It should also be made possible for NGOs to take legal proceedings in national and international courts on behalf of the groups they represented. In fact, participants emphasised that victims were frequently not in a position to apply to the competent bodies.

Several participants emphasised the importance which they attached to *national institutions* (national human rights committees and ombudsmen), which helped to monitor states' honouring of their human rights obligations. The existence of specialised national institutions did not prevent generalised national committees from being set up to take an overview of the problems, particularly at international level. These national institutions could also, in certain cases, play a role in the examination of complaints relating to human rights. They should in addition be able to make recommendations before a legislative text was adopted. Finally, they should also be able to submit reports to the organs of the United Nations and, if applicable, refer cases to domestic and international courts.

In order to promote, for those countries so wishing, the setting up and development of such independent national institutions for human rights protection, participants said that it would be appropriate to implement Recommendation No. R (97) 14 and Resolution (97) 11 of the Committee of Ministers of the Council of Europe, of 30 September 1997, as well as Resolution 48/134 of the United Nations General Assembly.

Most participants took the view that it was necessary to increase the role and resources of *ombudsmen* or similar institutions in the prevention of human rights violations, torture and ill-treatment, especially by facilitating:

- their inspection visits to prisons, psychiatric hospitals and other places of detention;
- the publication of their progress reports;
- their co-operation with the European Committee for the Prevention of Torture and Inhuman or Degrading Treatment or Punishment;
- the power to refer cases to national courts. Some participants also raised the question of whether ombudsmen or similar institutions could have their power to refer cases to the European Court of Human Rights recognised.

Theme 5: Protection: effective action at the international level

Rapporteur: Jeremy McBride

National legal orders are best placed to afford the fullest possible protection for human rights but they continue to provide ample opportunities for them to be violated, in many instances with impunity. This sad reality, manifested as much in obdurate disregard for the relatively limited concerns of some individuals as in barbarous acts traumatising whole populations, resulted in a gradual acceptance of the need for an international dimension to the protection of human rights. The adoption of the Universal Declaration has ensured that human rights have an unambiguous place on the international agenda, albeit one that has not always enjoyed an appropriate priority. Of course, the justifiable pre-eminence still accorded to domestic protection has been a restraining influence both on what measures are adopted at the international level and the expectations that can seriously be reposed in them. The primary concern must, therefore, be to maximise the effectiveness of the contribution that can be made within these limits, while recognising that they are not cast in stone; "domestic jurisdiction" is a clichéd mantra and a priori opposition to action at the international level where that can better secure human rights is no longer tenable.

The effectiveness of the contribution currently being made ought to be assessed by reference to a number of interrelated criteria:

- the unquestionable legitimacy of the normative standards which international action seeks to support;
- the degree of authority which international rulings enjoy;
- the relative promptness with which appropriate action is taken;
- the actual ability to secure the implementation of standards on a generalised basis and not just in particular cases, as well as to ensure that redress is afforded where those standards have not been observed;
- the extent to which international action is both seen to be, and genuinely is, coherent and integrated;
- the level of confidence which is reposed in international bodies by the community which they serve.

The unqualified fulfilment of these criteria, which are undoubtedly not exhaustive, belongs to an ideal world but they should also shape efforts to improve the one we are in.

Concern about the legitimacy of human rights norms relates not only to their formal status with respect to any state which may be the object of action at the international level but also to the strength of their authority both within it and in the wider international community. Although the establishment of primary human rights standards is now fairly comprehensive, there are still some important gaps and the applicability of those that do exist is by no means universal. The further elaboration of these standards, whether in supporting instruments or in judicial, quasi-judicial, expert and political rulings, is essential for their application in concrete situations and there can be no doubt as to the significance of the European contribution in this respect. Nevertheless such elaboration is most at risk of lacking the legitimacy needed to sustain effective action.

Almost all the rights proclaimed in the Universal Declaration have now achieved the status of international legal norms through the adoption of regional and global instruments and, to a lesser extent, the development of customary international law. Notable omissions from this process have been the right to a nationality and, at the regional level, a general prohibition on discrimination but efforts to repair these deficiencies are in hand. This does not mean that the identification of human rights, as opposed to their elaboration and application, is necessarily complete but there can be no doubts as to the availability of appropriate legal texts for most matters of current concern. Although it is now unusual to find a state that is not legally bound by a given human rights standard at either the regional or global level, there are many instances where states have failed to take on the same commitment at both levels. This is particularly true of rights of an economic, social and cultural character and there is no mistaking an apparent connection between the reluctance to accept the European regional commitment to such rights and the strengthening of its enforcement mechanism. Moreover, some reluctance to accept the additional protocols bringing the European Convention on Human Rights into line with a more exacting global standard regarding civil and political rights can also be discerned and again this would appear to be not unconnected with the issue of effective enforcement. The terms on which some instruments have been ratified also continues to a matter of concern since, through the device of reservations, states have limited the full application of some provisions. This is most evident in the case of commitments to civil and political rights at the regional level and on occasions this is despite the absence of any attempt to impose similar restrictions with respect to the commitment made to the comparable provision in a global instrument. There are certainly grounds for doubting the admissibility of this practice, particularly where the ratification of the regional instrument is subsequent to the global one, but such reservations will at the very least serve as an initial constraint on action against the state concerned at the most appropriate international level.

The more general guarantees are not, despite being legally binding, a sufficient basis for taking effective action as they are still not always specific enough to indicate what is needed. Even though instruments such as the International Covenants and the European Convention have considerably greater precision in their formulation than the Universal Declaration, their implications for specific situations still need to be clarified through a process of interpretation, as well as by their elaboration in instruments dealing with particular concerns. The role of the European Commission and Court of Human Rights in the former respect is not only of regional but of global importance. Such has been the volume of issues addressed by these bodies that the essential elements involved in securing many rights are now abundantly clear, although some rights remain underdeveloped because of a reluctance to address all the issues canvassed in a case. However, even where the Commission and Court's conclusions as to what particular provisions require may not be in doubt, the reasoning on which they are based is not always apparent. Although the specific outcome might be thought just by many, the risk of compliance being refused (or at best being perfunctory) is undoubtedly increased where no cogent argument for it is to be found in the ruling. Moreover inadequate or undeveloped reasoning will not only affect the disposition of the respondent state; other states may also be reluctant to amend their own laws on this basis and it may be harder to orchestrate pressure against a defaulting state in such circumstances. The interpretation of other instruments by non-judicial bodies can also give rise to the same concern, even if they do not always enjoy the same high profile. However, this does not occur where provisions in general instruments are elaborated in subsequent treaties. Nonetheless these face a related problem of legitimacy in that, despite their formal status, their standing may not be seen as comparable. This is partly a consequence of having inferior enforcement mechanisms but the accommodation of specialist concerns can also lead to marginalisation. There is a pressing need to demonstrate the indivisibility of human rights undertakings.

The prominence of the European Convention system is in part attributable to the nature of the issues brought before it but it is particularly a consequence of the fact that the rulings of the Court (both old and new) are binding in law. This is a remarkable strength, notwithstanding the problems of clarity just considered; the binding character of the Court's rulings is, when coupled with the general disposition of states to fulfil their legal obligations, usually sufficient to secure their implementation. Comparable authority has not, however, been conferred on any of the other bodies entitled to express opinions about compliance with the other human rights treaties of the Council of Europe. This is not significant where the bodies, such as the monitoring mechanisms are of a political nature (cf. the monitoring by the Committee of Ministers and the Parliamentary Assembly), but it undoubtedly reflects a lesser status for those bodies established by the legal instruments creating the obligations involved. Even in the new collective complaints system for the European Social Charter provision is only made for "conclusions" as to whether or not satisfactory application of a provision has been ensured which, in turn, may be followed by a recommendation by the Committee of Ministers. The character and logic of the reasoning of the Committee of Independent Experts may be of comparable quality to the Court but its standing in legal terms is evidently inferior. This particular reform is at most a tentative step away from the priority given to civil and political rights over all others when it comes to enforcement. Such an approach is inconsistent with the need to treat all rights on an equal footing and the failure to meet this requirement is the all the more apparent where the bodies have only an advisory and monitoring function (such as under the Framework Convention for the Protection of National Minorities). The issue of status for the opinions of such bodies is not only important at the international level; it will inevitably affect the respect accorded to them by national courts.

The length of time taken to process cases was a major concern behind the reforms of the European Convention now coming into effect. Whether this has been successfully addressed by them remains to be seen but it may be premature to think about further institutional reforms, as opposed to staunching the flow of cases by more effective domestic implementation. The understandable concern about delay was only to be expected given the high visibility of the Commission and Court's caseload but it also exists in respect of other mechanisms, even if it is less evident and harder to quantify, as well as not necessarily being directly attributable to them or the resources at their disposal. For example, in the case of the Social Charter a report from a state may miss a particular cycle and thus not be examined for a further four years. More significantly, perhaps, reporting procedures allow the time taken for implementation to be obscured; action may be requested and a report expected at the next cycle of review and, although this gives the impression of progress, substantial periods of time may have elapsed before any appropriate action is actually taken. These procedures do not, of course, focus on individual cases but these still exist behind the issues examined and the hardship endured as a result of delayed implementation will be just as keenly felt as if a communication procedure existed. Delay is, therefore, no less grave in this situation and should not be left unnoticed in the accumulating paperwork.

It is not always easy to establish that international action has had the required effect. In the case of the European Court of Human Rights there is the procedure for supervising the execution of its judgments of the Court by the Committee of Ministers. Its very existence is in some respects an incentive to act and action which is the subject of an approving resolution by the Committee can often be regarded as satisfactory, not least where the same issue is not ventilated in subsequent proceedings. Nevertheless the promptness and adequacy of what has been done is not always satisfactory. Interest on monetary awards prevents them from being devalued by delayed payment but the indulgence allowed for the time to make necessary administrative and legislative reforms can be excessive, particularly as what is needed is often readily apparent at a much earlier stage in the proceedings. Although many rulings are unproblematic as regards the consequential obligations arising for the respondent state, it is not always easy for the Committee of Ministers to assess whether enough has been done. It might, therefore, be appropriate to give the Court more power to require particular action to be taken. However, there is no reason for the Committee to be so loath to regard a state's proposed measures as inadequate where a continuous flow of similar cases points to more radical action being required. Nevertheless requiring a report on what has been done puts the onus on the state concerned to act before the matter is regarded as concluded. This contrasts favourably with the approach of the discretionary recommendation for action in other mechanisms; the issue of possible compliance is thus effectively left over to another cycle of supervision. The Committee for the Prevention of Torture and Inhuman or Degrading Treatment or Punishment can make a public declaration where there is a lack of co-operation but this has only occurred in extreme cases; it does not really help where there is apparent goodwill but no significant action.

Even the enhanced status given to applicants under Protocol No. 11 does not mean that the merits of applications will definitely be considered but the advantage of complaints mechanisms is that those affected by non-observance of standards can set in train efforts to deal with the problem. There is, of course, still scope for an unfavourable exercise of discretion along the way (not least at the admissibility stage) but a well-founded grievance cannot readily be ignored. However, persons with such grievances are not always prepared or able to initiate proceedings where that option exists and there must be concern that violations, some quite serious, are not being addressed. Regardless of whether victims of human rights violations are competent to waive the consequences of the latter in respect of themselves, the *erga omnes* nature of human rights commitments makes it inappropriate for them to be disregarded with impunity. Concern for the maintenance of friendly relations has inhibited the use of the Convention' s interstate procedure and alternative solutions are needed. The risk of significant issues being overlooked is reduced in the case of the Social Charter because of the systematic examination of reports and the knowledge of the experts. An even more explicit *proprio motu* role has been conferred on the Committee for the Prevention of Torture and the monitoring bodies but such an approach would be inappropriate for the Court. A commissioner for human rights could possibly be given a useful part to play in setting the agenda – whether in judicial or monitoring procedures – but it should not be exclusive since he or she would find it hard to evade the influence of political and resource considerations in taking up issues. A useful complement to such a role would be to give non-governmental organisations greater capacity to determine what matters should be taken up. In this connection the model of the collective complaints procedure under the European Social Charter might be an appropriate starting point for the Convention and minority rights instruments.

One of the most significant achievements of the European Convention is that a victim does have the prospect of some redress being afforded once a violation has been established. At present this is limited to damages and there is a good case for expanding the competence of the Court so that – like some similar regional and global mechanisms – it can specify a wider range of appropriate redress; this is, after all, an element of the existing obligation on states to provide an effective remedy. Such a possibility would not only benefit the individuals concerned but would also give important guidance to states generally for the action that ought to be taken in comparable situations. However, the present limitations are inconsequential when compared with the lack of specific power on this matter for the other instruments; there is no basis for international direction as to redress for individuals or groups when it comes to the violation of rights in the Social Charter or in the guarantees extended to minorities. Compliance with requirements about implementation tends to be prospective and general in character. This approach further underlines the inferior approach to protecting such rights at the international level.

The proliferation of procedures does not just result in unhappy comparisons between the action taken to protect different rights. It also leads to concern as to whether there is effective co-ordination both within the region's mechanisms and between them and others available. This is not just a matter of husbanding resources sensibly but of ensuring that the response to a problem is systematic and focussed rather than fragmented and haphazard. Co-operation and exchange of information is increasingly common between institutions and could be further developed without necessarily having to establish a commissioner. However, the principal test for introducing any further element such as that office into the system ought to be whether or not it will add to or reduce the procedures that have to be pursued before appropriate action (such as expulsion, sanctions and even enforcement measures) is taken to deal with gross and persistent violations of human rights; establishing the capacity for a speedier and less hesitant response must be the priority.

Confidence about effective action being taken is to an extent as important as the action itself; without it there may be a reluctance to use the system and the resulting cynicism engendered in respect of it will undermine its authority. Such confidence is in part derived from the evidence of past success but it also relies on openness and decision-making based on established criteria. The secrecy which comes with the friendly settlement procedure under the European Convention is acceptable because of the strict conditions governing the acceptability of proposals for bringing proceedings to an end and because of the status of the body involved in giving the necessary approval, as well as the publication of relevant details regarding the complaint and the action to be taken as part of the settlement. This cannot necessarily be said of the monitoring by the Committee of Ministers since, even though the same juridical standards may be being applied, any final determination will be taken by political figures and there will be no clear indication that particular action has been required of a particular country. This is not to question that results can be achieved, indeed might only be achievable, in this way but such procedures should at best be complementary to other more open and more strictly normative ones. There is certainly a danger that they might become, or be perceived as being, preferable from the viewpoint of states; the consequence of this would be to add to the risk of rights being negotiable by reference to political considerations. This remains a problem, undoubtedly unavoidable, when it comes to any form of enforcement action but it would be regrettable if it became a central feature of resolving problems that did not require that sort of response.

This paper has focused on problems in satisfying some criteria of effectiveness within the European context and, in so doing, there is an inevitable risk of losing sight of what has been achieved. The protection extended to human rights in this region has been considerably enhanced since the adoption of the Universal Declaration. Nevertheless the difficulties faced in securing human rights seem to increase rather than diminish and the value of the contribution made at the international level cannot be taken for granted.

Theme 5: Protection: effective action at the international level

Report on Discussion Group 5 by Jeremy McBride

Many members of the group had taken part in the earlier consideration of issues relating to prevention of and responses to structural or large-scale human rights violations. Points made in that group undoubtedly contributed to the context of the later deliberations.

The starting point of our discussion was a recognition both that most provisions in the Universal Declaration had been transformed into binding legal obligations for European states and that there was a particular value in relying on regional implementation mechanisms. However, it was also accepted that there were a number of lacunae in respect of both matters.

In terms of substantive rights it was noted that the Universal Declaration required a right to equality and protection against discrimination. Although the increasingly expansive interpretation by the European Court of Human Rights of the European Convention's non-discrimination provision was helpful in this respect, it was not considered to be an adequate substitute for a more general guarantee. Work on preparing an additional protocol to remedy this position was seen as a matter of priority. Another omission was the failure to give effect to the right to seek and enjoy asylum proclaimed in the Declaration; even though some protection for asylum-seekers and refugees is afforded by the absolute prohibition of torture in the Convention, people in this position do not always enjoy the full range of other human rights assured to others. There was some recognition that states consider that they cannot readily address this deficiency because of the economic and social implications. Nevertheless the development of protection in this field – as well as the issue of migration generally – was seen as a matter that had to be dealt with by European states collectively. Concern was also expressed about the need to build on the rights of all persons deprived of their liberty through the adoption of an additional protocol. Importance was attached to addressing the applicability of human rights norms to non-state actors in a variety of contexts, notably commerce and terrorism. Finally it was felt that the elaboration of human rights standards at the regional level should in no case be inferior to those established at the global level.

The group acknowledged the considerable contribution made by the European Court to the elaboration of standards through its case-law. It was noted that its rulings can be influential on courts outside as well as within the region. In addition, other regional tribunals and the United Nations treaty bodies rely on them. However, it was felt that the Court might also be assisted by considering the decisions of those bodies. Furthermore it was recommended that the Court and the other human rights treaty bodies of the Council of Europe should be more prepared to take into account their respective rulings so that coherence and consistency in the elaboration of standards is maximised. The group discussed the quality of the reasoning in judgments and appreciated the problems that could arise when attempting to draft something that reflected the common ground between judges. Nevertheless there was concern that the basis for rulings on some contentious matters could have been better expressed and that there was scope for giving clearer guidance on general principles, particularly in cases that turned on a specific set of facts.

There was general concern that implementation measures should keep pace with the elaboration of standards. However, these measures should respect the principle of subsidiarity as far as practical. It was also agreed that a cautious approach should be adopted to proposals to undertake further reform of the European Convention mechanism before the effects of Protocol No. 11 are fully digested. However, although it was recognised that generally states are well-disposed to respecting interim measures without any legal obligation to do so, some members of the group thought that these should become mandatory. There was also some support for the giving the Court power to specify the action required by a state pursuant to the finding of a violation. It was acknowledged that some issues may not be ventilated before the Court but there was a reluctance to allow it to consider complaints from other than the victim. However, it was thought that non-governmental organisations could assist in the bringing of cases by groups of victims and in addressing wider issues through third party interventions.

There was a wish to see the implementation of economic and social rights given more prominence and this was seen as linked to the status of the views of the supervisory bodies concerned. The collective complaints procedure was seen as an important advance and it was thought that the experience of its operation should be examined before considering any extension of the right of petition to individuals.

There was some hesitation about suggestions that rulings of the European Committee for the Prevention of Torture and Inhuman or Degrading Treatment or Punishment should become binding, but it was thought that the Committee of Ministers could play a greater role in ensuring that they are implemented. At the same time it was felt that political considerations should not influence implementation of human rights standards but that the risk of this would be minimised in the monitoring mechanisms of the Parliamentary Assembly and the Committee of Ministers so long as objective criteria were followed, clear recommendations were made and there was effective follow-up. It was also suggested that, while confidentiality in the Committee of Ministers mechanisms might have some advantages in securing compliance with human rights norms, there should be a willingness to use publicity as a pressure where progress is not being made. There was also support for facilitating the more active engagement of non-governmental organisations in the work of monitoring mechanisms. Indeed this was seen as only one instance where the Council of Europe could benefit from co-operating more closely with such organisations. In particular there was thought to be a need for a much more effective framework for consultation.

There was an extensive discussion on the idea of establishing a human rights commissioner for the Council of Europe. Although consideration of the appropriateness of such an initiative was to some extent foreclosed by the decision to establish one, the problem of defining a mandate left plenty of scope for discussion. There was general concern that this mandate should be clear and that it should dovetail with those of existing institutions in the region and at the global level. Such clarity would assist the general public to understand the commissioner's role and not result in any loss of opportunity to use an existing effective mechanism such as the European Court of Human Rights. It was also felt that the elaboration of the commissioner's mandate needed to involve non-governmental organisations in a much more extensive way, not least because these organisations will contribute to the success of the commissioner's work. A commissioner was seen as potentially useful in situations requiring a prompt response and in this context action to protect human rights defenders was cited. It was recognised that the effectiveness of the commissioner's efforts would be dependent on the political will of member states but it was thought that this new office could also be instrumental in promoting the human rights culture on which that will must depend. It was felt that the commissioner should work closely with national human rights institutions and ombudsmen. The commissioner might be assisted by a power to call for reports on human rights implementation in specific cases but a general reporting procedure was seen as unnecessary. The introduction of a commissioner was an opportunity to create a more integrated and systematic approach to human rights protection within the Council of Europe which should not squandered. There was no doubt that the creation of a commissioner should be accompanied by adequate additional resources.

Theme 6: The promotion of human rights: information, education and training

Rapporteur: Kaija Gertnere

Fifty years ago, the Universal Declaration of Human Rights was adopted to set a common standard of achievement for all peoples and nations "to strive by teaching and education to promote respect for these rights and freedoms and by progressive measures, national and international, to secure their universal and effective recognition and observance". One of the challenges that the international community must address collectively and as individual member states is whether or not such measures have been taken and what are the results of actions taken. While the United Nations and regional organisations such as the Council of Europe might set agendas and priorities for the protection and promotion of human rights, without the support and implementation of these on a national level, little or no progress can be made.

It is the responsibility of all of our countries to work together to set standards governing human rights and agree on ways to monitor the international implementation of these standards. At the same time, member states must ensure the respect, protection and promotion of human rights domestically. This requires political will, commitment from governments, national human rights institutions, national and international co-operation and NGOs.

The United Nations Decade for Human Rights Education beginning 1 January 1995 was proclaimed to "give new impetus to the task of addressing the many efforts that have already been initiated in the field of human rights education and to effectively supplement the numerous efforts that have been made to achieve the widest possible dissemination of human rights material".

The five main objectives of the decade are: the assessment of needs and the formulation of education strategies at all levels; the strengthening of programmes and capacities for education; the development of suitable education materials; the strengthening of the role of the mass media in the furtherance of human rights education and finally; the global dissemination of the Universal Declaration of Human Rights in the maximum possible number of languages.

In 1997, within the framework of the Decade for Human Rights Education, a group of experts working under the auspices of the United Nations drew up a set of guidelines on national plans of action for human rights education. Their definition of human rights education included "the enabling of all persons to participate effectively in a free society". The guidelines also state that "human rights are promoted through three dimensions of education campaigns:

- provision of information about human rights and mechanisms for their protection;
- promotion of a human rights culture through the development of values, beliefs and attitudes which uphold human rights;
- and encouragement to take action to defend human rights and prevent abuses".

The guidelines were prepared as a response to resolutions adopted by the General Assembly and the Commission on Human Rights calling upon states to develop national plans of action for human rights education. Member states not only agreed to develop such plans but also to involve all relevant actors on a national level. Unfortunately, for various reasons, few countries have developed such plans.

To be able to judge what future steps should be taken and what lessons can be learned from the past, it is important to address human rights information, education and training from the perspective of all relevant parties, including: the international community, individual countries, national human rights institutions and NGOs.

One of the concerns often expressed within the international community is the need for co-ordination and exchange of information relating to work being conducted on a national, regional and/or international level. International organisations should strengthen and rationalise their activities, so as to avoid duplication among other human rights initiatives. The Council of Europe, as a regional organisation can and should apply existing and well functioning mechanisms to complement the work and efforts of others. Resources are finite and priorities must be set to reflect needs.

International organisations should conduct their own needs assessment and measure the impact and effectiveness of their work. On a European level, a survey of the state of human rights education and training programmes could be conducted including resources allocated nationally and internationally for implementation. The experience and activities of the United Nations in regions other than Europe in the field of education could provide new ideas and impetus as well. Another area which is in need of co-ordination and exchange of information relates to existing human rights information and education materials. Human rights educational programmes, training and information are costly and very often seen to be a luxury that countries cannot afford. Although these activities are expensive, prevention of human rights violations by informing the public is by far more effective and less expensive.

The Vienna Declaration and Programme of Action adopted at the World Conference in 1993 reaffirmed the dignity and worth inherent in the human person, whose preservation and promotion are the basis of all human rights and fundamental freedoms. As the subject of these rights and liberties, the individual is the principal beneficiary and should participate actively in their realisation.

The Declaration also stipulates that states should be provided with technical and financial assistance upon request for "the elaboration and attainment of coherent and comprehensive plans of action". It was envisaged that these plans should: strengthen institutions that advocate human rights and democracy; reform penal and correctional institutions; provide legal protection for human rights; provide theoretical and practical training in the field of human rights for officials, lawyers, judges, officers of security forces and others; to educate and inform the public at large with a view to promoting respect for human rights; and to give preference to other activities which contribute to the smooth functioning of a rule of law society.

One of the aims of this colloquy is to examine the progress, problems and priorities in Europe in the implementation of the Vienna Declaration and whether Europe has progressed beyond talking about human rights education to doing something about it.

As mentioned previously, few countries have developed plans of action for the protection and promotion of human rights, including information and education plans. Reasons for this can include the lack of resources, commitment from responsible and interested parties, and know how. The development of a national plan is only a small part of the battle, it is the implementation that requires the greatest amount of work. Having said this, it does not excuse countries from doing so. It is the responsibility of each country to decide for itself what are the most appropriate means to fulfil its obligations.

I would like to share the experience of Latvia in its process of developing and implementing its National Programme for the Protection and Promotion of Human Rights. The development of Latvia's programme was similar to that recommended by the United Nations. As a result of this programme, in 1995 Latvia established a national human rights institution – the Latvian National Human Rights Office (LNHRO).

Under its enabling legislation, the Office has the mandate to:

- raise awareness and promote understanding and observance of human rights;
- inquire into allegations of individual human rights in both the public and private sectors;
- on its own initiative, investigate human rights related issues and problems in Latvia;
- advise on compliance of Latvia's laws and practices with its national and international human rights obligations; and
- co-ordinate programmes which promote observance of human rights.

By establishing an independent institution with a broad mandate, Latvia was able to incorporate within one institution, the responsibility to protect and promote human rights in accordance with Latvia's domestic legislation and international obligations in an accessible, transparent and cost effective manner.

Perhaps the most important role of a national institution or other responsible body, is to educate individuals that they have rights as well as responsibilities. This role can involve a variety of different activities including the collection, production and dissemination of information; the organisation of promotional events and the development and implementation of training programmes for a variety of professions. Judging from the experience of many central and eastern European countries, people understand that they have rights that the state is obliged to guarantee, but often fail to recognise that they themselves have responsibilities as well.

Where national institutions exist, they should play the key role in raising awareness of the law and its implications for all aspects of daily life – for people at work, school, in families and in public life. The principles enshrined in international human rights conventions and domestic law like privacy, the right to a fair hearing and the freedom of expression – have implications beyond the strict legal requirements which would be upheld before the courts. If governments with the assistance of national institutions, NGOs or any other actors are to succeed in promoting these principles, they will need to enhance awareness in at least three ways:

1. Firstly, by using the media for information and debate and providing reliable and comprehensive information for the media on human rights issues. Media has a huge impact in shaping society, influencing and changing public opinion and in setting acceptable standards of human rights within which a society operates. It is generally acknowledged that the use of media is a very important tool in the means available in the dissemination of information, education and the promotion of human rights. The two most important reasons for this are:

- It is a common source of information for most people in the community either through print, radio or television. Debate and discussion at all levels of society, in Parliament, within government, business and in local neighbourhoods, is often inspired and generated by the media;
- Large budgets for education and information campaigns are rare anywhere.

The cost of production and dissemination of materials is so costly that few can afford such luxuries. The Council of Europe and the United Nations have prepared good quality promotional, written, visual and audiovisual material that need only be translated and distributed. By co-ordinating materials produced, organisations can pool their resources and provide a materials which all member states use.

2. Secondly, through education, working with education authorities to ensure that human rights principles are discussed in schools. The general school system offers the most comprehensive audience for the promotion of human rights education: students from primary to university level. Including human rights into primary school curricula will guarantee that all children have an opportunity to become acquainted and begin to understand and apply the principles of human rights to their everyday lives. At a young age children need to be taught values, morals, tolerance and that being different does not justify discrimination. A child won't understand nor be interested in the meaning of a convention, but he/she can understand that a child with a disability is still a child just like him and should be treated as an equal.

At a university level human rights should be incorporated into all faculties, but priority should given to administrative, legal and social faculties. At the request of member states, the Council of Europe has developed and organised seminars on the European Convention, its protocols, the Social Charter and other topics at the request of member states that can be structured to meet the needs of formal education at all levels.

Professional groups (teachers, social workers, journalists, lawyers, officials and/or civil servants) must also be targeted in receiving human rights training and applying it to their everyday work. These groups can and do have a direct impact on the rest of society and should promote human rights by setting examples and through practice. By developing a human rights culture among professionals it will reflect upon the society that they are in contact with on a daily basis and broaden the understanding and respect of human rights.

Training programmes developed nationally or by international organisations can be tailored to fit the needs of professional groups and be conducted in all member states. Training trainers provides the ability to continue programmes on a national level and develop domestic capacity with the support of international organisations when needed. The Council of Europe has been active and successful in this area as well as in supporting national and regional initiatives based on information campaigns; seminars, conferences and contributing expert opinion on the human rights dimension of current debates. For the most part, these activities can and have been conducted on an ad hoc basis focusing on target groups or specific issues and organised in co-operation with relevant government bodies, NGOs or interest groups.

3. Thirdly, by promoting good practice, through the provision of advice and training, particularly to those institutions and professionals which have the greatest impact on vulnerable people – the police, prison and immigration services and institutions for the care of children, the elderly and the mentally and physically disabled. This is another area which would benefit from co-ordinated activities and materials prepared by the Council of Europe and other organisations.

   Effective promotion and protection of human rights does require a great deal of political will, commitment, co-operation, and resources, but an informed and educated public can help itself in preventing violations or discriminatory practices. On an international level, the United Nations has at its disposal the appropriate goals, guidelines and work programmes for the 21st century. However, on a European level concrete steps must be taken to guarantee that words and promises of commitment become a reality at the regional, national and local levels. The Council of Europe, its member states, national human rights institutions and NGOs should use the second "triennium" (1998-2000) of the Decade for Human Rights Education to work together and develop mechanisms and provide resources for the protection and promotion of human rights through education, information and training. After all, it is in our hands.

Theme 6: The promotion of human rights: information, education and training

Report on Discussion Group 6 by Kaija Gertnere

The Discussion Group on the promotion of human rights information, education and training discussed a broad range of issues. The composition of the group led discussions to focus on concerns of the NGO community. Unfortunately, governments constituted a small minority of the participants. It is ironic to recall the discussions of the previous days in other groups, where comments were often made on the need for education and information. Governments were quick to realise that education is important when discussing prevention of human rights violations, protecting social rights, women's rights, effective action on a national or international level, but failed to translate their commitments into action.

1. Plans of action for human rights information, education and training

Several NGOs stressed the importance of national plans, but were quick to acknowledge that few countries had national plans. However, this was not viewed as a deterrent for NGOs drafting plans of action themselves to better plan their work and to promote the need for human rights education. NGOs stressed the importance of national plans placing responsibility on governments to fulfil their commitments. Guidelines have been drafted and adopted by the UN to assist parties interested in preparing national plans. They include useful advice and annexes of relevant UN documents providing information on the political and legal basis for such plans.

Developing national plans for human rights education provides the opportunity to bring together people (government, NGOs, community groups) interested in the issue and includes a country needs assessment, sets priorities, identifies what has been done, and can provide the international community, including donors, with a comprehensive overview for possible co-operation.

2. Education and training

Participants reiterated the need for human rights education to be integrated or mainstreamed into the primary, secondary and university levels as was prescribed by the Committee of Ministers recommendation in 1985. It was felt necessary to review how far this recommendation has been implemented in member states.

Emphasis should also be placed on providing relevant and suitable information and training to professional or community groups (police, civil servants, social workers, etc.) and education authorities on human rights. Trade unions and other non-legal services should be used to channel information to the broadest public possible. Governments and organisations should use and share the experience of others on similar issues.

Interactive methodology should be used in human rights education by including the examples of everyday life to illustrate better the principles involved in an understandable manner.

3. The role of international organisations

Participants stressed the need for international organisations to co-ordinate their work, essentially at the national level, and be aware of each other's activities in areas relating to human rights information, education and training. Organisations should pool their resources (financial, technical and substantive) better to meet the needs of member states and other interested parties.

In view of concern expressed about the lack of communication which often exists between governments and NGOs, a number of participants supported the role of intergovernmental organisations acting as facilitators in bringing together the two parties.

A number of participants stressed the need for materials being suitable to a broad range of users. This would allow governments, NGOs and other activists to tailor information or programmes to suit their needs. It was suggested that a centralised information bank of human rights information and training materials be compiled and made accessible to interested parties. Such information could and should be made available via the Internet.

4. Role of NGOs

NGOs were recognised as playing a fundamental role in human rights education, information and training especially in countries that do not have a government policy or programme in this area. Some of the recommendations which were expressed focused on facilitating adequate training and dissemination of materials, using the internet, training community groups, facilitating co-operation among NGOs, national and local government and intergovernmental agencies and the need for new methodologies and teaching techniques.

5. Co-operation between NGOs and government

Co-operation between NGOs and governments is desirable and should be supported by governments. NGOs can provide expertise and information unavailable to governments and can ensure that the community's concerns are better reflected and represented. NGOs were critical of the lack of political will on the part of governments and in some instances considered that their government impeded their work. Lack of a legal basis for NGOs was mentioned specifically.

NGOs felt strongly that their views be taken into account by governments when reports to international treaty monitoring bodies are prepared. If such an opportunity is not possible, alternative reports have been submitted. NGOs expressed their willingness to work together with governments rather than apart from them.

6. Media and communication

Media is an inexpensive and powerful tool for conveying information to the general public. By working with the media, enabling them to view issues while wearing "human rights glasses", governments and NGOs provide a society access to information and can educate the public of its rights. The media must be interested and understand human rights so as to present every day issues with a human rights perspective.

Modern technology such as the internet provides access to a slew of information on human rights as well as a forum for distributing it and should be used as a tool for education and information dissemination. Even a small NGO can have impact by using the internet to promote its work.

Unfortunately, national authorities and local communities often fail to recognise human rights issues within their own geographical area and need to have a better understanding of domestic human rights concerns.

Closing session

General report. Presentation of the conclusions and recommendations of the colloquy

Hanna Suchocka

Over the last three days we have been meeting under the auspices of the Council of Europe in order to commemorate the 50th anniversary of the Universal Declaration of Human Rights, and to contribute to the 1998 review of the implementation of the Declaration and Programme of Action adopted at the World Conference on Human Rights in Vienna in 1993.

I should like to divide my presentation into three parts. First, I want to say a few words about where we stand generally fifty years after adoption of the Declaration. Second, I will refer to the results of the discussions on the six main themes of the colloquy. Finally, I will try to highlight a few issues, which, in my view, merit particular attention.

My task in so doing has been greatly facilitated by the respective rapporteurs of the discussion groups and their chairpersons, the support of the Secretariat, and the intensive "brainstorming" undertaken by participants in the discussion groups.

I. Fifty years later

Half a century has passed since the adoption of the Universal Declaration of Human Rights. At the time it was adopted, no-one envisaged the huge impact that this document would exert on peoples' awareness of human rights and on the importance placed on those rights in society.

Fifty years ago, the adoption of the Declaration resulted mainly from the need to react to the trauma, suffering and loss of confidence in human nature, resulting from the chaos and magnitude of the tragedies of the Second World War. The Declaration was a reaction to a war which had stripped people of all dignity, deprived them of all rights and resulted in a loss of self-respect and trust in other human beings.

Until quite recently we could delude ourselves that Europe would not depart from the principles of the Declaration. The war in the former Yugoslavia, however, deprived us of these delusions. It has transpired that societies, nations, and some individuals are still not sufficiently attached to the concept of human rights, to be prevented from inflicting pain, rape, torture and mass killings. It would appear that, without any inhibition, some people continue to destroy everything that others have tried to create in the last half century.

Europe looks very different now. The political situation has changed, new countries have emerged, some have vanished. But the Declaration has lost none of its currency. Even though its contents have not changed throughout these five decades, it is perceived today in a distinctly different manner than it was at the time of its adoption. Fifty years ago the Declaration was a breakthrough in establishing basic human rights, today it is viewed as an uncontested standard.

The main characteristics of the Declaration are its generality and universality. The United Nations must be credited with the creation of the most universal, globally accessible canon of human rights, consisting of the Declaration, the covenants, and the individual conventions. At the same time, it has transpired that practical enforcement of rights therein is more easily accomplished at the regional level than at the global level.

When one examines the way in which the international law of human rights has been developing, it becomes clear that the more signatories there are to an international treaty, the more difficult it is to find a compromise in establishing a common standard of human rights. While the desired standard forms a minimum for individual countries, it will, in reality, also constitute a maximum acceptable to member states. Difficulties in arriving at such a common standard arise in particular as a result of historical and cultural differences among nations. As some of the speakers have pointed out, regional instruments have proved more effective than global ones.

The regional conventions which set out detailed rights, and provide for substantial protective measures, have played a paramount role in achieving the security of person *vis-à-vis* the omnipotent state through their independent control mechanisms. Examples of such conventions are the European and American Conventions, the only human rights treaties to provide for judicial proceedings and to apply to countries which are closer to one another in history and legal culture.

The Declaration emphasises that a common perception of rights and freedoms is a precondition for full implementation of, and respect for, human rights. Formulating such a common understanding is a challenge to all judicial and quasi-judicial institutions, such as the European Court of Human Rights or United Nations human rights bodies. It is through their case-law, guidelines or general comments that a common interpretation of human rights is shaped. This process is a dynamic one, as the contents of any given right undergo constant evolution. The rights named fifty years ago by the Declaration now carry a richer (e.g. right to privacy) or even a different meaning. Censorship in prisons was once an inherent part of detention – its imposition today infringes the rights of those deprived of their liberty.

Significantly, the sets of rights contained in the European and American Conventions appear, at first glance, as rather modest compared to those contained in the documents whose implementation lack an effective protective mechanism. Governments sometimes sign conventions of the latter type for political and propaganda reasons without any intention of implementing their provisions. This was clearly illustrated by attitudes towards the ratification of the International Covenant on Civil and Political Rights and the Optional Protocol to the Covenant, two documents which, after all, were adopted simultaneously. While the majority of countries of central and eastern Europe bound themselves by the former in 1976, they were able to ratify the latter only after 1989.

As mechanisms for redressing individual violations, the preparation of periodic national reports and the practice of field monitoring have proved much less effective than judicial proceedings. Also, it has transpired that the potential of individual complaints procedures, as a form of initiating judicial proceedings, has, until now, been used to a fuller extent than that of interstate procedures. This can be illustrated by the case-law of the European Court of Human Rights as well by as the practice of the human rights bodies of the United Nations in cases where provision exists for complaints to be lodged by states.

The institution of individual complaint functions outside the political context and restrictions within which governments operate. However, individuals often cannot afford to pursue complaints before an international court, especially where they come from socially or economically vulnerable groups. Therefore, it may be advisable to increase the rights of non-governmental organisations to initiate and conduct proceedings within the framework of international human rights fora. Non-governmental human rights organisations, while pursuing the public good, may draw attention to gross violations of human rights which states find uncomfortable to expose for political reasons.

In this sense, the European solution, a solution advocating comprehensive protection of a more limited set of rights, has proved more effective than those instruments which contain a broad set of rights lacking protection mechanisms. This approach can be argued to have fulfilled the hopes of the authors of the Universal Declaration of Human Rights. A war is virtually unthinkable among countries in which human rights have been observed in the European manner over the lifespan of two generations. This state of affairs has been made possible, not through fear, or the maintenance of a balance of powers, but by curtailing the powers of those in a position of authority, in other words, by restricting the arbitrariness of the "rulers" *vis-à-vis* "the ruled". Unfortunately, this has not taken place in certain member states which still fail to provide for an appropriate infrastructure to limit abuse of power.

II. Themes discussed

This general report can only highlight some key conclusions reached in the discussions under the six topics of the colloquy. I will not attempt to duplicate the excellent reports which we have heard today.

1. Prevention of and responses to structural or large-scale human rights violations

In his written contribution, Vojin Dimitrijević compared Council of Europe and United Nations control mechanisms with respect to their ability to provide for prevention of and responses to structural or large-scale human rights violations. It appeared to him that the heart of the Council of Europe system, the one set up under the European Convention on Human Rights, was based on the assumption that Europe was a region where the general ideal of human rights was attained and remained only to be implemented in full detail by bona fide state authorities who sincerely co-operated with the international control bodies. Hence a control system which was based on individual complaints, where class action was not available and structural deficiencies could not as a rule be addressed and where states had proved to be extremely reluctant, for political considerations, to use the possibility of interstate complaints under Article 24 of the Convention. The system has remained "all but powerless" in the face of structural deficiencies.

According to Mr Dimitrijević, this problem is likely to become even more worrying in today's "reinstated" Europe, which is more heterogeneous. It comprises countries which have been influenced by cultures and political traditions and which are in social situations that western Europe has not lived with for almost half a century. Their situation – often characterised by low development, social inequality, lack of democracy, ethnic differences and armed conflicts – are much more likely to generate gross violations of human rights, that are not (only) due to bad law but to systematic misapplication and disregard of it.

Prevention of and responses to such large-scale human rights violations have always been a task for the United Nations, which has never known a homogeneous membership. Among the paths which appeared to be promising to Vojin Dimitrijević, were the non-conventional procedures of the United Nations Commission on Human Rights based on ECOSOC Resolutions 1235 (XLII) of 1967 and 1503 (XLVIII) of 1970. These procedures rely on the United Nations Charter and the Universal Declaration of Human Rights and thus neither depend on prior contractual consent of the state concerned, nor hinge on individual applications. Concern and resistance by member states against perceived "intrusion" have been met by the confidentiality of procedures and a thematic approach, where the focus is not on a given country but on a problem. According to Vojin Dimitrijević, however, the end results of the United Nations procedures have "tended to be disappointing", as the Commission has not been able to terminate a procedure by a clear statement that there was a violation, nor to address adequately cases where countries breached their obligation to report.

As acknowledged by Mr Dimitrijević, the Council of Europe's work for strengthening democratic institutions, building independent justice systems, fostering human rights education and addressing social problems was an important contribution to the prevention of human rights violations. Likewise, the preventive work done by a non-judiciary body of independent experts in the framework of the 1987 European Convention for the Prevention of Torture was judged "innovative" by him. However, with respect to the political monitoring done by the Committee of Ministers under its 1994 and 1995 Declarations, Vojin Dimitrijević regretted that no independent body of experts can initiate proceedings and that NGOs were kept outside the process. He considered that the exclusive use of the thematic approach and the absence of any action so far under Paragraph 4 of the 1994 Declaration directed towards specific situations in a member state "can mean either that there have not been any concerns or that there has been hesitance to test the sensitivities of governments". As regards field operations in the form of ad hoc or sedentary missions in the territory where gross violation are taking place, Dimitrijević considered them useful as parts of an effort to end conflicts resulting in gross violations of human rights. But he considered them "not truly preventive in nature" and did not seem to push the Council of Europe in that direction.

Peter Jambrek in his written contribution on individual complaints versus structural violence argued that increasing pervasive personal, institutional and social actions and policies that lead to massive, repetitive and persistent human rights violations may broadly be classified under a common category of "structural violence". The problem of structural violence in most of these cases could be associated with armed conflicts and intercommunal strife. In such circumstances the traditional "re-active" role of the European Court of Human Rights addressing individual cases could be seen as doing "too little too late". Hence, a new "pro-active" role of the Court should be developed, argued Jambrek. The European Court should not confine itself to ascertaining whether, in particular circumstances, the requirement of the Convention's provisions were satisfied or not. It should not hesitate, argued Jambrek, also to couch its findings in more general terms.

Peter Jambrek noted that although the European Court of Human Rights was empowered to deal with individual cases only, still the reasoning and the implementation of a judgment had a positive impact beyond the specifics of an individual case. Redress of an individual violation triggered change in a wider context, although the concrete judgment may lack an explicit *erga omnes* effect, Jambrek stated. Governments may be expected to display a certain lack of goodwill when highly politicised problems arise. At the same time, there are key obstacles which limit the efficiency of the European Court's response to applications.

In conclusion, Jambrek called for continued adherence to the doctrine of subsidiarity in view of the exhaustion of effective, purely domestic, remedies. Jambrek also saw a need for a strengthened constitutional method of adjudication for the European Court of Human Rights and recognition as well as articulation of the still hidden and unintended preventive and general functions of individual cases adjudication. Finally, he recommended a global approach in solving structural issues, relying upon links and bridges of the European Court to the other "supporting" Council of Europe mechanisms.

A main result of the discussions under Theme 1, of which we were informed by Mr Dimitrijević, was the broad consensus that the instruments and procedures that exist in Europe were useful but had often proved insufficient in preventing large scale human rights violations. In the Council of Europe, some of the root causes of gross violations must be addressed, and early warning provided. In this context, attention was drawn to the co-operation programmes, the work of the Committee for the Prevention of Torture and Inhuman or Degrading Treatment or Punishment, the supervisory work done under the European Social Charter, by the European Commission Against Racism and Intolerance and, in the near future the work of the Advisory Committee set up under the Framework Convention for the Protection of National Minorities.

However, intergovernmental action still needs to be shaped in such a way as to take account of, and react adequately to, early warnings received.

Here a crucial role has to be played by the Committee of Ministers which should ensure, in performing its functions under Article 54 of the Convention, that states take all appropriate steps to comply with judgments, including structural changes. In addition, there was a strong feeling that its monitoring procedures needed to be strengthened substantially and made more transparent.

The view was widely shared that attention should be focused on improving existing mechanisms and procedures rather than on creating new ones. The only exception considered was the proposed commissioner for human rights who might contribute to developing Council of Europe capacity to receive advance warning of threats to human rights and to take appropriate action. However, it was also suggested that such a role could be played by the Secretary General of the Council of Europe under the existing terms of his office.

A further point is the need for coherence between the actions of the various political and human rights organs of the Council of Europe. Streamlining and coordination of procedures would help gain more transparency and avoid contradictions and waste of effort and time.

The value of the NGOs' contribution to prevention of, and response to, structural human rights violations was hailed by many. Clearly, in the absence of active human rights groups at the domestic level, international initiatives will not have full effect. We must pay tribute to those who are engaged in the defence of human rights, often at a considerable personal risk.

2. *Social rights: the challenge of indivisibility and interdependence*

Aalt-Willem Heringa in his paper on social rights argued for the development of far-reaching "positive obligations" in connection with the rights and obligations guaranteed in the European Social Charter. Social rights, according to him, were still lagging behind political rights in development, implementation as well as public awareness within society at large. Professor Heringa focused on several "common" aspects of social rights in general but most importantly perhaps he underlined the interconnection between liberties and social rights; for example with respect to what he called "common denominators" such as the right to personhood and the equality-principle. However, he concluded that social rights are the ones that now require particular attention and promotion as a response to a present status quo of inadequate support for their development.

As a remedy to address this situation Heringa proposed a range of improvements and new policies. He stressed the importance of clear and non-discriminatory access to institutional human rights guarantees. Within the context of national structures he linked the above with a need for consistent state policy of compliance with the treaty obligations and the development of nation-wide institutions that would facilitate and activate such compliance as well as promote better access and greater understanding of human rights in society at large. In addition to the efforts of the state institutions, some non-governmental organisations should carry a part of a mission to bring people closer towards a full understanding of their rights. In terms of implementation, Mr Heringa stressed the importance of individual cases for rendering social rights more concrete and tangible, thereby demonstrating their enforceability.

Interestingly, discussions on Theme 2 as reported by Mr Heringa also emphasised the need for more coherence and synergies between different supervisory mechanisms. This would be a concrete expression of the indivisibility of economic, social and cultural rights on the one hand and civil and political rights on the other.

Concrete measures to improve the protection of social rights were identified. At the national level, efforts should be made, it was said, to render social rights more justiciable, especially by clearly defining core obligations non-respect of which would constitute a clear violation of the right in question. National human rights institutions and NGOs can play an important role in ensuring that social rights become much more part of public debate and policy in member states. Governments could consider involving them more directly in the preparation of reports under international treaty obligations.

Participants expressed the view that states should accept the European Social Charter's Collective Complaints Protocol and ratify the Revised Social Charter. The Protocol to the European Convention on Human Rights providing for a general prohibition of discrimination, now under preparation, was described as a "an essential step forward".

3. Effective implementation of women's rights

Significant improvements in ensuring women's rights in the course of the last fifty years have been achieved, wrote Katarina Tomaševski in her paper on effective implementation of women's rights, within a two-step framework: first, formal acceptance of equal rights for men and women and next, adequate implementation of this principle by ensuring equal access to the confirmed rights.

Ms Tomaševski noted that historical determinants and public conscience based on social heritage played an important role in stereotypes persisting in some places. She suggested that language-directed campaigns led to some improvement in the way society had allocated roles within the family or community. The author stressed, however, the fact that no terminological changes could be effective if they were not followed by concrete action to change the status quo. Ms Tomaševski saw the task of freeing women from their traditional role within the family, changing women's role within a society at large and adjusting historically determined public perceptions of women as one of the most important objectives. The international co-ordination of formulating women's rights was viewed by the author as a land of opportunity for promoting women's positions in society.

Ms Tomaševski also noted that violence against women should be regarded as structural violence – a result of a societal system that led to women's discrimination. The programmes against family violence were often superficial in their scope and operations as they failed to recognise the underlying financial, economic and legal dependence of women. In order to address this issue comprehensively, a far-reaching revision of law would be necessary – it would have to change such issues as the marital property law or parents' legal rights with respect to childcare. The author also addressed the particularly difficult situation of immigrant women.

Reforms must be encouraged with respect to the position of women on the job market. Ms Tomaševski claimed that women were unjustly discriminated against because of their lower productivity which she saw as a given because of women's family obligations. The author believed that the traditional legal approach, focused as it was on a greater protection for women, had actually led to their further separation from men on the job market.

In order to address these and other problems, Ms Tomaševski suggested a range of programmes and tasks including gathering information with regard to the situation of women, as well as further development of pro-women organisations (although she recognised the problem of potentially overlapping functions and conflicts of interests between such organisations).

It is highly significant that Ms Tomaševski's report on Theme 3 indicates a consensus on important points such as the meaning of human rights and women's human rights, and the fact that substantive equality between women and men should be the ultimate aim of national and international policies designed to achieve parity. We should be aiming at the effective enjoyment of human rights by women as well as by men. This does not exclude a gender sensitive approach, on the contrary. Effective realisation of human rights cannot be achieved in disregard of the realities of the situation of women.

The discussions on "mainstreaming" showed that much remains to be done to develop such gender sensitivity both in the work of national legislators, policy makers and courts, but also in that of the intergovernmental and human rights organs at the international level, including in the Council of Europe. Strong support was expressed for adopting a non-discrimination protocol to the European Convention on Human Rights, as well as for the protocol to the Convention for the Elimination of All Forms of Discrimination Against Women, as a tool for making the right of women to freedom from discrimination more enforceable.

4. Protection: effective action at the national level

Régis de Gouttes began his report on the protection of human rights at the national level by drawing on the conclusions of the January 1993 interregional meeting on human rights organised by the Council of Europe before the World Conference on Human Rights: a move from proclamations to actions is necessary in the field of human rights. In this, the state (each with its different culture, tradition and political history) should take a primary role and responsibility since the national level is the most effective policy level. The minimum for all states should be the protection and promotion of human rights as a counterbalance to any type of power: political, legal, media-based or economic, a preventive mechanism against abuse.

Mr de Gouttes believed that the state apparatus which becomes the protector of human rights rather than an oppressor, must be characterised by organisational and structural solutions for human rights promotion incorporated into each of the three main pillars of a genuine state governed by the rule of law: an independent and effective judicial system, a democratic and protective legislature, and accessible administrative authorities which are subject to control. The first pillar can be characterised as the one that secures access to justice for all, including access to law itself, legal advice, information, counselling, and legal aid; it also ensures independent and impartial justice incorporating institutions to protect judges; it provides effective justice and finally it is characterised by a judicial system that protects human rights according to a cross-European standard. The second pillar is based on a state legislature and its role in keeping with people's aspirations with regard to protection of their fundamental rights as well as ensuring that domestic law complies with international and constitutional law on human rights. The third pillar – the executive branch – should be based on full accessibility, awareness of human rights issues and be itself subject to control, both internal or hierarchical as well as external.

Apart from the state organisational structure and policy required to protect and promote human rights, the second part of the effort should be concentrated on the actors independent from the state. These should include national institutions for the promotion of human rights, non-governmental human rights organisations and, finally, the media. In conclusion, Mr de Gouttes stressed that effective human rights implementation can only be achieved if there is a co-ordinated effort on behalf of all these players acting together; this effort should be "interactive" in nature in order to arrive at the best possible protection and promotion of human rights.

In his report on Discussion Group 4, Mr de Gouttes presented many recommendations concerning the roles of national Parliaments, governments, courts as well as NGOs and national human rights institutions. The responsibilities of each of these actors were highlighted as was the importance of interaction between them in order to bring about effective respect for human rights in our societies.

With respect to the national authorities, several participants drew attention to the need to ensure that national courts and judges were truly independent, this independence being an essential element in ensuring the efficiency of justice. It was vital for judges, prosecutors, lawyers, representatives of the law, and officials responsible for public order to be granted adequate working conditions, as well as appropriate training in human rights. Specific recommendations were made on the role to be played by national ombudsmen and the need to speed up reform of judicial and penitentiary systems in certain countries.

Where the legislature is concerned methods of systematically examining the compatibility of draft legislation with the European Convention should be developed. The idea of attaching assessment reports to draft legislation specifically on the question of compatibility with the European Convention was put forward. NGOs and national human rights institutions can play an important watch dog role by drawing attention to possible contradictions between draft legislation and international human rights standards.

The self-executing nature of the European Convention was considered fundamental and states were recommended to incorporate the Convention into their domestic law. The recommendation was made that mechanisms should be developed at the national level to enable a re-opening of domestic proceedings following a judgment of the European Court of Human Rights.

5. *Protection: effective action at the international level*

In the opening paragraph of his report on protection at the international level, Jeremy McBride noted that the Universal Declaration has asserted a clear role for human rights protection on the international level. However, he argued, there are still concerns about the legitimacy of human rights norms, their applicability and the strength of their authority both within the states and in the wider international community. Mr McBride said that naturally there are limits of justifiable pre-eminence but at the same time "domestic jurisdiction" can no longer serve as a hard separator behind which international legal norms have no application. Mr McBride pointed at interesting differences in commitments of the same countries on the world level and their reluctance to accept equivalent standards on a regional basis.

The effectiveness of implementation of general guarantees was still limited, argued Mr McBride. Despite being legally binding, they are usually not specific enough to point at the set of actions that would be needed for implementation. He contrasted the more general Universal Declaration with the international covenants and the European Convention on Human Rights, which are set out with greater precision, though still requiring interpretation in order to make possible the application of their standards to specific situations. Mr McBride noted that the prominence of the European Convention system arises partly from the fact that the rulings of the Court are binding in law; this is a remarkable strength, the author notes. However, Mr McBride saw a problem in the fact that comparable authority has not been conferred on any of the other bodies entitled to express opinions about compliance with the other human rights treaties of the Council of Europe.

Other factors which have a negative impact on the effectiveness of such potential international actions in this field include the length of time taken to process cases, imperfection of execution and implementation supervision, inappropriate consideration of the entire scope of complaints in each case, inadequate a priori confidence in effective action being actually implemented, secrecy of procedures, and others. The protection extended to human rights in this region, wrote McBride in his concluding comments, has been considerably enhanced since the adoption of the Universal Declaration; nevertheless, the difficulties faced in securing human rights seem to increase rather than diminish.

As Mr McBride reported, Discussion Group 5 recognised that most rights contained in the Universal Declaration have nowadays been transformed into binding legal obligations for European states. However, there are still some lacunae concerning the prohibition of discrimination, protection for asylum seekers and refugees and the rights of all persons deprived of their liberty.

As concerns implementation it was stressed that international measures should respect the principle of subsidiarity. Indeed, the discussions of Group 4 have shown us how crucial is the primary role of national authorities. Caution was expressed in regard to further reforms of the European Convention mechanism at this stage. However, some practical suggestions were made with a view to enhancing the impact of judgments of the European Court of Human Rights.

Considerable attention was given to the proposed Commissioner for Human Rights. The debate focussed on aspects such as co-ordination with other international and regional institutions, relations with NGOs and perhaps, most importantly, the need for political will and adequate resources in order to allow the Commissioner to become truly effective, and not a token addition to the arsenal of existing institutions.

The hope was expressed that the monitoring procedures of the Committee of Ministers would become more open to input by NGOs. The point was also made that, in case of a clear lack of progress on a particular problem, the Committee of Ministers could usefully insert an element of publicity into the procedure.

6. The promotion of human rights: information, education and training

The co-operation between institutions promoting human rights on the international, national and regional level as well as effective implementation of such promotion policies at each and every one of these levels, separately, are the key themes of Kaija Gertnere's paper on the promotion of human rights via information, education and training. As she pointed out, the United Nations Decade for Human Rights Education (that began on 1 January 1995) recognises five main objectives for such policies: assessment of the current situation, strengthening of existing programmes, development of educational materials, strengthening the role of media, and global dissemination of the Universal Declaration.

With respect to the guidelines for the policies on the national level, Ms Gertnere recalled the study done by the United Nations experts who recognised three important priorities: provision of information, development of values and beliefs in support of human rights and encouragement to defend human rights when necessary. However the key to success, as Kaija Gertnere stressed repeatedly, is the co-ordination of efforts between the national, international and regional policies.

Within this context, the Vienna Declaration and Programme of Action adopted at the World Conference in 1993 stresses the need for assistance to states who wish to create or strengthen institutions that advocate human rights and democracy, reform penal and correctional institutions, provide legal protection as well as theoretical and practical training, and to educate and inform the public at large, particularly, as she stressed, with the aim of showing that people have rights as well as responsibilities.

Ms Gertnere wondered to what extent the policies mentioned above were implemented with respect to Europe and Latvia in particular. She mentioned the creation of the Latvian National Human Rights Office as one of the key projects in that respect and argues for this example as a case of incorporating in a single institution a broad responsibility for human rights protection and promotion. With regard to implementation policies, the author identified three essential areas for action: use of media, direct education at various age levels and education of professional groups, and, finally, promoting good practice within the institutions that have the greatest impact on vulnerable people.

If there is one area where partnerships between all players, national and international, governmental and non-governmental, are of the essence, it is that of human rights information, education and training. This came out very clearly from the report which Ms Gertnere presented on Discussion Group 6. More should be done to pool resources, to work closely with NGOs, to make good use of opportunities offered by the media and by modern technologies. In this respect, I can only echo the concern expressed by the Rapporteur at the apparent lack of interest by member states in the discussions under this theme and, more importantly, at the lack of progress in most member states, in devising and implementing national plans of action.

Governments must respond to the willingness to co-operate expressed by NGOs. International organisations can provide a framework for bringing together national authorities and NGOs to stimulate concrete action. It was recommended that the Council of Europe take initiatives in this regard. There is little doubt that training of key professional groups and of politicians, as well as raising awareness among the general public, are sound and indispensable long-term investments in human rights.

III. Human rights in Europe: the way forward

Acceptance of existing international standards on the world level is still of crucial importance. For example, the need for European states who have not yet done so to ratify both the United Nations' and the Council of Europe's main conventions in the field of human rights, including all protocols to the European Convention on Human Rights. Governments are also asked to re-examine reservations and withdraw them wherever possible.

This appeal to accept the human rights standards that exist in Europe is not only addressed to the governments, who do have a certain power to make practices change but who, in democracy, can only propose legislation; it is also addressed to national parliaments and – very importantly – to the citizens of Europe: they must signal to their elected representatives that they are expected to firmly commit the country to the respect of the whole range of essential human rights, by adopting the necessary national instruments in parliament (ratification laws, constitutional provisions, legislation, etc.). One sad example of how necessary it is to win public support for human rights is given to us by the ongoing struggle for the outlawing of death penalty in several member states of the Council of Europe. Here, the Council of Europe should not only remain very firm on abolition as a matter of human rights but also develop, together with local partners, concrete ways of informing public opinion on the need to end capital punishment.

Formal acceptance of standards by states is, as I just underlined, necessary. However, such a step is not sufficient. All actors must be fundamentally convinced of human rights. Here, participants in this colloquy underlined the need for manifold, serious and patient efforts in the fields of human rights awareness-raising and education. Overwhelming tribute was paid to the role of non-governmental organisations – international or national, big or small, famous or widely unknown – who do an enormous amount of precious work in direct contact with the members of the public.

But a key responsibility for protecting human rights at the national level remains in the hands of national authorities, especially the courts.

Allow me, at this juncture, to formulate some thoughts on the importance of the rule of law as a sine qua non for effective human rights protection, and on the notion of "rights". People who experienced communism are very sensitive to current definitions of rights, and for many the evolution of the language of rights has gone so far that we have begun to lose sight of what the real meaning of rights is. We must fight demagogical use of the term "rights", for, in the long run, this will make the notion of "rights" meaningless.

Many people seek to discuss rights in isolation, as if rights were possible without a whole host of other social and political institutions to support them. No rights, however noble, will have any practical meaning unless there is a rule of law to enforce them. The problem with communist totalitarianism was not that it eliminated the language of rights: after all, even Stalin's constitution of the Soviet Union was full of phraseology of "rights". Rather the problem is the inability to enforce them if there is no rule of law. The rule of law in itself is a complex concept, and I do not want to enter into a detailed discussion here. But for me, the rule of law includes the due process of law, which in itself requires the establishment of independent judges, an independent judiciary, a clear and transparent procedure, and so on. This set of institutions and practices are extremely complex, and cannot be established overnight.

Behind this idea of the rule of law inevitably lies the state. All too often, modern views of rights stress the need to defend the "individual" against "the state". That is an argument which is wrongly put, or at least a simplification. What we need to defend the individual against is not just "the state", but arbitrariness, lawlessness and abuse of power. Permit me to explain. Let us bear in mind that human rights can, and often are, violated by any person or institution having power over or dominating others. This includes non-state actors: think of domestic violence against women or abuse of children. The absence of stable, democratic institutions and situations of lawlessness are coupled with the worst violations of human rights, as tragically shown on our TV screens every day.

A last comment I would like to make on this topic concerns the risk that we may be losing sight of the very essence, object and purpose of human rights if we go too far in deriving very detailed requirements from them. Of course, it is important to provide a full guarantee of the right to a fair judicial process in criminal matters. However, an excessive accumulation of fair trial guarantees may lead to frictions with the need to ensure the right of every accused to be tried within a reasonable time as well as the right of the victim to obtain just satisfaction.

Protecting the stability of state institutions operating under the rule of law is crucial if rights are to have any coherent meaning for ordinary people. This is a particular problem in post-communist countries, where we are still struggling to restore the reputation of the courts and the police after the years when those institutions were weakened. Our citizens are fully aware that they have an entire catalogue of rights which are theirs: but above all they want those rights to be effectively enforced.

During the discussions many of you have spoken about the challenges facing the Council of Europe today and indeed, many of the recommendations from the discussion groups are about the role of this Organisation in promoting and protecting human rights.

While it would be unrealistic to think that all of these proposals can be implemented, I believe that this does show very clearly how high the expectations are that are placed in the Council of Europe and its human rights work in particular. Allow me, therefore, to offer you some reflections on where the Council of Europe should go from here, and to try to identify some key lessons which can be drawn from its experience so far.

A strong point of the Council of Europe has always been, and still is, its important *acquis* of legal standards in the field of human rights. A wide range of rights is firmly enshrined in the core human rights conventions. One may wonder whether there is still room for further development of new standards, and indeed some people, including myself, often warn against the unlimited proliferation of legal norms. Too many norms are likely to water down the significance and impact of each of them. Also, implementation of norms becomes increasingly difficult to monitor as they grow in number. Moreover, a world that is excessively governed by laws, legal rights and obligations entails the risk of rendering individuals largely irresponsible in terms of ethics and personal engagement.

However, giving more attention to implementation of human rights standards – I will deal with that shortly – should not become an alibi for refraining from further standard-setting in Europe in order to fill in certain lacunae or to face new challenges. A prime example for urgent standard-setting, is the ongoing work on a protocol to the European Convention on Human Rights providing a general prohibition of discrimination. The need for a rapid adoption of such a protocol was stressed by many participants in order to complement the current Article 14 of the European Convention, which falls behind United Nations' standards.

I would add that such a protocol would not only fill a gap but also enable the Convention system to respond better to the challenge of combating certain discriminatory practices on ethnic grounds, which were hitherto hardly known in the Council of Europe area.

Another example I would like to mention is that of extreme poverty. Clearly we must ask ourselves whether our human rights conventions offer sufficient protection against unacceptable situations where people are denied the right to the satisfaction of basic human needs: food, housing, clothing.

One of the main results of the colloquy is that more emphasis should be placed on the implementation of human rights norms and the monitoring of such implementation.

A most important achievement has just been reached in the field of judicial control where the new European Court of Human Rights faces the important challenge of maintaining standards. Improvements have also been made to the Social Charter's mechanism.

This colloquy – and the Forum of the non-governmental organisations which was held here in Strasbourg just on the day before the opening of this colloquy – did intensely deal with the question of additional, non-judicial ways of monitoring, and eventually ensuring compliance with human rights. The problem arises principally with regard to so-called structural violations of human rights. Participants acknowledged the Council of Europe's effort to prevent such situations from happening, by addressing the root factors. They also stressed, however, the insufficiency of the mechanisms currently available to put an end to such violations, once they occur, or to prevent them when they are imminent. What seems to be needed is a speedy, precise and strong political response.

Here I want to be very frank with you.

Three years ago, in a report to the 8th International Colloquy on the European Convention on Human Rights I said this (I quote):

> In the light of the experiences gained by the states which have liberated themselves from the totalitarian system during the five years which have passed since the beginning of the enlargement of the Council of Europe, one may, however, wonder whether mere adherence to such slogans, that is as general as "a return to democracy", to a state based on the "rule of law" and on "human rights", is a sufficient commitment to become a member of the Council of Europe and a party to the European Convention.

This year, in an article published in *La Semaine Juridique* on 7 January, Professor Sudre expressed the view that the Council of Europe (and I quote):

> [c]omposé aujourd'hui de 40 États ... s'est transformé de « club des démocraties » en un « centre d'apprentissage » de la démocratie et il est clair que nombre de nouveaux États membres sont incapables de respecter l'engagement fondamental inscrit dans l'article 3 du Statut du Conseil. L'abaissement des standards du Conseil de l'Europe est manifeste et la ratification de la Convention européenne des Droits de l'Homme par les nouveaux États semble relever de l'alibi, transformant la Convention, de « standard minimum exigeant », en une lointaine ligne d'horizon.

These are very harsh words which merit serious discussion within the Council of Europe.

Without at this juncture being able to analyse the situation fully, I feel that one must have the intellectual honesty to admit that the rapid enlargement of the Organisation poses a potentially serious threat to the Convention's acquis. Legal standards in a number of new member states often fall far below those required by the Convention control organs. A difficult (and daunting) balancing act is being attempted: high standards need to be maintained in the "old" democracies (in certain of which major problems have arisen) and at the same time standards substantially improved in several "new" democracies.

Let us face it: the classical human rights mechanisms at the Council of Europe have hardly been successful in addressing gross violations or major structural problems. In order to maintain its standards and its credibility, the Council of Europe should dispose of a scheme for dealing with such situations. Parallels have been drawn with the Collective Complaints Protocol of the Social Charter. Mention could also be made of the proposed commissioner for human rights and of the idea of creating special rapporteurs, which was floated at this colloquy.

On a more fundamental political level, conditionality is a concept which has hitherto been absent from the modus operandi of the Council of Europe. Enlargement of the Organisation has made it necessary to look at tools available to the Council of Europe in regard to states that clearly fall short of their commitments. As you know, the Statute envisages only the extreme step of excluding a state from the Organisation. It would, in my view, be useful if the Council of Europe would start looking at a range of warnings or sanctions that could be brought into play, if necessary through a statutory resolution.

The traditional structures of the Council of Europe, both intergovernmental and parliamentary, should refocus their activities much more on implementation questions. It is true that monitoring mechanisms have been set up both within the Parliamentary Assembly and the Committee of Ministers. In relation to the Committee of Ministers, the point was made that there is no independent body of experts involved in monitoring proceedings. Of course, some courage is necessary to conduct proceedings or have discussions directed at situations in a specific member states.

It is widely acknowledged that in the field of human rights, a broad range of activities, actors and mechanisms are necessary. However, a recurrent theme, initially emphasised in the Secretary General's opening address, is the need to improve coherence between the various human rights mechanisms, be they political, judicial or other, with a view to creating a true European "system" of human rights protection. As Mr Tarschys rightly underlined, the individual doesn't care where his or her rights are guaranteed, as long as he or she can effectively enjoy them. With the increase in the number of mechanisms, I think we should begin to consider this issue seriously, bearing in mind the experience of the United Nations. Especially where structural problems are concerned, a concerted effort by a variety of actors can perhaps mobilise sufficient pressure for reform. Political follow-up by the Committee of Ministers and the Parliamentary Assembly to general problems that have come to light in the context of the treaty mechanisms would seem essential.

The perceived distance between the human rights mechanisms and the day to day reality on the ground make these mechanisms seem somewhat theoretical in the face of certain situations. Reinforcing capacity for field operations, i.e. human rights monitoring in situ, may be a means of strengthening the Council of Europe's ability to tackle such problems. This presupposes, however, a capacity and a political will of the political institutions to follow-up. This work could render more coherent the efforts of European and Transatlantic institutions as a whole, operating in Europe, particularly in crisis situations. More should be done to arrive at mutually reinforcing institutional responses. I refer to the OSCE and to the European Union. Other institutions could usefully lean on the accumulated wealth of human rights experience of the Council of Europe. In this connection, new perspectives on co-operation with the United Nations were put forward by Mrs Mary Robinson, United Nations High Commissioner for Human Rights, in her keynote address to this colloquy.

Potentially, the Council of Europe is uniquely placed to ensure that its human rights work interacts with relevant actors at the national level. It is essential to reinforce dialogue between, for example, the European Court of Human Rights and national jurisdictions, to improve co-operation between the Council of Europe and national human rights institutions and Ombudsmen and to develop further contacts between NGOs and treaty bodies set up under the CPT, the Social Charter and the Framework Convention for the Protection of National Minorities. Here again, we should be building up a European network of interlocking relationships around our common European human rights standards. Such a strong network would contribute significantly to democratic security in our continent.

The task before us is impressive: building a Europe of human rights, a Europe where capital punishment belongs in the past, where torture has been eradicated, where the indivisibility of human rights, social as well as civil and political, is a reality, where respect for human rights is firmly embedded in the culture of our societies and the minds of their members and protected by the democratic process and the full operation of the rule of law.

The magnitude of this task may seem not only impressive, but even overwhelming. However, I firmly believe that it can be achieved, provided each of us is seriously committed and ready to move forward.

This colloquy has identified a whole range of possibilities for doing so. I could only mention a few of them in this report, but the discussions have yielded many more which merit close examination and follow-up. I express the hope that all of these ideas and proposals will receive, from governments, the Council of Europe and other international organisations, non-governmental organisations and all other actors involved, the attention they deserve in the coming months and years.

As far as the many suggestions directed at the Council of Europe are concerned, I believe that the contours of a rejuvenated Council of Europe are emerging from them: an organisation that is better adapted to changed circumstances and more closely focused on its raison d'être: pluralist democracy, the rule of law and human rights. I strongly recommend that these suggestions be studied carefully by the Committee of Wise Persons, the competent organs of this Organisation and, most importantly, by the governments of member states. After all, what the Council of Europe can do lies in their hands. A very concrete suggestion made at this colloquy is to examine, in eighteen months' time, what follow-up has been given to these various recommendations by the different organs of the Council of Europe to which they were addressed.

It is true that reinforcing the work of the Council of Europe in the field of human rights, according high priority to this work as the raison d'être of the Organisation, requires willingness by governments to invest in it, to give the Council of Europe the means for rapid intervention, field monitoring and for providing genuine assistance to help remedy structural problems. I believe the issues at stake are sufficiently serious to justify such commitments and investments.

A few moments ago I spoke, at some length, about the meaning of words. A society where words have lost their meaning is not a society where human rights are respected. Rule of law, democracy, human rights. These are very simple words indeed. Let us not forget that giving these simple words their true meaning requires a constant effort from all of us wherever we are, whatever our responsibilities in society may be. These words need constant action. I am reminded of what the Secretary General said at the opening of this colloquy, we do "never enough". This is not a sad conclusion; on the contrary it is a call on the responsibility of each of us to renew our commitment and to redouble our efforts.

Secretary General's closing words

During the past three days you have all contributed, in various ways, to our colloquy which, on the one hand, was devoted to the commemoration of the 50th anniversary of the United Nations Declaration of Human Rights and, on the other, to an important, although necessarily selective, follow-up of the implementation of the Declaration and Programme of Action adopted by the Vienna World Conference on Human Rights five years ago.

Allow me first to reiterate my gratitude for your participation. We are of course particularly grateful for the statements given by Mrs Mary Robinson, United Nations High Commissioner for Human Rights, and Mr Stelios Perrakis, Secretary General of the Greek Ministry of Foreign Affairs.

Furthermore I should like to thank Miguel A. Martínez, Hina Jilani, Jiří Dienstbier and Adama Dieng for their personal statements; and the rapporteurs, Professor Vojin Dimitrijević (from the University of Belgrade and the Belgrade Centre for Human Rights); Professor Aalt-Willem Heringa (from the University of Maastricht); Professor Katarina Tomasevski (from the Danish Centre for Human Rights in Copenhagen); Mr Régis de Gouttes (Avocat Général à la Cour de Cassation, Paris); Professor Jeremy McBride (from the Institute of European Law at the University of Birmingham) and Kaija Gertnere (former Director of the Latvian Human Rights Office) for their active contributions and their excellent reports on the main topics of our colloquy.

Thanks also to the chairpersons: Christian Strohal (Director of Human Rights, Austrian Ministry for Foreign Affairs); Nathalie Prouvez (International Commission of Jurists, Geneva); Elena Poptodorova (First Vice Chairperson of the Parliamentary Assembly's Committee on Equal Opportunities, member of the Bulgarian Parliament); Egbert Myjer (Deputy Procurator-General of the Court of Appeal, Amsterdam); Judge Thór Vilhjálmsson (European Court of Human Rights in respect of Iceland); Viacheslav Bakhmin (Executive Director of the Open Society Fund, Moscow) and Pierre-Henri Imbert (our Director of Human Rights) for their excellent management of the different sessions of our meeting.

Last but not least I express my great appreciation of the work performed by the preparatory committee under the chairmanship of Christian Strohal.

On this occasion I also wish to join Ms Hanna Suchocka in her very positive appreciation and summing up of the results achieved during this three-day meeting in Strasbourg.

We set out to provide a proper Council of Europe contribution to the 50th anniversary of the United Nations Declaration of Human Rights and we wanted you to have a thorough discussion regarding both current threats to human rights and appropriate initiatives for the future promotion and protection of human rights.

I am very happy to note that these goals were reached. No doubt this is thanks to the solid basis which the rapporteurs had provided for your debates, but also to the important input from NGOs, who met the day before this colloquy started so as to prepare their active contributions to the discussions. But I must thank all of you for your active participation in the discussions and for pointing to the various challenges facing human rights in the years to come. We are agreed that this is not the time to relax, that we cannot do enough, in particular concerning the implementation of texts and standards, for example to further confirm the indivisibility of all human rights by increasing the protection of social rights; to increase investments in training, education and awareness-raising; to enhance the fight against discrimination, racism and intolerance and to promote equality between women and men. As far as the Council of Europe is concerned we must also make sure that our human rights organs are adequately equipped – in terms of legal human rights standards, competences and resources – so as to be fully effective. In addition, we should strive for a better follow-up – in the framework of intergovernmental committees and activities – of lacunae and problems identified by our human rights organs.

As we approach the next millennium we will thus be able to draw useful lessons from this colloquy, both at national and international level. As I said in my opening address on Wednesday, success will largely depend on the concerted action taken by governments, by NGOs and by civil society in general. In closing this colloquy I wish finally to pay tribute to the indispensable role played by the NGOs in the tasks that lie before us.

Thank you again for your participation and attention.

Appendix

List of participants in the colloquy "In our hands": The effectiveness of human rights protection 50 years after the Universal Declaration

1. Analytical presentation

I. General rapporteur/Rapporteur général

Ms	**Hanna Suchocka**	Minister of Justice of Poland	Ujazdowskie 11, PL-00 950 Warsaw	Tel:	+48 22 628 73 6
				Fax:	+48 22 621 30 95

II. Commemorative speakers/Personnalités intervenant lors de la commemoration

Ms	**Mary Robinson**	United Nations High Commissioner for Human Rights	Palais des Nations 8-14 avenue de la Paix CH-1211 Geneva 10	Tel:	+41 22 917 31 34
				Fax:	+41 22 917 02 45
Mr	**Miguel Angel Martínez**	President of the Council of the Interparliamentary Union	Congreso de los Diputados Carrera de San Jerónimo E-28071 Madrid	Tel:	+34 91 390 65 18
				Fax:	+34 91 420 05 57
Ms	**Hina Jilani**	AGHS Law Associates	131-E-1 Gulberg III PK-Lahore	Tel:	+92 42 576 3234/3235
				Fax:	+92 42 576 3234/3235
Mr	**Jiří Dienstbier**		c/o Ministry of Foreign Affairs, Prague	Tel:	+42 02 2418 2658
				Fax:	+42 02 2418 2039
Mr	**Adama Dieng**	Secretary General, International Commission of Jurists	81*a* avenue de Châtelaine, PO Box 216, CH-1219 Châtelaine Geneva	Tel:	+41 22 979 38 00
				Fax:	+41 22 979 38 01
M.	**Stelios Perrakis**	Secrétaire Général des Affaires européennes	Ministère des Affaires étrangères 1 av. Vas. Sofias GR-10671 Athènes	Tél:	+30 1 339 42 81
				Fax:	+30 1 339 42 01

III. Rapporteurs

Mr	**Vojin Dimitrijević**	Professor of International Law and International Relations, University of Belgrade; Director, Belgrade Centre for Human Rights	Mlatišumina 26 YU-11000 Belgrade	Tel:	+381 11 43 25 72
				Fax:	+381 11 344 1203
Mr	**Aalt-Willem Heringa**	Professor of Public Law University of Maastricht	PO Box 616 NL-6200 MD Maastricht	Tel:	+31 43 388 31 07
				Fax:	+31 43 321 41 72

Ms	**Katarina Tomaševski**		Danish Centre for Human Rights Rørholmsgade 23 III DK-1352 Copenhagen K	Tel: +45 33 30 88 88 Fax: +45 33 30 88 00
M.	**Régis de Gouttes**	Avocat général à la Cour de Cassation	5 quai de l'Horloge F-75001 Paris	Tél: +33 1 44 32 74 77 Fax: +33 1 44 32 77 10
Mr	**Jeremy McBride**	Professor of Law	School of Law University of Birmingham Edgbaston GB-Birmingham B15 2TT	Tel: +44 121 414 6330 Fax: +44 121 414 3585
Ms	**Kaija Gertnere**	Former Acting Director of the Latvian Human Rights Office	Citadeles iela 5-5 LV-1010 Riga	Tel: +371 732 47 40 Fax: +371 732 47 40

IV. Chairpersons of discussion groups/Présidents des groupes de discussion

Mr	**Christian Strohal**	Director for Human Rights	Ministry for Foreign Affairs Ballhausplatz 2 A-1014 Vienna	Tel: +43 1 53 115 33 75 Fax: +43 1 53 185 212
Ms	**Nathalie Prouvez**	International Commission of Jurists	81*a* avenue de Châtelaine PO Box 216 CH-1219 Châtelaine Geneva	Tel: +41 22 979 38 16 Fax: +41 22 979 38 24 +41 22 979 38 01
Ms	**Elena Poptodorova**	First Vice-Chairman of the Committee on Equal Opportunities for Women and Men, Parliamentary Assembly of the Council of Europe	Member of the National Assembly Narodno Sobranye No. 2 BG-Sofia	Tel: +359 2 981 69 31 Fax: +359 2 981 31 31
Mr	**Egbert Myjer**	Deputy Procurator-General	Court of Appeal PO Box 1312 NL-1000 BH Amsterdam	Tel: +31 20 541 21 11 Fax: +31 20 541 33 51
Mr	**Thór Vilhjálmsson**	Vice-President of the European Court of Human Rights	Council of Europe F-67075 Strasbourg Cedex	Tel: +33 3 88 41 23 92 Fax: +33 3 88 41 27 91
Mr	**Vjacheslav Ivanovich Bakhmin**	Executive Director, Open Society Institute	Bolshoi Kozlovski pereulok 13/17 RU-107078 Moscow	Tel: +7 095 921 20 65 Fax: +7 095 288 95 12

V. Preparatory committee/Comité de préparation

Mr	**Christian Strohal**	Chairman of the Committee	*see under IV*	
M.	**Jean-Claude Couvreur**	Conseiller	Direction des droits de l'Homme Ministère des Affaires étrangères 13-15 rue des Petits Carmes B-1000 Bruxelles	Tél: +32 2 501 84 65 Fax: +32 2 501 38 23
M.	**Vitaliano Esposito**	Attaché juridique	Représentation permanente d'Italie auprès du Conseil de l'Europe 3 rue Schubert F-67000 Strasbourg	Tél: +33 3 88 60 20 88

Mr **Carsten Carlsen**	Adviser, Human Rights Section	Royal Ministry of Foreign Affairs Ulenriksdepartementet Postboks 8814 Dep N-0032 Oslo 1	Tel: +47 22 24 35 18 Fax: +47 22 24 27 87
Mrs **Heddy Astrup**	Executive Officer	Information Section Ministry of Foreign Affairs Ulenriksdepartementet Postboks 8814 Dep N-0032 Oslo 1	Tel: +47 22 24 36 00
Mr **Krzysztof Drzewicki**	Government Agent	Ministry of Foreign Affairs Aleja Szucha 23 PL-00-580 Warsaw	Tel: +48 22 62 39 683 Fax: +48 22 62 39 512
Mr **Miroslaw Łuczka**	Deputy to the Permanent Representative of Poland at the Council of Europe	2 rue Geiler F-67000 Strasbourg	Tel: +33 3 88 52 98 00 (ext. 237) Fax: +33 3 88 52 97 99
Mr **Oleg Malguinov**	Senior Counsellor, Permanent Mission of the Russian Federation	15 avenue de la Paix, CH-1202 Genève	Tel: +41 22 733 18 70 Fax: +41 22 734 40 44
Ms **Meral Çelikcan**	Human Rights Co-ordinator	Supreme Board Ministry of National Education Kizilirmak Sok 4 No: 14 Kat. 5, Kizilay, Ankara	Tel: +90 312 418 25 73 Fax: +90 312 417 39 74
M. **Pierre Boulay**	International Federation of Human Rights/Fédération internationale des Droits de l'Homme	Représentant FIDH auprès du Conseil de l'Europe 40 rue Principale F-67300 Schiltigheim	Tél/Fax: +33 3 88 83 27 29
Mr **Adama Dieng**	(see under II)		
Mr **Martin Eaton**	Steering Committee for Human Rights (CDDH)/ Comité directeur pour les droits de l'homme (CDDH)	Deputy Legal Adviser Foreign and Commonwealth Office King Charles Street GB-London SW1 2AH	Tel: +44 171 270 3786 Fax: +44 171 270 2767

VI. Council of Europe member states/États membres du Conseil de l'Europe

Mr **Arben Puto**, President of the Albanian Helsinki Committee	Albania/Albanie	Qendra Nderkombetare e Kultures Bulevardi Deshmoret e Kombit AL-Tirana	Tel/Fax: +355 42 274 90/336 71
Ms **Ingrid Kircher**, Adviser, Human Rights Department	Austria/Autriche	Ministry of Foreign Affaris Ballhausplatz 1 A-1014 Vienna	Tel: +43 1 531 15 45 53 Fax: +43 1 531 85 212
Mr **Christoph Lanner**, Member of the Constitutional Service	Austria/Autriche	Bundeskanzleramt Ballhausplatz 2 A-1014 Vienna	
Mr **Ullrich Hack**, Ambassador Extraordinary and Plenipotentiary, Permanent Representative of Austria to the Council of Europe	Austria/Autriche	29 Avenue de la Paix F-67000 Strasbourg	Tel: +33 388 36 64 04 Fax: +33 388 25 19 88

Mr	**Johann Fröhlich**, Deputy Permanent Representative of Austria to the Council of Europe	Austria/Autriche	29 Avenue de la Paix F-67000 Strasbourg	Tel: +33 388 36 64 04 Fax: +33 388 25 19 88
M.	**Michel Herckens**	Belgium/Belgique	Service du Conseil de l'Europe Ministère des Affaires étrangères 13-15 rue des Petits Carmes B-1000 Bruxelles	Tel: +32 2 501 82 96 Fax: +32 2 501 38 23
Ms	**Ludmila Bozhkova**, Deputy Director for International Organisations and Human Rights	Bulgaria/Bulgarie	Ministry for Foreign Affairs Alexander Zhendov 2 BG-Sofia 1113	Fax: +359 2 971 2881
Mr	**Slobodan Lang**, Special Adviser to the President for Humanitarian Affairs	Croatia/Croatie	Office of the President of the Republic Pantovčak 241 10000 Zagreb	Tel: +385 1 4565 192 Fax: +385 1 4565 188
Mr	**Vedrana Spajić-Vrkaš**, member of the Governmental Commission for Education on Human Rights and Croatian Commission for Co-operation with UNESCO	Croatia/Croatie	Department of Pedagogical Sciences Faculty of Philosophy University of Zagreb Trg burze 6 10000 Zagreb	Tel: +385 1 4556 510 Fax: +385 1 4556 510
Ms	**Thalia Petrides**, Ambassador Extraordinary and Plenipotentiary, Permanent Representative of Cyprus to the Council of Europe	Cyprus/Chypre	20 avenue de la Paix F-67000 Strasbourg	Tel: +33 388 37 18 18 Fax: +33 388 36 86 38
Mr	**Petinos Charalambos**, adjoint à la représentante permanente de Chypre	Cyprus/Chypre	20 avenue de la Paix F-67000 Strasbourg	Tel: +33 388 37 18 18 Fax: +33 388 36 86 38
Mr	**Jiří Mucha**, Ambassador Extraordinary and Plenipotentiary, Permanent Representative of the Czech Republic to the Council of Europe	Czech Republic/République tchèque	53 allée de la Robertsau F-67000 Strasbourg	Tel: +33 388 25 76 77 Fax: +33 388 37 63 62
Mr	**Richard Krpač**, Legal Adviser	Czech Republic/République tchèque	Ministry of Foreign Affairs Human Rights Desk Loretánské Nám 5 CZ-118 00 Prague 1	Tel: +420 2 24 18 31 78 Fax: +420 2 24 18 20 38

Mr **Arne Belling**, Ambassador Extraordinary and Plenipotentiary, Permanent Representative of Denmark to the Council of Europe	Denmark/Danemark	20 avenue de la Paix F-67000 Strasbourg	Tel: +33 3 88 35 69 49 Fax: +33 3 88 25 54 19
Mr **Erik Hedegaard**, Deputy Permanent Representative of Denmark to the Council of Europe	Denmark/Danemark	20 avenue de la Paix F-67000 Strasbourg	Tel: +33 3 88 35 69 49 Fax: +33 3 88 25 54 19
Mr **Marten Kokk**, Director, Human Rights Bureau	Estonia/Estonie	Legal Department Ministry for Foreign Affairs Rävala pst. 9, Tallinn EE0100	Tel: +.372 6317 415 Fax: +372 6317 099
Ms **Camilla Busck-Nielsen**, Legal Officer	Finland/Finlande	Unit for Human Rights Complaints Ministry for Foreign Affairs Legal Department PO Box 176 FIN-00161 Helsinki	Tel: +358 9 13 41 57 27 Fax: +358 9 13 41 59 51
Mr **Arto Kosonen**, Head of Unit, Co-Agent for the Government	Finland/Finlande	Ministry for Foreign Affairs Legal Department PO Box 176 FIN-00161 Helsinki	Tel: +358 9 13 41 57 29 Fax: +358 9 13 41 59 51
Ms **Anne Vasara**, Deputy Permanent Representative of Finland to the Council of Europe	Finland/Finlande	31 quai Mullenheim F-67000 Strasbourg	Tel: +33 3 88 15 44 44 Fax: +33 3 88 15 44 40
Ms **Sofie From**, Deputy to the Permanent Representative of Finland to the Council of Europe	Finland/Finlande	31 quai Mullenheim F-67000 Strasbourg	Tel: +33 3 88 15 44 44 Fax: +33 3 88 15 44 40
Mme **Geneviève Fraisse**, Déléguée interministérielle aux Droits des femmes, Chef de Délégation	France		
Mme **Nathalie Riomet**, Directeur du Cabinet de Mme Fraisse	France		
M. **Emmanuel Decaux**, Président de la sous-commission internationale de la commission nationale consultative des droits de l'homme	France	11 rue de Chartres F-92200 Neuilly-sur-Seine	Tel: +33 1 47 38 18 09 Fax: +33 1 46 41 04 31
M. **Gilbert Bitti**, Service des Affaires européennes et internationales (Ministère de la Justice)	France		

Mme	**Jocelyne Caballero**, Représentante permanente adjointe, Chargée d'affaires a.i.	France	40 rue de Verdun F-67000 Strasbourg	Tel: +33 388 45 34 00 Fax: +33 388 45 34 48/49
M.	**Harold Valentin**, Conseiller technique	France	Cabinet du Ministre Ministère des Affaires étrangères 37 quai d'Orsay F-75007 Paris	Tél: +33 1 43 17 57 93 Fax: +33 1 43 17 57 91
Mlle	**Ariane Trichon**, Adjointe au représentant permanent	France	40 rue de Verdun F-67000 Strasbourg	Tel: +33 388 45 34 00 Fax: +33 388 45 34 48/49
Mr	**Christian Much**, Deputy Head, Human Rights Department	Germany/Allemagne	Ministry of Foreign Affairs Auswaertiges Amt ASMR, Postfach 1500 D-53001 Bonn	Tel: +49 228 17 28 30 Fax: +49 228 17 39 15
Ms	**Diana Schröder**, Referentin	Germany/Allemagne	Bundesministerium für Arbeit und Sozialordnung Rochusstr. 1 D-53107 Bonn	Tel: +49 228 527 25 70 Fax: +49 228 527 11 76
M.	**Dimitri Constas**, Ambassadeur, représentant permanent de la Grèce auprès du Conseil de l'Europe	Greece/Grèce	21 place Broglie F-67000 Strasbourg	Tél: +33 3 88 32 88 18 Fax: +33 3 88 23 12 46
M.	**Stelios Perrakis**	Greece/Grèce	(voir sous II)	
M. M.	**Theocharopoulos** **Ayfantis**	Greece/Grèce Greece/Grèce	Représentation permanente de la Grèce auprès du Conseil de l'Europe 21 place Broglie F-67000 Strasbourg	Tél: +33 3 88 32 88 18 Fax: +33 3 88 23 12 46
Mr	**Thorsteinn Geirsson**, Secretary General	Iceland/Islande	Ministry of Justice 150 Reykjavík	Tel: +354 560 90 10 Fax: +354 552 73 40
Ms	**Emer Kilcullen**, Legal Adviser to the Council of Europe and Human Rights Sections	Ireland/Irlande	Department of Foreign Affairs 80 St Stephen's Green Dublin 2	Tel: +353 1 478 0822 Fax: +353 1 478 5923
Ms	**Kristine Krūma**, Head of Division of International Organisations and Human Rights Policy	Latvia/Lettonie	Ministry of Foreign Affairs Brivibas blvd. 36 LV-1395 Riga	Tel: +371 701 62 60 Fax: +371 783 00 75
Mr	**Andrius Namavičius**, Head of International Treaties Subdivision	Lithuania/Lituanie	Lithuanian Foreign Ministry Tumo-Vaižganto 2 LT-26000 Vilnius	Tel: +370 2 62 04 69 Fax: +370 2 61 69 63

Mr	**Joseph Filletti**, Judge at the Superior Courts of Malta, Head of the Delegation of the European Committee on Crime Problems (CDPC), Vice-Chairman of the Multi-Sectoral Group on Action against Trafficking in human beings for Sexual Exploitation (EG-S-TS)	Malta/Malte	c/o The Law Courts Republic Street Valletta	Tel: +356 223 281 Fax: +356 240 458
Mr	**Karel de Vey Mestdagh**, Head of the Regional and Global Organisations Division	Netherlands/Pays-Bas	Human Rights Department Ministry of Foreign Affairs The Hague	Tel: +31 70 348 48 93 Fax: +31 70 348 51 28
Mr	**Sten Lundbo**, Ambassador Extraordinary and Plenipotentiary, Permanent Representative of Norway to the Council of Europe	Norway/Norvège	20 avenue de la Paix F-67000 Strasbourg	Tel: +33 388 25 09 65 Fax: +33 388 25 10 44
Mr	**Halvar Saetre**, Deputy Permanent Representative of Norway to the Council of Europe	Norway/Norvège	20 avenue de la Paix F-67000 Strasbourg	Tel: +33 388 25 09 65 Fax: +33 388 25 10 44
Mr	**Slavomir Lodzinski**, Expert (sociologist)	Poland/Pologne	Ministry of Foreign Affairs ul. Falocka 5/7 m. 50 PL-02 547 Warsaw	Tel: +48 22 49 23 49
Mr	**Marek Lukaszewicz**	Poland/Pologne	Ministry of Justice Ujazdowskie 11 PL-00 950 Warsaw	Tel: +48 22 628 73 68 Fax: +48 22 621 30 95
Mr	**Piotr Nowotniak**, Legal Counsel	Poland/Pologne	Human Rights Office Ministry of Foreign Affairs Al. Szucha 23 PL-00 580 Warsaw	Tel: +48 22 623 96 09 Fax: +48 22 623 95 12
Mr	**Radoslaw Zubek**	Poland/Pologne	Ministry of Justice Ujazdowskie 11 PL-00 950 Warsaw	Tel: +48 22 628 73 68 Fax: +48 22 621 30 95
M.	**Álvaro Manuel Soares Guerra**, Ambassadeur extraordinaire et plénipotentiaire, représentant permanent du Portugal auprès du Conseil de l'Europe	Portugal	11 rue Fischart F-67000 Strasbourg	Tél: +33 3 88 60 16 77 Fax: +33 3 88 60 70 42
Mr	**Cristian Diaconescu**, Director General	Romania/Roumanie	Ministry for Foreign Affairs Modrogan Av. 16-18 RO-Bucarest	Tel: +40 1 230 75 71 Fax: +40 1 230 75 71

Mlle **Mihaela Silvia Babuşka**, Directrice des droits de l'homme	Romania/Roumanie	Ministère des Affaires étrangères Modrogan Av. 14 RO-Bucarest	Tél: +40 1 230 75 71 Fax: +40 1 230 75 71
M. **Andrei Magheru**, Directeur adjoint pour l'ONU	Romania/Roumanie	Ministère des Affaires étrangères 9a rue Logofatul Luca Stroici RO-70244 Bucarest 1	Tél: +40 1 230 75 94 Fax: +40 1 230 75 88
M. **Sabin Pop**, Ambassadeur extraordinaire et plénipotentiaire, représentant permanent de la Roumanie auprès du Conseil de l'Europe	Romania/Roumanie	64 allée de la Robertsau F-67000 Strasbourg	Tél: +33 3 88 37 01 60 Fax: +33 3 88 37 16 70
M. **Titus Corlatean**, Adjoint au représentant permanent de la Roumanie auprès du Conseil de l'Europe	Romania/Roumanie	64 allée de la Robertsau F-67000 Strasbourg	Tél: +33 3 88 37 01 60 Fax: +33 3 88 37 16 70
Mr **Yury Boychenko**, Head of the Human Rights Section	Russia/Russie	Ministry for Foreign Affairs Vozdvizhenka 9, RU-Moscow	Tel: +7 095 203 43 59 Fax: +7 095 290 0865
Mr **Mark Entin**, Chargé d'affaires	Russia/Russie	Permanent Delegation of the Russian Federation to the Council of Europe 75 allée de la Robertsau F-67000 Strasbourg	Tel: +33 3 88 24 20 15 Fax: +33 3 88 24 19 74
Mme **Barbara Tuhovčáková**, Directrice-adjointe	Slovakia/Slovaquie	Départment des droits de l'homme Ministère des Affaires étrangères Hlboká 2 833 36 Bratislava	Tél: +42 17 43 83 732 Fax: +42 17 43 83 739
Ms **Viera Strãznická**, Ambassador Extraordinary and Plenipotentiary, Permanent Representative of the Slovak Republic to the Council of Europe	Slovakia/Slovaquie	1 rue Ehrmann F-67000 Strasbourg	Tel: +33 388 36 57 17 Fax: +33 388 36 54 44
Ms **Eva Tomić**	Slovenia/Slovénie	Ministry of Foreign Affairs Gregorčičeva 25 1000 Ljubljana	Tel: +386 61 178 24 16 Fax: +386 61 178 22 49
Ms **Mary-Veronika Tovšak**, Deputy to the Permanent Representative of Slovenia to the Council of Europe	Slovenia/Slovénie	40 allée de la Robertsau F-67000 Strasbourg	Tel: +33 388 36 60 25 Fax: +33 388 37 14 44

M.	**Guillermo Kirkpatrick y Mendaro**, Ambassadeur extraordinaire et plénipotentiaire, représentant permanent de l'Espagne auprès du Conseil de l'Europe	Spain/Espagne	24 allée de la Robertsau F-67000 Strasbourg	Tél: +33 3 88 36 36 20 Fax: +33 3 88 36 70 63
M.	**Alejandro Abellan Garcia de Diego**, Adjoint au représentant permanent de l'Espagne auprès du Conseil de l'Europe	Spain/Espagne	24 allée de la Robertsau F-67000 Strasbourg	Tél: +33 3 88 36 36 20 Fax: +33 3 88 36 70 63
Mr	**Thomas Hammarberg**, Ambassador	Sweden/Suède	Ministry for Foreign Affairs Box 16121 S-10323 Stockholm	Tél: +46 8 40 55 646 Fax: +46 8 72 31 176
Ms	**Catherine von Heidenstam**, Ambassador for Human Rights	Sweden/Suède	Ministry for Foreign Affairs (International Law and Human Rights Department) Box 16121 S-103 23 Stockholm	Tel: +46 8 40 55 401 Fax: +46 8 72 31 176
M.	**Philippe Boillat**, sous-directeur	Switzerland/Suisse	Division des affaires internationales Office fédéral de la Justice Bundesrain 20 CH-3003 Bern	Tél: +41 31 32 24 140 Fax: +41 31 322 78 64
M.	**Alain Guidetti**, Représentant permanent adjoint de la Suisse auprès du Conseil de l'Europe	Switzerland/Suisse	9-11 Bd Président Edwards F-67000 Strasbourg	Tél: +33 3 88 35 00 72 Fax: +33 3 88 36 73 54
M.	**Stefan Nikolovski**, Ministre-adjoint, Secteur multilatéral	"The former Yugoslav Republic of Macedonia"/« l'ex-République yougoslave de Macédoine »	Ministère des Affaires étrangères ul. Dame Gruev 6 91 000 Skopje	Tél: +389 91 115 379 Fax: +389 91 115 790
Mr	**Osman Yavuzalp**, First Secretary	Turkey/Turquie	Ministry of Foreign Affairs T.C. Disisleri Bakanlği Balgai Ankara	Tél: +90 312 287 25 55/18 26 Fax: +90 312 287 15 81
Mr	**Özkan Suat Özmen**	Turkey/Turquie	Ministry of Labour and Social Security Calişma ve Sosyal Güvenlik Bakanliği Yik Genel Müdürlügü Invönü Blvari No. 40 Ankara	Tel: +90 312 212 97 00 Fax: +90 312 212 19 63
Ms	**Meral Çelikcan**	Turkey/Turquie	(see under V)	
Mr	**Thor Mysyk**, Représentant permanent adjoint de l'Ukraine auprès du Conseil de l'Europe	Ukraine	30 bld de l'Orangerie F-67000 Strasbourg	Tel: +33 388 61 44 51 Fax: +33 388 60 01 78
Ms	**Audrey Glover**	United Kingdom/Royaume-Uni	Brussels	Tel: +32 2 231 0454 Fax: +32 2 287 6355

VII. Non-member states having observer status at the Council of Europe/États non membres ayant le statut d'observateur aupres du Conseil de l'Europe

Mr **Akira Ando**, Consul	Japan/Japon	Consulate General of Japan "Tour Europe" 20 place des Halles F-67000 Strasbourg	Tel: +33 388 52 85 00 Fax: +33 388 22 62 39

VIII. Non-member state having the status of permanent mission to the Council of Europe/État non membre ayant accredité un observateur permanent aupres du Conseil de l'Europe

M. **Giorgio Filibeck**, Conseil Pontifical « Justice et Paix »	Holy See/Saint-Siège	Cité du Vatican I-Rome	Tél: +39 6 698 871 91 Fax: +39 6 698 872 05
Mr **Michael Courtney**, Special Envoy of the Holy See to the Council of Europe	Holy See/Saint-Siège	Permanent Mission 2 rue Le Nôtre F-67000 Strasbourg	Tel: +33 388 35 02 44 Fax: +33 388 24 78 05

IX. Non-member states having special guest status at the Parliamentary Assembly of the Council of Europe/États non membres dont les parlements ont le statut d'invité spécial auprès de l'Assemblée parlementaire du Conseil de l'Europe

M. **Safet Pasic**, Vice-Ministre	Republic of Bosnia-Herzegovina/République de Bosnie-Herzégovine	Ministère de la Justice de la Fédération de Bosnie et Herzégovine Sarajevo	
Ms **Elene Goguadze**, Head of the Department on Human Rights of the Apparatus of the National Security Council for Georgia	Georgia/Géorgie	Ingorokva 7 State Chancellery Tbilisi	Tel: +995 32 931 322 Fax: +995 32 92 35 58

X. Council of Europe/Conseil de l'Europe

European Court of Human Rights/ Cour européenne des Droits de l'Homme

M. **Jean-Paul Costa**	Juge à la nouvelle Cour européenne des Droits de l'Homme	7 rue Sébastien Mercier F-75015 Paris	Tél: +33 1 45 77 99 75 Fax: +33 1 45 71 00 03
Mr **Peter Jambrek**	Judge at the European Court of Human Rights, Professor of Law	Constitutional Court of Slovenia Beethovnova 10 1000 Ljubljana	Tel: +386 61 17 76 453 Fax +386 61 210 451
Ms **Wilhelmina Thomassen**	Judge at the new European Court of Human Rights, Justice in the Court of Appeal, The Hague	Frankenslag 353 NL-2502 HP Den Haag	Tel: +31 70 355 92 46
Mr **Pieter van Dijk**	State Counsellor, Judge at the European Court of Human Rights	Gregoriuslaan 16 NL-3723 KR Bilthoven	Tel: +31 30 228 54 89 Fax: +31 30 228 54 89
Mr **Thór Vilhjálmsson**	(see under IV)		

European Commission of Human Rights/Commission européenne des Droits de l'Homme

Mr	**Evert Alkema**	Member of the European Commission of Human Rights, Professor of constitutional law	Cobetstr. 28 NL-2313 KC Leiden	Tel: +31 71 514 3162 Fax: +31 71 527 7600
M.	**Corneliu Birsan**	Membre de la Commission européenne des Droits de l'Homme	Palais des Droits de l'Homme F-67075 Strasbourg Cedex	Tél: +33 388 61 96 21 (Strasbourg) +40 1 687 75 57 (Roumanie)

Committee of Independent Experts of the European Social Charter/Comité d'experts indépendants de la Charte sociale européenne

Mr	**Rolf Birk**	President of the Committee of Independent Experts of the European Social Charter	Institüt für Arbeitsrecht und Arbeitsbeziehungen in der Europäischen Gemeinschaft Postfach 18 12 30 D-54263 Trier	Tel: +49 651 9666 211 Fax: +49 651 9666 200

Governmental Committee of the European Social Charter/Comité gouvernemental de la Charte sociale européenne

Ms	**Lenia Samuel**	Chairperson of the Governmental Committee of the European Social Charter, Director of Administration	Ministry of Labour and Social Insurance Lord Byron Avenue 7 Nicosia	Tel: +357 2 307 246 Fax: +357 2 450 993
Mr	**Juraj Dzupa**	Head of the Multilateral Co-operation Department	Ministry of Labour, Social Affairs and Family Špitálska 6 81643 Bratislava	Tel: +421 7 59 75 24 19 Fax: +421 7 362 150
Ms	**Riitta-Maija Jouttimäki**	Counsellor of Legislation	Ministry of Social Affairs and Health Snellmaninkatu 4-6 PO Box 267 FIN-00171 Helsinki	Tel: +358 9 160 38 06 Fax: +358 9 160 38 09
Ms	**Pirjo Kaartinen**	Government Secretary	Ministry of Labour Eteläesplanadi 4 PO Box 524 FIN-00101 Helsinki	Tel: +358 9 18 56 80 22 Fax: +358 9 18 56 80 13
Ms	**Zala Rakovec-Bitenc**	Advisor to the Government	Ministry of Labour, Family and Social Affairs Kotnikova 5 SL-1000 Ljubljana	Tel: +386 61 178 33 37 Fax: +386 61 178 33 55

European Committee for the Prevention of Torture and Inhuman or Degrading Treatment or Punishment/Comité européen pour la prévention de la torture et des peines ou traitements inhumains ou dégradants (CPT)

M.	**Constantin Economides**	Professeur de droit international	5 Odos Asklepiou GR-14563 Politia-Athènes	Tél: +30 1 620 35 93 Fax: +30 1 360 80 53

Advisory Committee of the Framework Convention for the Protection of National Minorities/Comité consultatif de la Convention-cadre pour la protection des minorités nationales:

Mr	**Rainer Hofmann**	Chairman of the Advisory Committee, Professor of International Law	Walther-Schücking Institute of International Law University of Kiel Olshausenstrasse 40 D-24098 Kiel	Tel: +49 431 880 1733 Fax: +49 431 880 1619

European Commission Against Racism and Intolerance/Commission européenne contre le racisme et l'intolérance (ECRI)

Mr	**Nikos Frangakis**	President of ECRI, President of the Hellenic League on Human Rights	6 Kriezotou Street GR-10671 Athens	Tel: +30 1 36 26 888/32 671 Fax: +30 1 36 31 631
Mr	**Michael E. Head**	Second Vice-Chair of ECRI	Byways The Ridge GB-Woking GU22 7EE	Tel: +44 1483 77 29 29 Fax: +44 1483 77 29 29

Parliamentary Assembly/Assemblée parlementaire

Ms	**Elena Poptodorova**	First Vice-Chairperson, Committee on Equal Opportunities for Women and Men/Commission sur l'égalité des chances pour les femmes et les hommes	(See under IV)	
Mr	**Jerzy Jaskiernia**	Chairman of the Committee on Legal Affairs and Human Rights	Sejm ul. Wiejska 41618, MM-S PL-00902 Warsaw	

Steering Committee for Human Rights/Comité directeur pour les droits de l'homme (CDDH)

Mr	**Martin Eaton**	(See under V)		
Mr	**Jens Meyer-Ladewig**	Chairman of the CDDH	Auf dem Köllenhof 74 D-53343 Wachtberg	Tel: +49 228 34 14 31

European Committee on Crime Problems/Comité européen pour les problèmes criminels (CDPC)

Mr	**Joseph Filletti**	(See under VI)		

Congress of Local and Regional Authorities in Europe/Congrès des pouvoirs locaux et régionaux de l'Europe
Local Democracy Agencies (LDA)/Agences de la démocratie locale (ADL)

Ms	**Nadia Cuk**	Delegate a.i. of the LDA of Subotica	Trg cara Jovana Nenada 15/I YU-24000 Subotica	Tel: +381 24 554 587 Fax: +381 24 553 116
M.	**François Friederich**	Délégué de l'ADL d'Osijek/Vukovar	4 rue du Tramway F-67400 Illkirch	Tél: +33 388 67 95 18 Fax: +33 388 84 77 16
Ms	**Antonella Valmorbida**	LDA	S.i.A. Radiga ZA Sisak	Tel: +385 44 521 227 Fax: +385 44 521 231

Information and Documentation Centres on the Council of Europe/Centres d'Information et de Documentation sur le Conseil de l'Europe

Ms	**Andela Bartosova**	Director	Information and Documentation Centre on the Council of Europe Senovazne nam. 26 CZ-11000 Prague 1	Tel: +42 2 243 98 315 Fax: +42 2 243 98 315
Mr	**Vladimir Ristovski**	Director a.i.	Information and Documentation Centre on the Council of Europe Bul. Krste Misirkov bb Law Faculty MK-91000 Skopje	Tel: +389 91 130 032 Fax: +389 91 130 032

Human Rights Grouping of NGOs having consultative status with the Council of Europe/Regroupement des ONG ayant le statut consultatif auprès du Conseil de l'Europe et s'intéressant aux droits de l'homme

M.	**Pierre Boulay**	Président	(voir sous V)	

Staff of the Council of Europe/Agents du Conseil de l'Europe

Mr	**Bosse Hedberg**	Private Office of the Secretary General/Cabinet du Secrétaire Général		Tel: +33 388 41 29 70 Fax: +33 388 41 27 99

Mr	**Andrew Drzemczewski**	Secretary General's Monitoring Unit/Unité de « Monitoring » du Secrétaire Général	Tel: +33 388 41 23 26 Fax: +33 388 41 37 67
Mme	**Fatoş Araci**	Secretariat of the European Commission on Human Rights/Secrétariat de la Commission européenne des Droits de l'Homme	Tel: +33 3 88 41 32 75 Fax: +33 3 90 21 49 72
M.	**Michel de Salvia**		Tel: +33 388 41 23 68 Fax: +33 388 41 27 92
Mr	**Akiko Ejima**		Tel: +33 390 21 42 60 Fax: +33 388 41 27 92
Mme	**Danielle Coin**	Parliamentary Assembly/Assemblée parlementaire	Tel: +33 388 41 21 05 Fax: +33 488 41 27 02
Mme	**Agnès Nollinger**		Tel: +33 388 41 22 88 Fax: +33 488 41 27 76
M.	**Klaus Fuchs**	Directorate of Social and Economic Affairs/Direction des Affaires sociales et économiques	Tel: +33 388 41 21 68 Fax: +33 388 41 27 85
M.	**Franco Millich**		Tel: +33 388 41 23 31 Fax: +33 388 41 27 31
Mr	**John Murray**		Tel: +33 388 41 21 67 Fax: +33 388 41 27 31
Mr	**Michael Neurater**		Tel: +33 390 21 42 31 Fax: +33 388 41 27 31
Mme	**Patricia Nicli**		Tel: +33 388 41 48 80 Fax: +33 388 41 27 18
Mr	**Simon Tonelli**		Tel: +33 388 41 21 62 Fax: +33 388 41 27 18
Ms	**Birgit Bertsch-Sansotta**	Directorate of Education, Culture and Sport/Direction de l'enseignement, de la culture et du sport	Tel: +33 388 41 29 44 Fax: +33 388 41 27 50
Mr	**David Crosier**		Tel: +33 3 88 41 30 58 Fax: +33 3 88 41 27 06
Ms	**Olivia Dorricott**		Tel: +33 388 41 29 30 Fax: +33 388 41 27 06
Mr	**Maxim Ferschtman**		Tel: +33 3 88 41 36 55 Fax: +33 3 88 41 27 53
Ms	**Himka Ziga**		Tel: +33 3 88 41 36 56 Fax: +33 3 88 41 27 53
Mme	**Maguelonne Dejéant-Pons**	Directorate of the Environment and Local Authorities/Direction de l'environnment et des pouvoirs locaux	Tel: +33 388 41 23 98 Fax: +33 388 41 37 51
Mlle	**Sandra Jen**		Tel: +33 388 41 22 56 Fax: +33 388 41 37 51
Ms	**Danuta Wisniewska-Cazals**	Directorate of Legal Affairs/Direction des affaires juridiques	Tel: +33 388 41 28 51 Fax: +33 388 41 39 55
Ms	**Marjorie Farquharson**	Directorate of Human Rights/Direction des droits de l'homme	Tel: +33 388 41 30 66 Fax: +33 388 41 39 88
Mme	**Sophie Piquet**		Tél: +33 388 41 21 96 Fax: +33 388 41 27 93

XI. Other international and regional organisations/Autres organisations internationales et régionales

United Nations/Nations unies

Ms	**Mary Robinson**	High Commissioner for Human Rights	(see under II)	
Mr	**Eric Tistounet**	External Relations Officer	Palais des Nations CH-1211 Geneva	Tel: +00 41 22 917 39 65 Fax: +00 41 22 917 04 04

United Nations High Commissioner for Refugees/Haut Commissaire des Nations Unies pour les réfugiés

Mr **Rick Towle**	Senior Liaison Officer (Human Rights Liaison)	Division of International Protection Case Postale 2500 CH-1211 Geneva 2	Tel: Fax:	+41 22 739 76 64 +41 22 739 75 53
Mr **Salvatore Lombardo** Ms **Ida Huussen**	Liaison Officer Legal Assistant	Council of Europe Office, F-67075 Strasbourg Cedex	Tel: Fax:	+33 388 41 28 69 +33 388 41 39 79

United Nations Educational, Scientific and Cultural Organisation/Organisation des Nations Unies pour l'Education, la Science et la Culture

Mr **Vladimir Volodine**	Chief of the Human Rights Unit	Division of Human Rights, Democracy and Peace Sector of Social and Human Sciences 7 place de Fontenoy F-75732 Paris	Tel: Fax:	+33 1 45 68 10 00 +33 1 45 67 16 90

International Labour Office/Bureau International du Travail

M. **Alessandro Chiarabini**	Chef du Programme droits de l'homme	Centre International de Formation de l'OIT Corso Unitá d'Italia 125 I-10127 Turin	Tél: Fax:	+39 11 693 66 46 +39 11 693 69 06
Mr **Lee Swepston**	International Civil Servant, Chief of the Equality and Human Rights Coordination Branch	International Labour Office 4 route des Morillons CH-1211 Geneva 22	Tel: Fax:	+41 22 799 71 51 +41 22 799 63 44

Organisation for Security and Co-operation in Europe/Organisation pour la securité et la coopération en Europe

Mr **Jean-Daniel Ruch**	Personal Adviser to the Director of the Office for Democratic Institutions and Human Rights	OSCE/ODIHR 19 Ujazdowskie Al. PL-00557 Warsaw	Tel: Fax:	+48 22 520 06 00 +48 22 520 06 05

European Communities, European Union/Communautés européennes, Union européenne

Ms **Nathalie Davies,** Commission of the European Communities/Commission des Communautés européennes	Administrator, Human Rights and Democratisation	DG IA A2, European Commission Rue de la Loi 200, (Char 11/90) B-1049 Brussels	Tel: Fax:	+32 2 296 49 33 +32 2 299 53 96
Mr Eamonn Noonan, Official, European Parliament/Parlement européen		MON 404 European Parliament Rue Wiertz B-1047 Brussels	Tel: Fax:	+32 2 284 23 83 +32 2 284 90 70
Ms **Benita Broms**	Legal Officer, Office of the European Ombudsman		Tel: Fax:	+33 388 17 24 23 +33 388 17 90 62

Council of the Baltic Sea States (CBSS)

Ms **Magdalena Sykulska**	Assistant to the Commissioner of the CBSS on Democratic Institutions and Human Rights, including the rights of persons belonging to minorities	Amagertorv 142 PO Box 1165 DK-1010 Copenhagen	Tel: Fax:	+45 33 91 22 88 +45 33 91 22 96

International Committee of the Red Cross/Comité international de la croix rouge

M. **Stéphane Jeannet**	Conseiller juridique	19 avenue de la Paix CH-1202 Genève	Tél: Fax:	+41 22 330 2596 +41 22 733 2057

XII. Ombudsmen and national institutions for the promotion and protection of human rights/Ombudsmen et institutions nationales pour la promotion et la protection des droits de l'homme

Mr **Kerstin André** Mr **Jan Pennlöv**	Parliamentary Ombudsman Parliamentary Ombudsman	Riksdagens Ombudsmän Box 16327 S-10326 Stockholm	Tel: +46 8 786 40 00 Fax: +46 8 216 558
M. **Fermín Barceló**	Delegado del Ararteko	Bureau de l'Ombudsman des Pays Basques Dato 20-2° dcha E-01005 Vitoria	Tél: +34 45 13 51 18 Fax: +34 45 13 51 02
Mr **Ivan Bizjak** Mr **Jakob Štunf**	Ombudsman of Slovenia Public and International Relations Officer	Office of the Ombudsman Dunajska Cesta 56 1109 Ljubljana	Tel: +386 61 175 00 00 Fax: +386 61 175 00 40
Ms **Inger Claesson Wästberg** Ms **Jenny Olausson**	Director General Legal Adviser	Handikappombudsmannen PO Box 7779 S-103 96 Stockholm	Tel: +46 8 20 17 70 Fax: +46 8 20 43 53
Mr **Giorgio de Sabbata**	Ombudsman Région Marche	Via Giusti 6 I-61100 Pesaro	Tel/fax: +390 721 30382
Mr **Paul Donaghy**	Trade Union Training Officer	Standing Advisory Commission on Human Rights Temple Court 39 North Street GB-Belfast BT1 1NA	Tel: +44 1232 243 987 Fax: +44 1232 247 844
M. **Gerard Fellous**	Secrétaire Général	Commission nationale consultative des droits de l'homme 35 rue Saint-Dominique F-75007 Paris	Tél: +33 1 42 75 77 09 Fax: +33 1 42 75 77 14
Ms **Jenny E. Goldschmidt**	Chair of the Equal Treatment Commission, Professor in Women and Law	State University of Leiden Commissie Gelijke Behandeling PO Box 16001 NL-3500 DA Utrecht	Tel: +31 30 233 51 51 Fax: +31 30 230 06 06
Ms **Gret Haller**	Human Rights Ombudsperson for Bosnia and Herzegovina	PO Box 627 CH-3000 Bern 8	Tel: +387 71 666 006 Fax: +387 71 666 007
Ms **Vera Jovanović** Mr **Esad Muhibić** Ms **Branka Raguz**	Federal Ombudsmen of Bosnia and Herzegovina	Valtera Perića 15 71000 Sarajevo	Tel: +387 71 667 929 Fax: +387 71 653 461
M. **Georges Kaminis**	Médiateur adjoint	8 rue Hadjiyanni Mexi GR-Athènes	Tél: +30 1 33 93 111
Ms **Ewa Matuszewska**	Lawyer	Office of the Commissioner for Civic Rights Protection Al. Solidarnosci 77 PL-00090 Warsaw	Tel: +48 22 827 0849 Fax: +48 22 827 6453
Mr **Oleg Mironov** Mr **Marat Bashimov**	Plenipotentiary for Human Rights of the Russian Federation Adviser to the Plenipotentiary for Human Rights of the Russian Federation	47 Myasnitskaya ul. Moscow 103084	Tel: +7 095 207 39 26 Fax: +7 095 292 74 81

Mr **Branko Naumoski**	Public Attorney-Ombudsman of the Republic of Macedonia	"Dimitrie Čupovski" br. 2 91000 Skopje	Tel: +389 91 129 351 Fax: +389 91 129 359
Mr **Jens Olsen**	Legal Adviser	Folketingets Ombudsmand Office of the Danish Ombudsman Gydelandsveg 2 DK-3400 Hillerod	Tel: +45 33 13 25 12 Fax: +45 33 13 07 17
M. **Antonio Sequeira Ribeiro**	Adjoint de Cabinet du Médiateur	Rua do Pau de Bandeira, 7e9 P-1200 Lisbonne	Tél: +351 1 397 91 07/8 Fax: +35 1 396 12 43
Mr **John Tate**	Deputy Parliamentary Commissioner for Administration and Legal Adviser	OPCA 15th Floor Millbank Tower GB-London SW1P 4QP	Tel: +44 171 217 4081 Fax: +44 171 217 4000
Mr **Heimo Tröster**	Official in charge of Social Matters	Austrian Ombudsman Office Volksanwaltschaft Singerstrasse 17 A-1015 Vienna	Tel: +43 1 51 505 125 Fax: +43 1 51 505 160

XIII. Human rights institutes/Instituts des droits de l'homme

Mme **Nicole Derhy** Mme **Azoux-Bacrie** M. **Lunel**	Institut des droits de l'homme du Barreau de Paris	98 Bvd St Germain F-75005 Paris	Tél: +33 1 42 80 49 54 Fax: +33 1 48 74 15 00
Mr **Tamás Bán**	Hungarian Centre for Human Rights	c/o Ministry of Justice Kossuth tér. 4 H-1055 Budapest	Tel: +36 1 268 39 83 Fax: +36 1 268 39 82
Ms **Paloma Durán y Lalaguna**	Head of International Relations	Instituto de la Mujer Condesa de Venadito 34 E-Madrid 28027	Tel: +34 91 347 7903 Fax: +34 91 347 80 76
Ms **Vera Klopčič**	Institute for Ethnic Studies	Erjavzeva 26 Ljubljana	Tel: +386 61 21 08 23 Fax: +386 61 21 09 64
M. **Silvio Marcus-Helmons**	Centre des Droits de l'Homme UCL	Place Montesquieu 2 (Collège Thomas More) B-1348 Louvain-la-Neuve	Tél: +32 10 474 766/78 Fax: +32 10 47 30 58
M. **Jean-Bernard Marie**	Secrétaire Général, Institut International des Droits de l'Homme	2 allée Zaepfel F-67000 Strasbourg	Tél: +33 388 45 84 45 Fax: +33 388 45 84 50
M. **Patrice Meyer-Bisch**	Institut interdisciplinaire d'éthique et des droits de l'homme	Université de Fribourg 6 rue St-Michel CH-1700 Fribourg	Tél: +41 26 300 73 44/43 Fax: +41 26 300 97 07
Mme **Irina Zlatescu**, Directrice M. **Emil Marinache**	Institut roumain pour les droits de l'homme	Piata Charles de Gaulle nr. 3 Sect. 1 Bucarest	Tél: +40 1 222 72 29 Fax: +40 1 610 21 11/222 42 87

XIV. Non-governmental organisations having consultative status with the Council of Europe/Organisations non gouvernementales ayant le statut consultatif aupres du Conseil de l'Europe

Ms **Yvonne Terlingen**	Amnesty International	1 Easton Street GB-London WC1X 8DJ	Tel: +44 171 413 5836 Fax: +44 171 956 1157
M. **Patrick Peguet**	Association Internationale des Jeunes Avocats	22 rue du Général de Castelnau F-67010 Strasbourg	Tél: +33 388 56 54 49 Fax: +33 388 35 54 77

Mme Ms	Claudine Haenni Audrey Vogel	Association pour la Prévention de la Torture (APT)	Route de Ferney 10 CH-1202 Genève	Tél: +41 22 734 20 88 Fax: +41 22 734 56 49
M.	Louis Bloch	Conseil Consultatif des Organisations juives	14 rue Silbermann F-67000 Strasbourg	Tél: +33 3 88 60 72 93 Fax: +33 3 88 60 72 93
Mr	Richard Fischer	Conference of European Churches (KEK)	EECCS 8 rue du Fossé des Treize, F-67000 Strasbourg	Tél: +33 3 88 15 27 60 Fax: +33 3 88 15 27 61
M.	Marc Feix	Colloque Européen des Paroisses (CEP)	2 rue du Presbytère F-67810 Holteheim	Tél: +33 3 88 78 06 61 Fax: +33 3 88 78 06 61
M. M.	Gérard Fonteneau, Conseiller Klaus Lörcher	Confédération européenne des syndicats (CES)	155 Boulevard Emile Jacqmain B-1210 Bruxelles	Tél: +32 2 224 04 61 Fax: +32 2 224 04 54
M. M.	Gilbert Roos Jean-Pierre Weil	Congrès juif européen	23 quai Rouget de Lisle F-67000 Strasbourg	Tél: +33 3 88 35 12 44
M. M.	Victor Bolley Bert van Caelenberg	EUROFEDOP	rue de Trèves 33 B-1040 Bruxelles	Tél: +32 2 230 38 65 Fax: +32 2 231 14 72
Ms	Ruth Brand	European Anti-Poverty Network	Rue Belliard 205 Bte 13 B-1040 Brussels	Tel: +32 2 230 44 55 Fax: +32 2 230 97 33
Mr	Nikolaus Schwaerzler, President	European Ombudsman Institute	Salurnerstrasse 418 A-6020 Innsbruck	Tel: +43 512 56 69 10 Fax: +43 512 57 59 71
Mr	John Evans	FEANTSA	1 rue Defacqz B-1000 Bruxelles	Tel: +32 2 538 66 69 Fax: +32 2 539 41 74
Mme	Elisabeth Marie	Fédération internationale de l'action des Chrétiens pour l'abolition de la torture (FIACAT) – Paris	8 rue des Tourterelles F-67800 Hoenheim	Tél: +33 3 88 83 46 50
M.	Antoine Bernard, Directeur Exécutif	Fédération Internationale des ligues des droits de l'homme	17 passage de la Main d'Or F-75011 Paris	Tél: +33 1 43 55 25 18 Fax: +33 1 43 55 18 80
M.	Lul Rudolph	FIFSP	18 rue J. Leirotes F-67000 Strasbourg	Tél: +33 1 39 07 17 00
M.	Claudio Zanghì	Intercenter	via Casale Ghella 45 I-00 189 Rome	Tél: +39 6 30 36 17 30 Fax: +39 6 30 36 17 30
Mr Ms Mr	Adama Dieng Nathalie Prouvez Matthias Kloth	International Commission of Jurists	81a avenue de Châtelaine CH-1219 Châtelaine Genève	Tel: +41 22 979 38 23 Fax: +41 22 979 38 01
Mme	Annelise Oeschger	Mouvement International ATD Quart Monde	Krozingerstrasse 58-10 D-79114 Freiburg	
Mr Mr	David Gee Richard Seebohm	Quaker Council for European Affairs	Square Ambiorix 50 B-1000 Brussels	Tel: +32 2 230 49 35 Fax: +32 2 230 63 70
M.	Jean-Yves Ouevy	Union internationale de la propriété immobilière (UIPI)	8 rue A. Warocqué B-7100 La Louvière	Tél: +32 7 532 18 65 Fax: +32 6 421 23 85
Ms	F. Ursula Hahn	University Women in Europe	Haardterstrasse 3 D-67433 Neustadt	Fax: +49 6321 82 972

XV. Other non-governmental organisations/Autres organisations non gouvernementales

Ms	Kozara Kati	Albanian Centre for Human Rights	Rr. Kont Urani 10 Tirana	Tel: +355 42 30 630 Fax: +355 42 39 369
Mr	Nikolay Khramov	Anti-militarist Radical Association	Nagatinskaja nab. 88-2-119 Moscow	Tel: +7 095 923 91 27 Fax: +7 095 923 91 27
Ms	Vesna Teršelič, Network Coordinator	Antiwar Campaign Croatia (ARK)	Gajeva 55 10000 Zagreb	Tel: +385 1 431 374 Fax: +385 1 432 456

Ms **Helen Darbishire** Mr **Predrag Sekulić**	Article 19	67 rue de la Verrerie F-75004 Paris	Tél: +33 1 40 29 94 05 Fax: +33 1 40 29 94 50
Ms **Teoroda Kaleynska**	Association of NGOs "Agenda 21"	PO Box 345 BG-5000 Veliko Turnovo	Tel: +359 62 30 048 Fax: +359 62 30 048
Ms **Elmira Alekperova**	Association for the protection of women's rights in Azerbaijan	9 Shamsi Badalbeyli str. 370005 Baku	Tel: +994 12 973 492 Fax: +994 12 973 492
Mr **Vojin Dimitrijević** Mr **Vladimir Djerić**	Belgrade Centre for Human Rights	Mlatišumina 26 YU-11000 Belgrade	Tel: +381 11 43 25 72 Fax: +381 11 344 1203
Ms **Guenoveva Ticheva**	Bulgarian Centre for Human Rights	PO Box 433 BG-1000 Sofia	Tel: +359 2 987 76 21 Fax: +359 2 987 76 21
Ms **Veronika Rešković**	Centre for Direct Protection of Human Rights	Kri aničeva 1/III 10000 Zagreb	Tel: +385 1 46 22 704 Fax: +385 1 46 11 704
Mr **Balázs Hidvéghi**, Secretary General	Civitas International	8 rue des Ecrivains F-67000 Strasbourg	Tel: +33 3 88 24 71 00 Fax: +33 3 88 24 71 09
Mr **Martin Weightman**	Church of Scientology European Human Rights Office	61 rue du Prince Royale B-1050 Brussels	Tel: +32 2 502 37 30 Fax: +32 2 511 84 39
Ms **Fiona Doherty**	Committee on the Administration of Justice	45/47 Donegall Street, GB-Belfast BT1 2FG	Tel: +44 1232 232 394 Fax: +44 1232 246 706
Mr **Károly Bárd**	Constitutional and Legislative Policy Institute/ Open Society Institute-Budapest	Nádor u. 11 H-1051 Budapest	Tel: +36 1 327 31 02 Fax: +36 1 327 31 03
Mr **Werner Lottje**	Diakonisches Werk der Evangelischen Kirchen in Deutschland (EKD)	PO Box 101142 D-70010 Stuttgart	Tel: +49 711 215 95 01 Fax: +49 711 215 93 6
Mr **Kinga Ga'l**	European Centre for Minority Issues	Schiffbruecke 12 D-24939 Flensburg	Tel: +49 461 14 14 961 Fax: +49 461 14 14 969
Ainhitze Bizgalagorra Mr **Thomas Tichelmann**	European Youth Forum	120 rue Jospeh II B-1000 Brussels	Tel: +32 2 230 64 90 Fax: +32 2 230 21 23
Ms **Sarah de Mas** Mr **Stephen Ronald Jakobi**	Fair Trials Abroad Trust	Bench House Ham Street GB-Richmond	Tel: +44 1223 319 009 Fax: +44 1223 355 679
M. **Ioannis Ktistakis** Mme **Alice Marangopoulos**	Fondation Marangopoulos pour les droits de l'homme	1 rue Lycavittou GR-10672 Athènes	Tél: +30 1 361 35 27 Fax: +30 1 362 24 54
Prof. **Grigore Ungureanu**, Président	Fondation roumaine pour la jeunesse	CP. 4-49 RO-Bucarest	Tél: +40 1 687 13 48 Fax: +40 1 242 07 18
Mr **Archil Ordenidze**	The Georgian Committee against Human Torture	162 Tsinamdzgvrishvili str. 380012 Tbilisi	Tel: +995 32 950 730 Fax: +995 32 221 099
Ms **Sabine Marquardt**	German Commission for Justice and Peace	Adenauerallee 134 D-53113 Bonn	Tel: +49 228 103 217 Fax: +49 228 103 318
Mr **Eldar Zeinalov**	Human Rights Centre of Azerbaijan	165-3 Bäşir Säfäroğlu Street 370000 Baku	Tel: +994 12 97 32 33 Fax: +994 12 94 24 71
Ms **Felisa Tibbitts**	Human Rights Education Associates	PO Box 382396 Cambridge MA 02238-2396 USA	Tel: +1 617 661 02 78 Fax: +1 617 249 02 78
Mr **Yavuz Önen**	Human Rights Foundation of Turkey (HRFT)	Menekse 2 Sok. No. 16/6 06440 Kizilay Ankara	Tel: +90 312 417 71 80 Fax: 90 312 425 45 52

Mr	**Mioara Micu**	Independent Human Rights League of Romania/La Ligue indépendante roumaine pour les droits de l'homme	Bd. Alexandru Chregia No. 3, RO-Bucharest	Tel: +40 1 684 16 07
Ms	**Aynur Demirel**	Insan Hak ve Hürriyetleri ve Insani Yardim Vakfi (IHH)	Macar Kardesler Caddesi Hulusi Noyan Sokak no. 23, Fatih-Istanbul	Tel: +90 212 631 33 68 Fax: +90 212 621 70 51
Ms	**Sarah Spencer**	Human Rights Programme, Institute for Public Policy Research	30-32 Southampton Street GB-London WC2E 7RA	Tel: +44 171 470 6100 Fax: +44 171 470 6111
Mr	**Piret Multer**, Project Manager	Jaan Tõnissoni Instituut	Endla 4 EE-0001 Tallinn	Tel: +372 62 63 154 Fax: +372 62 63 152
Mr Ms	**Ramazan Dyryldaev** **Nazira Sopieva**	Kyrgyz Committee for Human Rights	Kievskaya St. 96-A, apt 713-714 Bishkek 720030	Tel: +996 3312 66 13 42 Fax: +996 3312 66 01 83
Mr	**Bodgan Constantin Secelean**	Lawyers' Association for the Defence of Human Rights	Bd. 15 Noiembrie No 45 RO-2200 Brasov	Tel: +40 94 566 465 Fax: +40 68 410 279
Mr	**Paul Strutzescu**, President	The League for the Defence of Human Rights in Republic of Moldova (LADO Moldova)	PO Box 8744 MD-2068 Chisinau	Tel: +373 2 733 255 Fax: +373 2 733 621
Mr M.	**Ishak Saoi Garsancakli**, President **Nuri Yasar**	Mazlumder	Kiztaşi Caddesi Malbant Demir Sokak No. 12/5 Istanbul	Tél: +90 212 539 29 90 Fax: +90 212 532 17 55
Ms	**Jana Kviecinska**	Milan Simecka Foundation	Hviezdoslavovo nam. 17 81102 Bratislava	Tel: +421 7 533 05 07 Fax: +421 7 533 05 07
M.	**Giovanni Caso**, Juge à la Cour de cassation de Rome	Mouvement Focolari	Via Quattrucci 117 I-00046 Grottaferrata	
Ms	**Fernanda Bruna**		Via di Val Cannuta 32 I-00166 Roma	Tel: +39 06 66 22 695
Ms	**Esther Salamanca Aguado**, Professor of Public International Law at the University of Madrid		c/ Zurbano 58, 3° F E-28010 Madrid	Tel: +34 91 394 56 00 Fax: +34 91 394 57 05
Mr Mme Mme	**Kalende André Bigirinama** **Anne Depardon** **Maria Voce**, Vice-President	New Humanity	23 chemin des Palettes CH-1212 Geneva	Tel: +41 22 794 64 44 Fax: +41 22 794 64 47
Ms	**Brindusa Ionescu**	Romanian Family Forum	sos Stefan cel Mare no. 38 RO-Bucharest	Tel: +40 1 610 211
Ms	**Monica Luisa Macovei**	Romanian Helsinki Committee	str. Cercului no. 6 bl. 5/7, sc. B ap. 64, Sector 2 RO-Bucharest	Tel: +40 1 619 1975 Fax: +40 1 619 1975
M.	**André Jacques**	Service International pour les droits de l'homme	1 rue de Varembé Case postale 16 CH-1211 Genève	Tél: +41 22 733 35 123 Fax: +41 22 73 30 826
Ms	**Zalikha Tagirova**	Women's Rights Monitoring Group	150-9 165-3 Bäşir Säfäroğlu Street 370000 Baku	Tel: +994 12 94 75 50 Fax: +994 12 94 75 50

XVI. Other participants/Autres participants

M.	**Vincent Delattre**	Avocat stagiaire à l'Université de Strasbourg	11a rue du Fossé des Treize F-67000 Strasbourg	Tél: +33 388 15 14 26 Fax: +33 388 15 19 85
Mr	**Cees Flinterman**	Professor of international law	Faculty of Law University of Maastricht PO Box 616 NL-6200 MD Maastricht	Tel: +31 43 38 83 124 Fax: +31 43 32 57 818
M.	**Carlos Flores**	Professeur de droit constitutionnel	Université de Valencia Santa Maria Micaela 18, pta 138 E-46071 Valencia	Tél: +34 96 384 38 09 Fax: +34 96 382 81 19
Ms	**Gordana Genadieva**	Adviser of the Public Attorney of the Republic of Macedonia (interpreter)	"Dimitrie Čupovski" br. 2 91000 Skopje	Tel: +389 91 129 351 Fax: +389 91 129 359
M.	**Laurent Hincker**	Avocat, professeur à l'Université de Strasbourg	11a rue du Fossé des Treize F-67000 Strasbourg	Tél: +33 388 15 14 26 Fax: +33 388 15 19 85
Mr	**Neven Pecelj**	Translator to the Federal Ombudsmen of Bosnia and Herzegovina	Valtera Perića 15 71000 Sarajevo	Tel: +387 71 667 929 Fax: +387 71 653 461
Mme	**Mady Schaffer**	Directrice, Centre régional de formation professionnelle des avocats d'Alsace	3 quai Jean Sturm F-67000 Strasbourg	Tél: +33 388 37 12 99
M.	**Christophe Speckbacher**		2 rue des Lis F-67100 Strasbourg	Tél: +33 388 84 45 19
M.	**Maurice de Thevenard**	Magistrat	Ministère de l'Industrie DGAF/SDAJC 113 rue de Grenelle F-75353 Paris 07 SP	Tel: +33 1 43 19 23 47 Fax: +33 1 43 19 34 27

XVII. Secretariat/Secrétariat

Mr	**Daniel Tarschys**	Secretary General/Secrétaire Général
M.	**Pierre-Henri Imbert**	Director of Human Rights/Directeur des Droits de l'Homme
Ms	**Jane Dinsdale**	Deputy Director of Human Rights/Directrice Adjointe des Droits de l'Homme

Directorate of Human Rights (organisation of the colloquy)/Direction des Droits de l'Homme (organisation du colloque)

Mr	**Jeroen Schokkenbroek**	Head of the Human Rights Section/Chef de la Section Droits de l'Homme	Tel: +33 3 88 41 22 79 Fax: +33 3 88 41 27 93
Ms	**Maggie Nicholson**	Head of the Human Rights Awareness Unit/Chef de l'Unité de sensibilisation des droits de l'homme	Tel: +33 3 88 41 28 25 Fax: +33 3 88 41 27 36
Mme	**Françoise Mantion**	Principal Administrative Assistant/Assistante administrative principale	Tél: +33 3 88 41 23 33 Fax: +33 3 88 41 27 93
Ms	**Heather Stewart**	Administrative Assistant/Assistante administrative	Tel: +33 3 88 41 35 63 Fax: +33 3 88 41 27 93
Ms	**Christina Nicolaidou**	Administrative Assistant/Assistante administrative	Tel: +33 3 88 41 28 18 Fax: +33 3 88 41 27 36

Assistants to the rapporteurs/Assistants aux rapporteurs

Mr	**John Darcy**	Directorate of Human Rights	Tel: +33 388 41 31 56 Fax: +33 388 41 37 00
Ms	**Isobelle Jaques**	Directorate of Human Rights	Tel: +33 388 41 23 49 Fax: +33 388 41 39 87

Mr	**Markus Jaeger**	Secretary General's Monitoring Unit	Tel: +33 388 41 23 34 Fax: +33 388 41 37 67
Mr	**Antti Aaro Korkeakivi**	Directorate of Human Rights	Tel: +33 388 41 29 56 Fax: +33 388 41 27 93
M.	**Christophe Poirel**	Direction des Droits de l'Homme	Tel: +33 388 41 23 30 Fax: +33 388 41 27 05
M.	**Patrick Titiun**	Direction des Droits de l'Homme	Tel: +33 388 41 32 76 Fax: +33 388 41 39 88
Ms	**Veronica Williams**	Directorate of Human Rights	Tel: +33 388 41 47 78 Fax: +33 388 41 37 00

2. Alphabetical presentation

The figures in Roman numerals after the names correspond to the headings in the above list.

Alekperova, Elmira	XV
Alkema, Evert	X
Ando, Akira	VII
André, Kerstin	XII
Araci, Fatoş	X
Astrup, Heddy	V
Ayfantis	VI
Azoux-Bacrie	XIII
Babuşka, Mihaela Silvia	VI
Bakhm, Vjacheslav Ivanovich	IV
Bán, Tamás	XIII
Barceló, Fermín	XII
Bárd, Károly	XV
Bartosova, Andela	X
Bashimov, Marat	XII
Belling, Arne	VI
Bernard, Antoine	XIV
Bertsch-Sansotta, Birgit	X
Bigirinama, Kalende André	XV
Birk, Rolf	X
Birsan, Corneliu	X
Bitti, Gilbert	VI
Bizgalagorra, Ainhitze	XV
Bizjak, Ivan	XII
Bloch, Louis	XIV
Boillat, Philippe	VI
Bolley, Victor	XIV
Boulay, Pierre	V, X
Boychenko, Yury	VI
Bozhkova, Ludmila	VI
Brand, Ruth	XIV
Broms, Benita	XI
Bruna, Fernanda	XV
Busck, Camilla	VI
Caballero, Jocelyne	VI
Carlsen, Carsten	V
Caso, Giovanni	XV
Çelikcan, Meral	V, VI
Charalambos, Petinos	VI
Chiarabini, Alessandro	XI
Coin, Danielle	X
Constas, Dimitri	VI
Corlatean, Titus	VI
Costa, Jean-Paul	X
Courtney, Michael	VIII
Couvreur, Jean-Claude	V
Crosier, David	X
Cuk, Nadia	X
Darbishire, Helen	XV
Darcy, John	XVII
Davies, Nathalie	XI
de Gouttes, Régis	III
de Mas, Sarah	XV
de Sabbata, Giorgio	XII
de Salvia, Michel	X
de Thevenard, Maurice	XVI
de Vey Mestdagh, Karel	VI
Decaux, Emmanuel	VI
Dejéant-Pons, Maguelonne	X
Delattre, Vincent	XVI
Demirel, Aynur	XV
Depardon, Anne	XV
Derhy, Nicole	XIII
Diaconescu, Cristian	VI
Dieng, Adama	II, V
Dieng, Adama	XIV
Dienstbier, Jiří	II
Dimitrijević, Vojin	III, XV
Dinsdale, Jane	XVII
Djerić, Vladimir	XV
Doherty, Fiona	XV
Donaghy, Paul	XII
Dorricott, Olivia	X
Drzemczewski, Andrew	X
Drzewicki, Krzysztof	V
Durán y Lalaguna, Paloma	XIII
Dyryldaev, Ramazan	XV
Dzupa, Juraj	X
Eaton, Martin	V, X
Economides, Constantin	X
Ejima, Akiko	X
Entin, Mark	VI
Esposito, Vitaliano	V
Evans, John	XIV
Farquharson, Marjorie	X
Feix, Marc	XIV
Fellous, Gerard	XII
Ferschtman, Maxim	X
Filibeck, Giorgio	VIII
Filletti, Joseph	VI, X
Fischer, Richard	XIV
Flinterman, Cees	XVI
Flores, Carlos	XVI
Fonteneau, Gérard	XIV
Fraisse, Geneviève	VI
Frangakis, Nikos	X
Friederich, François	X
Fröhlich, Johann	VI
From, Sofie	VI
Fuchs, Klaus	X
Ga'l, Kinga	XV
Garcia de Diego, Alejandro Abellan	VI
Garsancakli, Ishak Saoi	XV
Gee, David	XIV
Geirsson, Thorsteinn	VI
Genadieva, Gordana	XVI
Gertnere, Kaija	III
Glover, Audrey	VI
Goguadze, Elene	IX
Goldschmidt, Jenny E.	XII
Guerr, Álvaro Manuel Soares	VI
Guidetti, Alain	VI
Hack, Ullrich	VI
Haenni, Claudine	XIV
Hahn, F. Ursula	XIV
Haller, Gret	XII
Hammarberg, Thomas	VI
Head, Michael E.	X
Hedberg, Bosse	X
Hedegaard, Erik	VI
Herckens, Michel	VI
Heringa, Aalt-Willem	III
Hidvéghi, Balázs	XV
Hincker, Laurent	XVI
Hofmann, Rainer	X
Huussen, Ida	XI
Imbert, Pierre-Henri	XVII
Ionescu, Brindusa	XV
Jacques, André	XV
Jaeger, Markus	XVII
Jakobi, Stephen Ronald	XV

Ollscoil na hÉireann, Gaillimh
3 1111 40036 9821

Sales agents for publications of the Council of Europe
Agents de vente des publications du Conseil de l'Europe

AUSTRALIA/AUSTRALIE
Hunter publications, 58A, Gipps Street
AUS-3066 COLLINGWOOD, Victoria
Fax: (61) 33 9 419 7154
E-mail: jpdavies@ozemail.com.au

AUSTRIA/AUTRICHE
Gerold und Co., Graben 31
A-1011 WIEN 1
Fax: (43) 1512 47 31 29
E-mail: buch@gerold.telecom.at

BELGIUM/BELGIQUE
La Librairie européenne SA
50, avenue A. Jonnart
B-1200 BRUXELLES 20
Fax: (32) 27 35 08 60
E-mail: info@libeurop.be

Jean de Lannoy
202, avenue du Roi
B-1060 BRUXELLES
Fax: (32) 25 38 08 41

CANADA
Renouf Publishing Company Limited
5369 Chemin Canotek Road
CDN-OTTAWA, Ontario, K1J 9J3
Fax: (1) 613 745 76 60

CZECH REPUBLIC/RÉPUBLIQUE TCHÈQUE
USIS, Publication Service
Havelkova 22
CZ-130 00 Praha 3
Fax: (420) 2 242 21 484

DENMARK/DANEMARK
Munksgaard
PO Box 2148
DK-1016 KØBENHAVN K
Fax: (45) 33 12 93 87

FINLAND/FINLANDE
Akateeminen Kirjakauppa
Keskuskatu 1, PO Box 218
SF-00381 HELSINKI
Fax: (358) 9 121 44 50
E-mail: akatilaus@stockmann.fi

GERMANY/ALLEMAGNE
UNO Verlag
Proppelsdorfer Allee 55
D-53115 BONN
Fax: (49) 228 21 74 92
E-mail: unoverlag@aol.com

GREECE/GRÈCE
Librairie Kauffmann
Mavrokordatou 9, GR-ATHINAI 106 78
Fax: (30) 13 23 03 20

HUNGARY/HONGRIE
Euro Info Service
Magyarország
Margitsziget (Európa Ház),
H-1138 BUDAPEST
Fax: (361) 302 50 35
E-mail: euroinfo@mail.matav.hu

IRELAND/IRLANDE
Government Stationery Office
4-5 Harcourt Road, IRL-DUBLIN 2
Fax: (353) 14 75 27 60

ISRAEL/ISRAËL
ROY International
41 Mishmar Hayarden Street
PO Box 13056
IL-69865 TEL AVIV
Fax: (972) 3 6499469
E-mail: royil@netvision.net.il

ITALY/ITALIE
Libreria Commissionaria Sansoni
Via Duca di Calabria, 1/1
Casella Postale 552, I-50125 FIRENZE
Fax: (39) 0 55 64 12 57

MALTA/MALTE
L. Sapienza & Sons Ltd
26 Republic Street
PO Box 36
VALLETTA CMR 01
Fax: (356) 233 621

NETHERLANDS/PAYS-BAS
De Lindeboom Internationale Publikaties b.v.
PO Box 202
NL-7480 AE HAAKSBERGEN
Fax: (31) 53 572 92 96

NORWAY/NORVÈGE
Akademika, A/S Universitetsbokhandel
PO Box 84, Blindern
N-0314 OSLO
Fax: (47) 22 85 30 53

POLAND/POLOGNE
Głowna Księgarnia Naukowa im. B. Prusa
Krakowskie Przedmiescie 7
PL-00-068 WARSZAWA
Fax: (48) 22 26 64 49

PORTUGAL
Livraria Portugal
Rua do Carmo, 70
P-1200 LISBOA
Fax: (351) 13 47 02 64

SPAIN/ESPAGNE
Mundi-Prensa Libros SA
Castelló 37, E-28001 MADRID
Fax: (34) 915 75 39 98
E-mail: libreria@mundiprensa.es

SWITZERLAND/SUISSE
Buchhandlung Heinimann & Co.
Kirchgasse 17, CH-8001 ZÜRICH
Fax: (41) 12 51 14 81

BERSY
Route d'Uvrier 15
CH-1958 LIVRIER/SION
Fax: (41) 27 203 73 32

UNITED KINGDOM/ROYAUME-UNI
TSO (formerly HMSO)
51 Nine Elms Lane
GB-LONDON SW8 5DR
Fax: (44) 171 873 82 00
E-mail: denise.perkins@theso.co.uk

UNITED STATES and CANADA/
ÉTATS-UNIS et CANADA
Manhattan Publishing Company
468 Albany Post Road
PO Box 850
CROTON-ON-HUDSON, NY 10520, USA
Fax: (1) 914 271 58 56
E-mail: Info@manhattanpublishing.com

STRASBOURG
Librairie Kléber
Palais de l'Europe
F-67075 STRASBOURG Cedex
Fax: +33 (0)3 88 52 91 21

Council of Europe Publishing/Editions du Conseil de l'Europe
Council of Europe/Conseil de l'Europe
F-67075 Strasbourg Cedex
Tel. +33 (0)3 88 41 25 81 – Fax +33 (0)3 88 41 39 10 – E-mail: publishing@coe.fr – Website: http://book.coe.fr